CHINESE CHARACTERS

Sarah Lloyd was born in London. She trained as a landscape architect and has practised in London and the West Indies. She has travelled widely in Africa, Asia and America – spending two years in South America, and two years in India. Between travels, she lives and writes in Staffordshire. In 1984 she published *An Indian Attachment* (Harvill) which was widely acclaimed. This is her second book.

CHINESE CHARACTERS

A Journey through China

SARAH LLOYD

FLAMINGO
Published by Fontana Paperbacks

First published by William Collins 1987

This Flamingo edition first published in 1988 by Fontana Paperbacks,
8 Grafton Street, London WIX 3LA

Flamingo is an imprint of Fontana Paperbacks, part of the
Collins Publishing Group

Typeset in Linotron Sabon by
Rowland Phototypesetting Ltd, Bury St Edmunds, Suffolk
Made and printed in Great Britain by
William Collins Sons and Co. Ltd, Glasgow

For my father

Contents

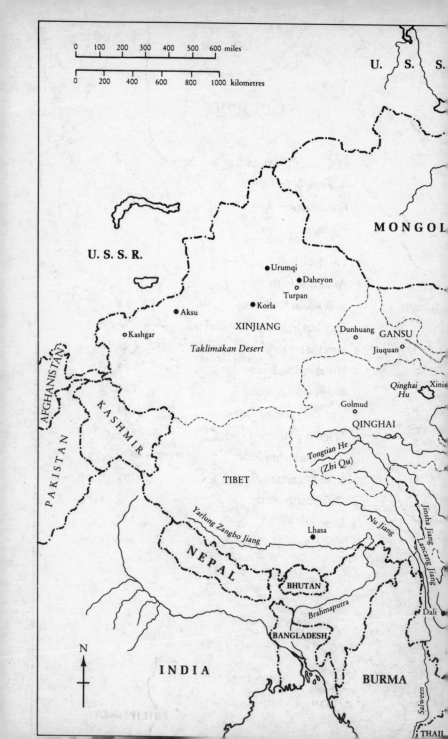

List of Illustrations

Acknowledgements

If I were able, I would thank by their real names those Chinese who helped and trusted me and told me their tales. Since I am not I can only acknowledge them in my heart. There have been instances of Chinese being held in labour camps or shot for indulging anti-communist beliefs in the presence of foreigners, and while this would be unlikely under the current regime a swing back to the left could threaten the safety of those concerned. I would also like to thank my editor and agent, my friends in Hong Kong who put me up, and the foreign expert Jan, who had also to be given a pseudonym. Of the names appearing prominently in this account (with the exception of well-known political figures), only Rosy is real.

Introduction

TRANSLITERATION

The new Pinyin system, a phonetic romanization of Chinese characters that replaces the British Wade-Giles system, has been used throughout, with the exception of names that would otherwise be hard to recognize, notably Confucius and Chiang Kai-shek. Sounds are phonetic, apart from the following:

c approximates to the *ts* in vats,

q is like *ch*, as in Qing (Ching) dynasty,

x is like *sh*, as in Deng Xiaoping,

z is like *ds*, as in Mao Zedong,

zh is like *j*, as in Zhou Enlai.

e is sometimes pronounced *u* as in Deng ('dung'),

i as the *er* in fern,

and *a* as the *e* in ten.

ui is pronounced *way*, as in sway.

PRONUNCIATION OF PLACE NAMES

Anhui	*Aanhway*	Haikou	*High-ko*
Chengdu	*Chungdu*	Hangzhou	*Hangjo*
Daheyon	*Da-her-yon*	Lanzhou	*Lanjo*
E Mei	*Er may*	Kunming	the *u* is the same as
Fujian	*Foojien*		in *kung* of *kung fu*
Guangxi	*Guangshee*	Quanzhou	*Chwenjo*
Guangzhou	*Guangjo*	Shantou	*Shanto*
Guilin	*Gwaylin*	Shenzhen	*Shunjun*

Suzhou	*Sujo*	Zhangzhou	*Jangjo*
Xiamen	*Shiamen*	Zhanjiang	*Janjaing*
Xian	*Shee-an*	Zhengzhou	*Jungjo*
Xinjiang	*Shinjiang*		

NOTE ON CURRENCY

The unit of currency in China is the yuan, three yuan being roughly equivalent to £1 sterling, or two to the US dollar. The yuan is divided into ten jiao, worth a little over three pence each, and one hundred fen. Visitors to China receive Foreign Exchange Certificates (FEC), an alternative system of Chinese currency supposed to be for their sole use and consisting of notes of the same denominations as ordinary 'people's money', or renminbi.

Prologue

I climbed through the fence and entered another world. As if in a dream, an old woman in black came swaying down the path, bent beneath the weight of a shoulder pole. She swung off left and into a field, a vision from the past in side-fastened tunic and calf-length trousers with a wide straw hat upon her head. From the brim of her hat a black cotton pelmet blew gently in the breeze, shielding her eyes from the sun.

Her face was in shadow. She contrived to keep her back to me as she watered the growing vegetables, as if eyes, like cameras, could steal a person's soul. She steadied the big wooden buckets with her hands, the muscles drawn taut like cords on her neck. Water flowed in arching rosettes, catching the sun like silver thread.

All that day, my first in the Orient, I wandered the coast of this outlying island, one of the complex that make up Hong Kong. I moved along tiny earth-trodden field paths, climbing headlands, descending to the brim of the salt-scented sea. The waves slapped sullenly on the bouldery beach, at the dragon-humped line of red-brown seaweed stranded by the tide. A group of men were mending a net; boys waded the shallows, fishing with spears.

I wandered through villages, their tended hinterland enfolded by thickets of tall grass and bamboo and backed by grave-scattered hills. The low grey houses with shallow tiled roofs gathered tight about paths that were thoroughfare and living room, public and private, shaded by awnings and used as extensions of kitchens and storerooms and yards. So close were the houses, so domestic the activity that I felt like a trespasser in a family scene. I trod quickly and softly so as not to impose upon the old woman sewing, the man splitting wood, the girl threading cabbage leaves on strings to dry, the children playing with stones. Birds were singing in bamboo cages; washing was dangling from bamboo poles. Against the walls there were stacks of firewood and large round baskets and dove-cotes and pot plants and tables and stools. Doors were protected by miniature shrines and offerings of incense and guardian posters and the faded red banners from the previous New Year. Pigs grunted in sties; hens clucked in coops: dogs barked a warning of personal domain.

But though the passages were public the houses themselves were secretive. Doors were ajar but the rooms were dark, betraying no clue of interior style. Windows were small, curtained by dust. Imagining altars and ancestral tablets and scrolls of calligraphy, I longed to see inside.

I wandered among the vegetable plots, the most perfectly tended, intensively cultivated land I'd ever seen, the long earth strips raised like chocolate bars with twelve-inch paths between the strips and careful watertight rims. Women weeded by hand or hoe; men bore buckets from the wells on poles. It was a garden landscape, textured by a tapestry of vegetable green. Pumpkins grew on pergolas, peas on wigwams, arrowhead and taro in water-filled fields, celery and carrots in a feather-froth of leaves. Between the plots were compost pits and reservoirs and large glazed jars for storing night soil. There were scarecrows on sticks in black peasant shirts and rags of pink polythene flapping from strings. Birds twittered in thickets and balanced on wires. There were shrines to the earth gods with troughs for the proferring of incense sticks. Water spirits resided in springs; farm gods presided in fields. There were man-sized temples with figures on the roof ridge and faded red satin embroidered with flowers. The graves, the shrines and the temples faced the sea.

The wind bends the Melaleuca trees. The hillsides are desecrated, their flesh ripped open by marauding machines. Beyond Sheung Shui we enter the closed zone. There are watercress beds and rivers and ponds. The train stops: people stare at the rain. Goods wagons wait in a lonely siding, their porcine cargo squealing and crashing against the bars. Then Lo Wu. An arrow points to China.

I look at the faces as I cross the barrier, the soldiers in green, round-cheeked, shy-eyed, the girls checking passports in large peaked caps. Their look of innocence is strangely disquieting, betraying nothing of their past, nor yet of the country that lies ahead.

On the Road

It was still half-dark as we crossed the river and left Guangzhou for the open fields. The urban blocks became rural cropland across a curious no-man's-land, neither city nor country, a dynamic zone where concrete and farmland mingled in an unplanned interim. Clouds hung low and grey and cold. It was early February, the Chinese New Year.

Day dawned on a stubble of flat fields. A duckherd tended his flock in a pool. Buffaloes munched on a field of cut cane. Away from the road traditional villages clustered tightly in on themselves about bed-wide alleys and thickets of bamboo; apart from the slender roadside trees it might have been pre-Liberation China. That people were poor there was ample indication in the mud-brick walls and reed-mat shacks and hand-worked fields and battered straw hats. The sagging roofs, the compost heaps, the strips of mud wheel-rutted on the roadside defied order and control. When we came to a river we stopped. We got out of the bus and crossed by boat.

On our twelve-hour journey south to Zhanjiang we moved alternately between low rounded hills dotted with pine trees and gently terraced rice fields that rippled and nudged at their base. This was to be the predominating pattern over much of South China, a coherent landscape, human in scale and execution. For the first few days I watched it compulsively, following the jigsaw of unfenced plots, picking out the elegant red-brown grasses and lettuce-green ferns and dark rhododendrons that fuzzed the hills beneath the pines. So irregular and wide-spaced and stunted were the trees that at first I thought the forest was self-sown. So sparse were their branches that my eyes travelled through successive corrugations of undulating hills to a distant crest of miniature pine trees etched against the sky in a dark stencilled line. For four thousand years these hills had fed the plains, had had their herbage gathered and their soil removed to replace the starved earth in the fields below.

Only once that day was there a vista evocative of my Western-based image of China, of pine-topped hills receding into mist, of bamboos like giant ferns tufting the banks of a broad silver river on which sampans and bamboo rafts floated like insects on a pane of glass. Mostly the landscape reminded me of India. I was back in Punjab among the dry brown earth and coarse vital texture of clay dug by hand, among the rice fields and rape and plots of high cane. There were the same kinds of trees and the same roadside pools and the same piebald myna birds pecking in the soil. But here in China was a vegetable opulence lacking in India, a more careful husbandry, and the hills were forested and the pools stocked with fish.

This mirroring of India was as startling as the elegance of building style, expressing an instinct for rhythm and harmony and changing from hour to hour. I noticed wok-shaped gable ends of ex-officials' houses, dragon friezes on fascia boards and carved wooden brackets on former temples; I saw whole villages of upswept roofs, that deliberate ploy of lightening appearance, linking home with heaven and balancing yang with a gesture of yin.

It was not what I'd expected. Revolutionary posters portrayed the countryside as a perfection of order and selfless production, as a grid of canals and pylons and power lines, a regulated land ruled by gated communes and people herded in whitewashed blocks. They shifted the reality of unplanned villages and irregular plots to gangs of industrious rosy-cheeked workers addressing themselves to rectangular fields, and tractors working the perfect soil and trailers laden with the cabbages thereof, and rural factories and hydroelectric dams, but they were as naive and idealized as the proverbial package tour. In eight months in China I was never to see a tractor working the fields; small walking tractors, buzzing machines with two front wheels and an attachment arm, plied the roads instead, transporting loads. I was never to see a commune of the kind the posters portrayed. The fields were small and bare of crops. The rosy-cheeked comrades were nowhere in sight.

The term 'commune' still carries sinister undertones in the West, although in China officially it was no longer in use. A commune was never a visible entity but an administrative area, with a provincial market-town as its central headquarters and forty or fifty or a hundred thousand people within its control. The lone hut on a distant hillside might be twenty miles from the nearest building, but it had still formed part of a people's commune. Had I dropped from a parachute I might not have known which land I was in, could not have discerned that the system of tenure was not a feudal regime of farmer and tenant or landlord and serf. Communism was invisible in the countryside, as if China's whole recent history was no more than a dream.

In the four hundred kilometres between Guangzhou and Zhanjiang, a city and sea port in southern Guangdong – the province of which Guangzhou is the capital – I scarcely saw a town. That four-fifths of the population lived in the countryside made immediate sense. Where the land was tended, villages were spaced a mile or so apart, with earth-trodden field paths between. There were no other roads, no road signs or verges. Traffic was light, a few buses and bicycles and the occasional deep green Liberation truck. This major road linking two big towns was the width of an English country lane.

In spite of our tickets having numbered seats there'd been a panic getting on. People burrowed through the scrum before their tickets had been checked, to be hauled back out by their jacket tails in a manner undignified to both passenger and conductor. They scrambled to their seats and piled their sacks and hold-alls in the aisle while the driver and his mate, in layers of blue cotton and soft peaked caps, made a bed in the front with a box for their legs and a grimy quilt. While one of them drove the other lay in comfort and puffed on a bong, a bamboo water pipe, and passed it round those sitting at the front.

Most of the passengers were men. They generated a blue-green-grey neutrality in their clothes of baggy proletarian conformity, smoking and talking and dozing on the rail of the seat in front. I sat at the rear, sharing a seat with a peasant girl with rough-hewn hair and a baby on her back. When the baby made a sound she undid the ties of the cloak enfolding it, pulled off the straps that held it in place, pushed my knees to the side and held it up to add its mite to the peanut shells and melon-seed husks and cigarette butts massing in damp heaps on the floor. The bus smelt of mud and nicotine, and garlic breath and the sudden sharp tang of mandarin peel.

A retired teacher sat in front of me, travelling with his wife to spend a few days of the New Year holiday with his son in Zhan-jiang. He spoke a little English – or rather, he qualified quickly and justifiably, he had spoken some forty years previously. Frowning in concentration he excavated words from his failing memory, and having garnered sufficient he presented me with a gift of three or four words. I, meanwhile, was hanging to the rail on the back of his seat, for the driver was speeding and the road wasn't up to it, and we in the back were being thrown in the air to land with loud cursings and bruising of bones. Except for the final fifty miles where the road was unsurfaced, and nice and smooth.

At nine o'clock we stopped for food. Imagining that therefore we would be stopping quite frequently, I dashed up the road to a village set back across fallow fields and thereby missed my lunch, for it proved the only meal stop all day. Even the teacher, who like everyone else had stocked up on dumplings and clods of steamed rice, was grumbling to his wife by mid-afternoon: 'What's the matter with this bloody driver? Doesn't he ever eat?'

But the village was worth it. Its dark charcoal brickwork was splashed by the scarlet of New Year couplets around the doors and the symbols of New Year prosperity above: a lantern, a mandarin and a wilting Chinese onion. A confetti of spent firecrackers speckled the alleys; a woman was kneeling before a shrine. At the side of a creek shacks wavered on stilts, and boat people strung fish on the roofs of their sampans to dry.

Soon after our meal break we entered a zone of densely built villages dominated by houses in the form of towers. Plain and fortress-like for three or four storeys they blossomed out on the fifth and sixth in a confection of balustrades and domes and cupolas, even turrets in the manner of baronial castles. I supposed them to be watchtowers, a defence against bandits and the armies of warlords, but there was no telling for sure. At this point the teacher swivelled round in his seat and fixed me once more with his doleful gaze. I returned his look in anticipation, for if anyone knew the history of these houses, a product of such lurid fairytale imagination, then here was the man.

'This is countryside,' he announced with deliberate emphasis. 'Not city.'

Bowling along the road in the battered country bus I felt an intimacy with the landscape that would elude me when travelling by train. For a train was a habitat within itself, cut off from the countryside unfolding beyond the windows by its own life unfolding within; but the bus was a part of the land through which it passed, in direct relationship with the people on the road – old men walking, their trouser legs tied with string, young men on bicycles or pulling hand-carts, pigtailed girls in twos or threes – swerving, hooting, responding to its geography and physically on the level of the fields. Trains followed the course of least resistance, tunnelling through hills, skirting villages and towns, rumbling along embankment or cutting, a superficial overlay across an age-old pattern of hills and rivers, canals and fields that the road was forced to obey. In the bus there was no community. The ride was noisy, the road was bumpy, the seat was uncomfortable; attention turned outwards to the land.

The Chinese word for landscape is *shan-shui*, mountains and water. It is a humbler term than the English one, for 'landscape' implies rights. It implies man, its viewer, its proprietor; it implies the Christian philosophy of dominion as opposed to the Daoist one of harmony, of following natural laws.

Paradoxically, while Western nations were struggling to conserve their remaining wildlife the Chinese seemed intent on wiping theirs out. Since only one-eighth of China's terrain is cultivable and only then under irrigation (the rest being mountain or desert or hill tract), the battle against nature is still fundamental so it is essential that none be wasted. Within tended areas there isn't room for cattle or sheep or nature reserves: nor can the farmers, desperately poor, afford to share their crops with birds or beasts. During the fifties and sixties the Party campaigned against the so-called four pests: flies, mosquitoes, rats and grain-eating birds. Everyone carried fly swats and birds were kept flying by a mobilized population beating pots and pans until they fell to the ground with exhaustion and died.

Never had I seen so few birds. Habitats were there between the fields – pond and riverside, scrub and crag – but the skies were empty, the waters silent. People still shot what birds there were; I would see them in noodle stalls laid out in plucked rows. Once again people trapped them and kept them as musical ornaments in cages. There was widespread use of insecticides.

In the Botanical Gardens outside Guangzhou I'd been dismayed by the absence of plant labels. I asked one of the botanists, a bristle-haired man with an impish grin called Yao.

'We used to have porcelain labels,' he replied, 'but people shot them.'

'Shot them?'

'Well they used to come to the gardens to shoot birds, to eat mostly, but also for fun. When the Party forbade the killing of wildlife in parks and sanctuaries the people got angry and shot the labels instead.' Elsewhere there was no means of enforcing the rule. Wild plants were uprooted for sale as ornamentals and certain species were almost extinct. 'Then we used aluminium labels,' Yao went on, 'but people stole them. So now we have plastic ones. No one wants those.'

Even the trees in China were regimented, socialist trees held prisoner in rows or in state plantations on eroded hillsides: alien species in alien formation. Of indigenous forest, the subtropical woodland containing fishtail palm and fronded bamboo, and giant horsetail and rattan and fern that I saw on a hillside west of Guangzhou, there was none along the main road south and little anywhere in China's south-east. No flowers bloomed; even insects were scarce. Nothing was safe, not plant nor bird nor fish nor animal; nor, as I would later discover, even man.

Since my visit an environmental protection agency has been set up under the Forestry and Wildlife Ministry and attitudes have at last begun to change. But in 1984 there was just one exception to the widespread notion that everything existed for the benefit of man. The giant panda, living in the mountains of Western Sichuan, was a matter of international prestige. Only a thousand remained, of which half were at risk owing to the disappearance after flowering of the arrow bamboo, the pandas' staple food. Zoologists were attempting to move the pandas but in so doing would have to resettle a reluctant Tibetan community. Meanwhile the pandas were being kept going on sheep's heads and the people's own favourite, pork chops.

In 1905 an American soil specialist, Dr F. H. King, sailed around China on what was then its major transport network, an extensive system of inland waterways. He wrote his observations in *Farmers of Forty Centuries*. Little had changed in the time since his visit; the peasants were using the same techniques that they had used for the past four thousand years. Almost every task was still performed by hand. Canal banks, road verges and field bunds were cultivated in addition to the fields, and pools were fertilized and stocked with fish. Every leaf and stalk was composted and ploughed back into the land. Herbage was carried down from the hills, water hyacinth was skimmed from pools, fallen leaves swept up from roads, aquatic plants sieved from lakes and sea. Into the compost went mud from canals and thatch from leaking roofs and bricks from dismantled earth walls, and manure and wood ash and stubble and weeds and amounts of human and household waste. I saw depots by the roadside for recycling metal, plastic, paper and glass. Feathers went to dusters; rags to paper and patches and mops and the padded soles of cloth shoes; bones to buttons, jerseys (unpicked and reknitted) to long johns; hair to wigs; coal-dust to briquettes. Silkworm dung became compost and medicine, the chrysalids were eaten and waste silk was used for quilts. Multi-purpose crops; multi-cropped plots: no opportunity was overlooked.

Poverty forced an even greater endeavour in 1905 to get the ultimate out of the land. The Guangdong countryside through which I was travelling produced four crops annually, and one-sixth of a fertile acre was sufficient for the maintenance of one Chinese. Dr King saw peasants exchanging the soil between rice plots and orchards in the belief that each would profit the other. He saw six-foot stacks of fresh-cut clover decomposing between layers of mud. He saw canal silt spread thickly over the soil, and terraced fields no bigger than a napkin.

Had I been travelling this same road then it would have been an earth road no wider than a cart track, trafficked by sedan chairs, by coolies pushing one-wheeled barrows fitted with sails to speed their propulsion (and still in use, according to reports) and by farmers and traders with shoulder poles. Deforestation had already been in progress for hundreds of years; few trees shaded the narrow earth paths and the hills were eroded and bare. Temples and small shrines sprinkled the fields and grave mounds occupied much cultivated land. The average size of a family farm was then an acre, forcing the poor to infanticide and the poorest of the poor to roam as bandits. Survival engendered brutality; clan wars raged, bandits looted, warlords strove to increase their domain.

For centuries the Chinese had believed that the landscape teemed with supernatural powers which they venerated, placated and feared. The world had a soul; trees, pools, rocks, springs, even the soil was alive. According to the ancient science of *feng-shui*, literally 'wind-water', currents of energy travelled through the universe in a network of forces, influencing the fortunes of men. Destiny could be favourably affected by manipulating the environment and timing events to concentrate the good and deflect the bad, from the siting of the city in which people lived to the position of their graves and the arrangement of furniture in their rooms. Yet when I asked if *feng-shui* was still practised I was met with rebuffs or denials of its existence. It had been driven underground in the Cultural Revolution and its practitioners had been persecuted or had fled to Taiwan or Hong Kong. Educated Chinese had no time for *feng-shui*, representing as it did the antithesis of the philosophy of scientific thought they were now encouraged to believe.

'How could it be,' scoffed my botanist friend Yao, 'that just because you bury your grandmother in a favourable *feng-shui* site on an auspicious day you will become prosperous? This is all *feng-shui* is, the blind following of unfounded superstition that has no base in either science or common sense. People's respect for it in the past has been purely materialistic. And as for the yin-yang principle,' Yao continued, 'you could apply that to anything. If you laugh it's yang. If you cry it's yin. Where does that get anyone?'

I eventually established what a powerful force *feng-shui* remained in the lives of the peasants, though no practitioner would speak to me directly. Instead I searched for its visible expression in the siting and layout of villages on the road, but it proved as illusive as the legendary ideal commune. Villages gave no hint of being built according to the specifications of the local geomancer, but appeared to have been governed by topography and defence. The requirements of *feng-shui* were frequently synonymous with practical considerations, whatever Yao and the pragmatists might suppose, and conformed with what a designer might propose as a matter of course: grave plots on well-drained slopes, and for the living the shelter of evergreen trees or hills from cold north winds, an entrance facing south and water flowing nearby. Was *feng-shui* a means of externalizing what the landscape planner knew by instinct? Or was the planner's analysis founded on awareness of the earth's vital energies, the existence of which he would probably deny?

Fields lined the road, fallow brown fields, each one a different shape and size. We slowed and swerved round a small procession encircling a village to ward off evil in the coming year. Its leader wore a dragon mask and a dozen behind him writhed and cavorted, bearing the scaly patchwork tail aloft on poles. Others waved flags, beat drums, clashed cymbals, let off firecrackers and brandished tridents and spears. Their stamping feet threw up clouds of dust like galloping horses' hoofs.

I had stayed in Guangzhou over Chinese New Year, or Spring Festival as it was properly called. As dusk fell on New Year's Eve the streets, for once, were almost deserted. The older neighbourhoods were built along alleys that twisted and intersected between grey brick and wood-panelled walls. The last of the shoppers were hurrying home, girls with new perms, a woman with a chicken hanging from a string. A man was finishing painting his door. Shops and street stalls were closed and shuttered, as if in the curfew of a city under siege. Firecrackers sputtered in ritual extravagance, their poppy petal fragments lying exhausted on the stones. The smell of gunpowder lingered in the air.

The sky was purple. Up on the roofs dark shaggy tufts of night-blooming cereus poked long cacti feelers down grey and white walls. Each door was framed by a welcoming trilogy of New Year mottoes, scarlet-lettered gold. Through open windows I saw families dressed in bright new clothes, gathered round feasts of goose or duck, their rooms fresh-papered, bright with cut-outs and New Year crafts, exploding with bowls of fragrant narcissus, and kumquat bushes baubled with fruit, and spreading peach trees, pink flowers on bare stems. The scent of flowers and roasted meat mingled with the spice-smell of incense on doorsteps. Offerings of fruit were laid out for the gods and spirit money set alight for the ancestors. Along the canal the multi-paned windows of balconied buildings gleamed in lozenges of winegum light. That night nobody would sleep.

New Year's Day brought well-groomed crowds buying biscuits and candy, being carried along pavements by the pull of the tide and being marshalled in buffeting queues. That people could look so ecstatically happy shuffling round a city on a cold wet day, posing for portraits in pavilions in parks, admiring flowers at the entrances of restaurants, merely with the memory of last night's meal and the promise of three days' holiday ahead was a measure of the hardship of their daily lives.

Towards Zhanjiang the grey villages turned pink, and the earth grew red and dry. It undulated in eroded folds supporting here a plantation of sisal or oil palm, there a hedge of screw pine. Beside the memory of New Year Guangzhou everything seemed poor and thin: the land, the men, the crops, the trees. Only the pigs were plump and pink, snouting for tubers in stony fields.

As dusk approached we reached Zhanjiang. Having spent ten days exploring Guangzhou, finding my feet on Chinese soil but in the city most affected by the outside world, atypical of China as a whole, I was looking forward to what I supposed was the real New China, the China of Mao. But I soon got over that idea. Totalitarian concepts displayed their all in a single blow, in wide empty streets flanked by large grey buildings and abbreviated trees, in wasted space that went so against the principles of the Chinese cultivator, and in the rosy posters of single-child families gazing faithfully into a sanitized future. My obligatory hotel for foreign guests stood in watchful dominion at the end of the street, as large and forbidding as every other building but fluttering with a row of little red flags.

Even within the few hotels permitted to outsiders there was one set of rules for 'foreign friends', quite another for ordinary Chinese. While Chinese could select the accommodation they preferred, Western tourists had to occupy the upper-grade rooms and pay more for the privilege than anyone else, whether foreign expert or student or high-ranking Chinese. More than usually irritated one night months later in Sichuan when the beds allocated to foreigners were full and I was left with no option but to cross a large city late in the evening to a yet more expensive establishment, I followed a Chinese who had arrived after I had – who had secured a bed for a quarter the price I would have been paying had I got in – down a corridor, round a corner, out into a courtyard, up some steps, right, then left, then left again into another building and a room containing one hundred and ten beds and seven televisions. At least eighty beds were still unoccupied; I would have been happy in any one.

But on arrival in Zhanjiang the hotel was half-empty. My room overlooked a barren quadrangle flanked on all sides by prison-like walls. Accommodation was spartan but adequate, a prototype for the fifty hotel rooms to come. A hard wooden bed with a folded quilt laid diagonally at its foot. A towel-covered pillow stuffed with dried leaves. A mosquito net hanging in a knot from a hoop; squashed mosquitoes on the whitewashed walls. A terrazzo floor and blue rubber shoes. A desk and chair, a bucket, a spittoon, a mirror, an ashtray, a fan (but no heater), a string for drying washing, some teacups, a thermos and an enamel washing bowl.

This hotel room spoke chapters about the customs of China: about Mao's goals of austerity, about the passion for learning, about the onus on hygiene and public frugality, and about the national addictions of smoking and tea. Folded bedding was a legacy of overcrowding where beds were in living rooms and visitors sat on them; quilts were displayed to show off their covers embroidered with dragons and peonies. Shoes were essential in a land plagued by snail fever, and still infested with unwashed floors: since the concept of floor equated with ground, it got spat on and littered but was rarely carpeted and never soaped clean. The placement of furniture at right angles to walls was a Confucian tradition of propriety and order; the casualness of Western arrangement was still offensive to most Chinese. The clumpy design – nothing old and therefore feudal, nothing elegant and therefore bourgeois, nothing comfortable and thereby sensual – presented an ideal of solid and disciplined utilitarianism to inspire thoughts and actions in a strictly circumscribed way.

Most of the visitors were men. Travelling on state business and unaccustomed to being away, they seemed strangely inhibited and lost. Whereas Westerners would truly inhabit a room, spreading out belongings, moving the furniture to suit their needs and treating the place as if it were home, the Chinese occupied the hotel gingerly and wondered how to fill their time. They hung over service desks, riffled through pictorial propaganda magazines, pored over papers in their glass-panelled stands, slopped along corridors with empty flasks, slumped on their beds or lounged on landings in front of TV. Their doors were ajar, no matter the temperature or the noise outside. Perhaps they felt lonely. Perhaps they wanted to demonstrate that nothing suspicious was happening within. Or perhaps it was purely to let out the smoke.

The noise was intolerable even with the door shut: voices reverberated through the open grille, water grumbled through pipes beside my bed, iron-clad footfalls sounded in the corridor and boisterous card games echoed from next door. Not until midnight was everything quiet. Then at four in the morning the litany recommenced: the getting up, packing bags and catching buses; the hooters, loudspeakers, radios, engines and New Year firecrackers, the loudest and meanest of all.

I was, after all, in a communist state. Much on my journey south from Guangzhou and in Guangzhou itself had hinted otherwise but the hotel staff in Zhanjiang and elsewhere made it plain they weren't there to serve their guests or solicit their custom, but to perform their duty laid down by the State. If my Chinese was inadequate that was my problem, not theirs. They came in without knocking, at seven in the morning before I was up. They thumped on the door when I was asleep, reminding me to check that it was properly locked. If I left it open while fetching hot water they would reprimand me for my casual attitude. When my key wouldn't turn the girl said cursorily, 'I can't open it,' and left me standing helpless in the corridor. Most often I couldn't get in at all because the girl with the keys was nowhere to be found. I would pace up and down and bash on doors till she appeared at the end of the corridor, walking slowly with those precise Chinese steps, with a stack of spittoons or a mop made of rags, the blues and olives of Chinese clothes.

After two dismal nights under damp musty quilts and two rain-filled days walking dour grey streets and living off rape and rice I was on the road and heading south. It was the greyest, mistiest, drizzliest day yet. On the six-hour journey down the Leizhou peninsula I saw little of the land beyond a shroud of trees and signs of greater poverty borne out by villages of mud and thatch and sweeps of barren, rolling land. At the tip of the peninsula I boarded a tanker for the two-hour crossing to the city of Haikou in the north of Hainan Island.

I went to Hainan to exchange the cold weather that was harassing the mainland for the tropical beaches of the island's south coast. But apart from Haikou, Hainan Island was officially still closed, the authorities informed me smiling over cups of tea. They could, however, offer me a car and a private driver for £30 a day with a special endorsement on my alien's permit which they would arrange. The bus station refused to sell me a ticket on an ordinary bus since I hadn't a permit to visit the south, but in the end I discovered a mini-bus company that wasn't concerned about regulations just so long as I paid the fare.

As we travelled south along the island's east coast the increasing heat was signalled by a succession of tropical crops. Fallow fields gave way to pineapple and pepper. Low folds rose to rubber-clad hills which in turn relaxed to a flatter geometry of rich black earth, where matt-black buffaloes and basalt-built villages shimmered in a silver haze, and beds of young rice pushed up pale thin spears the colour of primroses in bud. An hour further south the seedling rice was being planted out in snail-trail rows, and blue-shirted peasants in conical hats were bent double over sky-filled fields.

Across the creek from the small port of Sanya where women in black sarongs dried fish on the quay, the guest-house occupied its own private world. Walled in from outside were rooms off verandahs in the herringbone shade of coconut palms, patronized by high-grade cadres (party officials) and foreign students on holiday from northern towns. During the Cultural Revolution the whole compound had been the personal domain of Mao's widow Jiang Qing. She now paid the price for her past excess in a prison on the north-east outskirts of Beijing where she was still better off than most other Chinese.

Through a tousled fringe of casuarinas a sickle of white coral sand sliced the waves of the grey-green sea. Cadres came in bands and stood at the tide mark in their high-buttoned suits. They gazed at the sea, turned back to their comrades, gesticulated, passed platitudes and went away. The foreigners stretched out on the sharp white sand and reddened their limbs under burning clouds. But the local villagers embraced the sea, caught fish from sewn boats, plucked winkles from coral flats and dug for cockles in the low-tide strand. All knees and straw hats, they hunkered on the shore, moving without rising like a colony of crabs.

Between the village and the guest-house was a six-foot wall and as wide a gulf of unequal privilege as I would find anywhere in the land. The cadres in the guest-house ate six-dish banquets at every meal, snake and octopus, fish and crab, duck egg and aubergine, chicken and prawn, while they of the village ate plain boiled rice. The guest-house was walled, each room had its key, but in the village there was little to steal. A gentle place of palm-thatched mud huts its rhythm was determined by the canopy of palms casting shifting rosettes of shade upon the sand. The absence of walls denoted trust; fruit hung for the taking from the trees. Were it not for the hats, the Asiatic faces and the New Year couplets framing the doors it might have been Haiti rather than China. There was the same vegetation, the same sun-scorched hills, the same slow succour of life made rich by colour and warmth and the fruits of land and sea. I touched the plants for I knew their feel, stored up heat against the cold to come; I sniffed the sea and listened to the slop of the waves on the beach, for soon I would be far from all these things.

After three more days of rickety bus rides on rickety roads I arrived in Nanning, capital of the province of Guangxi. Ten miles from its boundary it signalled its proximity with wider roads and smoking stacks and acres of wasted land. Then came factories, power lines and bus queues, and raw new buildings among the vegetable fields. Grey block after waste plot after telegraph pole after heap of stone after dust track after mat shack. People clustered round food stalls and scavenged for rubbish in municipal heaps. But the centre of Nanning expressed a colourful enterprise and its streets were blotted by inky trees.

In Nanning it was winter, and had been raining for a month. The damp had penetrated people's quilts so they dreaded going to bed and drank *mao tai*, a vodka-like spirit, to sleep, but still lay rigid, unable to get warm. Yet I, in passage, enjoyed the rain, the polished streets, the puddled reflections of buildings and bicycles, the dripping trees shiny like newly washed bottles, the plastic rain capes in ravishing pastels – pink and blue and aquamarine – glistening like opals in the underwater wet of silver and grey. I put up my hood and paddled unnoticed to the big free market selling fluorescent shoes, and filmy scarves like fairies' wings, and striped string bags and coats and ribbons and bags and buttons and socks that defied rainbows. And string and sacks and saws and saddles and fishing nets. And steamed rice wrapped in banana leaves, and gongs and cymbals and coins and jade bangles and salted vegetables in plastic bowls. And Chinese chopping-boards that were slices of tree, and eggs and meat and fish and fruit, and dogs and chickens and ducks and monkeys and doves and turtles and owls and lizards and snakes and cats and pangolins. And after a month the sun came out, and the breeze blew the leaves in a shower from the trees and a man stood alone on the roof of the tallest building and faced the sun. Spring had come to Nanning.

2

At Home with Xiuying

There was a knock on the door of my room. A girl stood in the corridor, her hair clamped in bunches, apprehension in her eyes.

Her words tumbled out in a stream. 'I'm sorry to disturb you – I'm translating a short story from a magazine but it has words and expressions that aren't in my dictionary. I work in the university library – look, here's my identification card.' She extracted the card from its scarlet holder and held it forward for me to see. 'Your name was in the hotel register, but they tried to prevent me from coming to find you. "What do you want with a foreigner?" they asked. So I told them how I'd been searching for help, and that you were the only chance I had. I was desperate, you see.'

'Come in,' I said. We sat side by side on the edge of my bed. She placed a folder on her lap, a collection of stories from *Asian Magazine*, mimeographed by a friend in Beijing. She introduced herself as Yen Xiuying. (Yen is the surname; Xiuying is pronounced 'Shyooying'.)

'This is the only translation material I have.' She flounced through the pages of smudged grey type and pursed her lips. 'Since the Cultural Revolution no new literature has emerged in China except works analysing the mistakes of the ultra-left policies. The rest of the world must be full of books, but we can't get good ones here. When my parents' books were seized and burnt I was still a young child.' The most recent campaign was in autumn 1983 when, in a renewed drive to rid China of 'spiritual pollution', in other words its corrupting Western and feudal influence, libraries and bookshops were closed and searched for romances and other counter-revolutionary material. Western dress, Western disco and Western habits – short skirts, moustaches and writers describing human problems – were similarly outlawed in a temporary Maoist comeback.

32

'There were some reasonable paperbacks in the hotel bookshops in Guangzhou,' I recalled. 'Though I don't suppose they would allow you in to buy them?'

'No,' she agreed. 'They won't let us in. They think we'll do some mischief.'

'What sort of mischief?'

'We might disturb the foreign guests. Some Chinese would ask them for foreign currency or exchange certificates.' Foreign exchange certificates were the currency in which visitors were supposed to deal. Most travellers swapped them at a growing premium into people's money, or renminbi. 'They think we will dirty the sofas and carpets and throw cigarette ends on the floor,' she continued. Then she came to the real point. 'There are girls who make money by sleeping with foreigners.' This revelation was later supported by a New Zealander who'd caught gonorrhoea from just such a girl.

I was surprised and attracted by Xiuying's frankness. I was surprised she had the courage to mention sex at all; in their legendary prudishness, unmarried girls were supposed not to know such a thing existed. It was not that they were told that sex was bad, but that they weren't told anything at all. But these revelations came later. We spent the first two hours of our acquaintanceship going through the text of her translation, a story about a young Indian immigrant in Kuala Lumpur and his difficulty getting into university with its small quota for non-nationals. The story was published in 1962.

Not only did Xiuying want to understand the precise meaning of every word and phrase in her text – no small task in itself since it contained expressions in Malay, the names of Hindu festivals, references to archaic examination systems and words like burger, which took drawings and ten minutes of cultural background to explain because she wanted to be quite sure – she also wanted to know the underlying point of the story. Each time she understood something new she would smile and look pleased. 'You are my saviour!' she exclaimed. But when she asked me to elaborate on the Malay school curriculum, and why Chandra got angry when he failed to get a place, my explanations were less satisfactory.

'If his results weren't good enough why should he have a place?' she sniffed.

33

'His results were reasonable but competition was high and places for immigrants too few.'

Chandra's teacher had advised him to resit the entrance exam, to which Chandra's reaction was to curse the teacher. This was quite beyond Xiuying.

'He's just lazy,' she repeated.

'Not necessarily,' I told her. 'The point of the story is that the system was unfair.'

'But he wasn't good enough to get in,' she insisted. She had taken exception to Chandra, I could tell, to his disrespect and lack of application. But the principal source of her indignation was that however small Chandra's chances were they were very much higher than her own had been. Yen Xiuying was brought up in the knowledge that only three in every hundred pupils would have access to further education and for that they had to work with their whole heart and soul in a full-time frenzy of dedication. Some who failed committed suicide, because learning, after rice, had for two thousand years been the most important thing in life, the ladder to success. She had no sympathy for Chandra.

Only a bold and determined Chinese would have had the gumption to enter a large hotel and knock on a foreigner's door. Only a peasant or something of a rebel would dispense with formality and ask without preamble what she wanted to know. I respected her for it and already we got on well.

'Are you married?' she enquired.

'No, I'm not married.'

'Do you not believe in marriage?'

'I do, but not necessarily for myself. I know it's different for you.'

'In China almost everyone marries. Even blind people, deaf people. It is only those with a physical deformity whom nobody wants. Like myself.'

She touched her face. A slate-grey birthmark covered the entire left side. It was the first thing that had hit me when I opened the door, but having talked with her and warmed to her it was her sincerity and vitality I noticed now, and her slanting eyes and peach-smooth skin, each feature in perfect proportion to the rest. Her birthmark no longer registered.

The anti-beauty cult continued to be fostered by the communist regime but Xiuying wanted none of it. In official magazines like

Women of China peasant girls and plain-faced workers posed for the photographer in stark unflattering light. Mao's idolization of the robust, bronzed peasant girl fell flat among the intellectual classes, obsessed with slim figures and good looks. Pale skin meant status when not attached to foreigners, and remained a major hallmark of beauty.

'You have a very pretty face,' I told Xiuying. 'Even if you hadn't, someone would want to marry you for what you are.'

'No,' she countered. 'Men want a beautiful woman whom they can show off to others. But I don't care!' she continued defiantly. 'I won't get married. I will absorb myself in my work.'

'Tell me about your library.'

'I will tell you how I come to be working there. When I left school I was sent to the countryside for a year, like everyone else. We all hated it. I was fortunate in being let off field labour to teach English to the village children. After that I studied English at the university. My teachers were all Chinese, so my English has many mistakes,' she added apologetically. I denied this, as I was meant to. Xiuying was staring straight ahead, at the whitewashed wall. 'I wanted to become an English teacher. My academic level was good enough, but the cadres in my department said I couldn't be a teacher because of my appearance.'

'They actually said that in your presence?'

'They said my birthmark was unattractive. They said they were doing me a favour by giving me a position in the library. Would people call me names in England?'

'Not like that. A few in the street might say unkind things.'

'I get that here too.'

'And the library?'

Had I asked Xiuying if she liked her work eight, or even five years earlier she would have replied: 'It is the job my country needs me to do.' She would not have dared admit that one job was preferable to another. Now she replied: 'It's tedious. The people I work with are uninteresting, which is why I put all my efforts into translation. While the others in my dormitory sit and gossip in the evenings I translate stories so that others should be able to read them too.'

'What do the other girls think of that?'

'They find me aloof because I don't join in. But I dislike their gossip. It's endless, malicious, all about who said what and what went on in their colleagues' families.' The sexes rarely mixed. While the boys played games and practised on their instruments, the girls knitted sweaters and talked. Each of their victims was dissected in detail, her character, her behaviour but especially her looks. A girl was 'fat' if her cheeks were round or if she was fatter than another who was thin.

The *Asian Magazine* had its limitations and Xiuying needed stories to translate. I couldn't think of anything offhand. She once met an American who had sent her copies of the *Reader's Digest*. 'But then he stopped sending them,' she pouted. 'I don't know why he stopped.'

Next day it was raining. I caught a bus out through the suburbs to the university to meet Xiuying. Slips of teenage girls were commandeering the passengers, screeching with what authority their positions could muster: 'Buy your tickets! Buy your tickets! Who hasn't bought a ticket? There's a foreign guest on board; mind you don't crush her!' It was up to these conductresses, sitting vigilant in control of the doors, to decide if and when they should be opened to allow yet more people to heave and muscle their way inside. Marooned in the centre of the standing passengers I could see little of the city through which we passed.

The library was an imposing building approached through a gateway and a garden limp with last year's leaves. Marx, Engels, Lenin and Stalin stared down from dark frames across a long empty hall: they were portrayed as men intent upon a purpose, as men who would not hesitate to mow down anything that got in their way. I climbed a broad staircase to the upper floors. One room held a card-index filing system which a handful of students was leafing through; another a counter and a queue of borrowers filling in forms. A third was a reading room of papers and periodicals, all apparently different and all out of date. I glanced at a few of the fifteen hundred titles: *Stomatology, Tianjin Journal of Oncology, The Chinese Journal of Otorhinolaryngology, Microcomputer Applications, Oil Geophysical Prospection* and, one of the few semi-scientific publications, *Edible Fungi*. Nothing was frivolous; the arts and humanities were barely touched upon; science was god.

I passed a locked room on the first-floor landing marked 'Exspozicio Esperantajo', a reminder of what a few Chinese still held as the world language of the future, and entered the final hall where for the first time I saw books. They were not displayed on shelves about the room, but glimpsed through a hatch with a coterie of peasants on guard. A book must be requested, everything noted down. If you had no knowledge of a book's existence, why should you wish to borrow it?

The reading room was large and silent, with grape-green curtains knotted at the hems and sieving the light from church-high windows. Students entered its sanctity on tiptoe, hung their bags on the backs of chairs, sat at the tables in padded coats and immersed themselves in books. In the hallowed, crypt-cold air of reverence, no one spoke. No one noticed the presence of an outsider. No one paused in his communion with words to gaze about idly, to see who'd come in or to look through the window. So much scholarship: a fever of sacred study. Learning for the sake of learning, learning for the sake of forgetting, escaping reality, obliterating the cold.

Next day was Sunday and Xiuying was going home. During the week she lived at the university, loath to waste an hour each day travelling to and fro. 'You must come and visit my family,' she stated firmly. 'My mother will cook for you.'

'Won't she be afraid to have a foreigner in the house?' During the ten years of the Cultural Revolution communication between Chinese and foreigners was banned. Even now invitations were rare.

'She will be pleased to welcome you. It is only other people who may think it strange.'

There was more involved than prohibition. I remembered hearing of a family in Hong Kong who had an English girl to stay in their home, their daughter's best friend. In any other circumstances, they said later, they would never invite a foreigner to the house, because of the disparity of manners and views.

'Be sure to come as you promised,' said Xiuying.

Her house was in the old city quarter, gentle in its welcome of mellowing brickwork and the texture of hand-made tiles. I climbed a staircase to a first-floor courtyard awash with wet laundry. Women were scrubbing at a tap in the wall and cleaning vegetables for the five o'clock meal. In the centre of the courtyard a light-well afforded views of similar activity below.

Xiuying was there to meet me, clapping her hands with pleasure.

'How brave of you to come here all on your own,' she laughed, leading me to the kitchen to meet her mother. Her father worked three hundred miles away.

Blackened by the cooking fires of the three families who shared it, the walls dissolved into cave-like gloom. Woks and cleavers glimmered in steam-billowed light. Sieves and baskets wove a bamboo tapestry. An antique table stood dusty in the corner, supporting jars of pickled cabbage and bags of coal. Rice bubbled in cooking pots and aproned ladies gave welcoming beams.

'It's a terrible, dirty place,' said Xiuying, who, had I shown her a picture of a model Western kitchen in a women's magazine, all sparkling units and hygienic surfaces, would have been likely to mistake it for a chemical laboratory. She bore me away before I noticed any more, across the courtyard to her parents' quarters, one of several small rooms on the opposite side. Shabby wooden furniture elbowed for space, cupboard against wardrobe, table concealing foodsafe, crowded by objects in casual disarray. Through a curtained partition was a windowless cell barely larger than its bed where her parents slept. Xiuying apologized again.

'My mother wishes she could talk to you, but she doesn't know English.' With that distinctive Chinese gesture she pointed towards her mother with her chin. Standing smiling in the doorway with her short, swept-back hair pinned down by clips, her baggy cotton trousers, blue apron and sleeve guards, she looked the epitome of Chinese motherhood, warm-hearted, hard-working, with an unassuming dignity born of discipline and restraint. Brought up in an era when women's expectations were much less grand, she seemed placid and accepting, finding fulfilment in the achievements of her family.

'Please tell her I would have loved to talk to her too.' What couldn't Xiuying's mother have told about her privileged childhood, her marriage at fifteen to a man she didn't know and the political swings since the communists came to power? Looking at her now in this humble room it was hard to imagine the teenage girl coiling her hair with lacquer and pins, whitening her face and rouging her cheeks, dressing in embroidered satin gowns, embarking on a marriage at best of servitude, at worst a nightmare of frivolity and tedium, of gambling and gossiping, mahjong and opium and managing servants, sharing her husband with whores and concubines (the Western system of getting rid of a woman before taking on another was considered impractical), a slave in her turn to husband and mother-in-law, to VD and sex (for which all 'virtuous' women expressed repugnance), and the soul-eroding niceties of social propriety. Whereas men, who were yang, were seen as positive, fiery, living and moving, women were yin: dark, soft, wet, cold, still, negative and deadly. Women's ignorance was their virtue.

For Xiuying's grandmother life had meant virtual imprisonment in the house where her descendants now occupied two small rooms. When male visitors called she had remained in retirement, and whereas her daughters had normal or 'big feet', her own had been bound.

It was my turn to be shocked. I had not as yet seen any bound feet, the south being a relatively progressive part of China.

'Did you ever see her feet unbound?'

'Yes,' replied Xiuying sadly. 'It was terrible; her toes were all compressed.' She scrunched up her hand to demonstrate the deformation, arching her knuckles and pressing her fingers against her palm. 'The skin of her feet was white and unhealthy, for the bandages stayed on all the time.'

'How did your grandmother feel about it?'

'When she was five years old and her mother and grandmother began to bind them she screamed and screamed. But they *forced* her. Her feet hurt for years, though by the time I knew her she had learnt to accept it. They say they did it because men at that time found small feet attractive, and to prevent their wives from leaving the house.'

In the thirty-five years since 1949 the lives of Chinese women had changed more radically than in the previous twenty-five centuries. Their emancipation, however incomplete, was possibly the greatest of the communists' achievements. The 1950 Marriage Law gave women the freedom to marry whom they chose, and in theory to divorce. There was a subsequent ban on child betrothal, the sale of women, female infanticide, prostitution, polygamy and concubinage, all common practice and long condemned by Western missionaries. Women were given 56 days' paid maternity leave, free nurseries and kindergartens where available and the right to equal pay for equal work. In 1953 a network of Women's Federations was set up to tackle resistance to this radical change through the combined re-education of women and men. The Women's Federations stressed female equality, encouraged men to help in household tasks and women to exercise their rights. They later concentrated on birth control and household hygiene before being disbanded in 1978.

This was the theory. But evidence that equality was still far from universal was explicit all around, in the elderly woman staggering on to a bus weighed down by baskets slung from a shoulder pole to grab the last seat so her empty-handed husband could sit down. It was explicit in the men who beat their wives, who blamed them for the birth of a female child and refused to help at home. It was explicit after the fall of the so-called Gang of Four when many men said: 'See what happens when a woman gets in power!' It was explicit in the resurfacing of prostitution, of female infanticide and the sale of girl children, proof of which was to be found on court-house notice boards, in the current campaign against infanticide and in the woman who tried to sell me her child. The equality of post-Liberation women may not have been as real as it sometimes seemed.

Emancipation held different meanings depending on who you were. In as much as they thought of it at all, to Xiuying's mother's generation liberation might signify an inside tap and toilet, pork for dinner and the right to stay at home. To Xiuying and her friends it meant the right to read, to do satisfying work, to have decent housing and fashionable clothes, most of all, perhaps, to love whom they chose.

Xiuying seemed untouched by the tyranny of her past. While her parents' generation still remembered the days before the revolution, Xiuying could only compare the present with what it might and ought to have been, and invest all her hopes in the years to come. For the present she escaped the hardship of reality in a personal intensity of love and work and family and friends. She helped her younger brother with his English. She sorrowed for her mother who had cataracts, the only effective medicine for which, according to the doctor, was unavailable in China. Would it be too much to ask me to buy some in Hong Kong? While I was about it, Xiuying added quickly, her elder sister had a problem too; having been married for two years with no sign of pregnancy she was assailed by feelings of worthlessness and her husband's threats to leave her.

While her mother cooked our meal on the small coal stove Xiuying gave me fruit, a costly commodity bought only for guests or on special occasions. A meal was the greatest of Chinese gifts, and etiquette prevented any skimping of food. There were bowls of spiced spinach, of stir-fried egg, of tomatoes with sugar, of clams so briefly boiled they were still alive, a banquet by comparison with my usual meals. Seated as honoured guest in the only chair, I ate of each while Xiuying, on a stool, picked daintily at some spinach and her mother and sister – who, I imagine, got no share of this feast – hovered in the background by the door.

'Eat, eat!' cajoled Xiuying's mother. 'Maybe the food is not to your liking that you don't eat more?' I ate, and assured her that it was good.

After the meal Xiuying led me to her bedroom, a world away at the end of a passage. Its floorboards creaked as we squeezed past eight bunk beds pushed up against the wall.

'What are the bunks for?'

'This is a hotel.'

'A hotel?' I had assumed all hotels to be state-run megaliths of terrazzo and orthodoxy. What we were passing was a sleazy doss-house of the Indian kind. Between each pair of bunks a door in a partition wall opened into a compartment containing five or six bedsteads with a mat for a mattress and a mug and washing bowl half-hidden under each. Voices mingled in a smoky half-light and sunflower-seed shells were scattered on the floor. Had it not been Xiuying's grandmother's old home it seemed the kind of place that might once have been an opium den, suggestive of ghosts and all the desolation addiction implied.

The final door opened on to the room Xiuying shared with her younger sister and brother. Its walls swept up to a scaffolding of rafters and a scaly incline of overlapping tiles. Undiluted sounds of hooters and shouting and undiluted smells of frying chilli came through the windows from the street. A family of six sharing two small rooms, I thought, chastened by the memory of my sole use of five.

'Compared to the disturbance at night this is nothing,' observed

41

Xiuying dryly. 'Each night there are different people in the hotel. Every night there is noise!' The six-foot partition wall that divided her room from the row of dens did little to muffle the heated discussions, the stacking of trunks, the crying of infants and the banging of doors. Though few buses or trains left before dawn, people were sometimes so anxious lest they miss their transport that they got up as early as midnight. 'Sometimes I ask them to make less noise, and sometimes they do, but never very much. Even now they are gossiping about you, wondering what business a foreigner has here. There will be plenty of talk,' she said. New customers were claiming the bunks in the corridor. For eight jiao a night, about twenty-five pence, a Chinese could sleep in a family home whereas I, as a foreigner, was paying five times that in a large and anonymous state hotel.

I thought how intolerable it would be living as Xiuying did in the middle of a hotel, passing beds full of strangers to reach the kitchen or your parents' room or the loo down the street, sharing a room at twenty-two with a brother and sister, with noise all evening and half the night. Even Xiuying found it tiresome, preferring the university to the absence of sanctuary at home. Not every Chinese enjoyed noise. Its traditional function of frightening spirits and its un-realized modern one of drowning despair were irrelevant when salvation lay in academic work.

We sat in one corner on Xiuying's bed. My heels touched the front of a cardboard box in which her belongings were stored. The walls were lined with a skin of white paper which had yellowed with time and puckered as it dried like the parchment brow of an aged sage. Against this background Xiuying's brother's bicycle, bound in the bandages of its brown paper wrappings, rested on its stand in the centre of the floor. Rather less prestigious was a small bamboo chair. It was tucked in a corner gathering dust, slotted and wedged without any nails. I admired it. It glowed deep gold with age and use, smooth but angular, very Chinese.

'I think it's awful. The peasants make them.' She said this not with pride but scorn. 'You can take it with you.'

I would have, had I been able to carry it.

Xiuying's dislike of anything made by hand and her respect for machines was our greatest clash of views.

'Machines displace people! Millions in England are out of work

42

because so much is automated. The same will happen here in China,' I said.

And as with the kitchen, the beautiful baskets of woven bamboo and the hand-made chair, so with my clothes.

'Why do you wear those clothes?' she demanded. I had experienced the same censure in India. 'You foreigners always wear such cheap, baggy, old-fashioned clothes. You dress like the peasants!'

'We need comfortable, practical clothes for travelling,' I said in defence. To me this seemed logical, but the Chinese only went out in their best. Many travellers dressed quietly so as not to stand out. They thought it distasteful to show wealth in a country where people were poor. Chinese who had been overseas had no such sensitivity, returning to their villages with expensive watches and smart Western clothes, flaunting their status and deriding their 'backward' friends.

Xiuying was not impressed. 'But your shirt! It's so rough!' The cotton was handwoven. 'And your trousers; only workers wear corduroy!' That I hadn't realized. But the diatribe was not yet over. 'Your scarf! Do you really like it?'

'Don't you?'

'No.'

But at least I washed my clothes by hand, with a bar of hard soap on a slab in the washroom, or when there was one on the floor of the shower. Xiuying was surprised and fractionally mollified: 'I didn't think foreigners ever washed clothes themselves.'

Last time we met Xiuying had been wearing the standard Chinese trousers and jacket with lapels similar to those popular in Britain in the fifties. I told her so.

'You think we're backward!' she accused me, blushing. Such clothes were the height of fashion in China, and Xiuying applied herself to the ritual of being modern and young. 'But we think you're backward too!'

'In what way?'

'Your clothes!' Ever afterwards in China I was conscious of a universal approbation of my clothes.

This time Xiuying wore a shiny top the colour of tomato soup and sky-blue tracksuit trousers, both stretch synthetic. I couldn't really blame her; her taste for all that was bright and new as beautiful and her abhorrence for all that was natural and old as ugly was a response to prevailing Chinese attitudes just as my preferences were a product of mine. It was a logical outcome of a socialist revolution to make everyone dress down to the practical conformity of the industrial worker – sombre colours, plain styles and loose cuts that concealed the form. Xiuying's taste in clothes was a reaction against compulsion, against rationed cotton (five metres per person per year), against the shabby old clothes that went in and out of trunks, preserved just in case. In the mid-fifties and again in the early sixties stronger colours and styles had been permissible for a while, only to be crushed by the Great Leap Forward and the Cultural Revolution. In 1984 they were blossoming once again, along with greater choice and exposure to the West.

'What do your cadres think of the way you dress?' I asked.

'I have to be careful to avoid being criticized – I wouldn't wear these things at work. The more left-wing cadres believe fashionable and colourful clothes denote a low political level and an unwillingness to make sacrifices for higher ideals. To identify with the workers one must wear loose blue jackets and trousers. Poof!' said Xiuying.

Her wardrobe was limited. Two-thirds of her salary went on food at the university canteen ('Good food?' 'No, it's awful'), and the remainder she tried to save. She had saved for a year to buy her bicycle and now she was saving for a watch. 'They cost a hundred yuan,' she said wistfully, 'but my daily routine is programmed to precise times. Without a watch I sit about waiting.' When three months later I met a man whose watch cost a pound from a man in the street I thought of Xiuying and groaned in sympathy. Prices in China were becoming more stable, necessities having been held very low and 'luxuries', like watches, ridiculously high. Xiuying's greatest pride was a summer dress sent by a friend in Taiwan, a short-sleeved sheath of shimmery cream nylon adrift with pleats and frills, the envy of her friends and ghastly beyond words. She held it up against herself. Did I like it? I didn't, I told her.

She wore it dancing in the summer. 'We dance the waltz to a tune called "The Blue Danube".' Her eyes were unfocused, remembering hot nights when she danced her sadness away.

'Don't your parents object?'

'They are less puritanical than most.'

The memory of dancing reminded her of men. At twenty-two she

44

was nearing the age when she'd be expected to find a husband. Once again I told her that her birthmark was not the obstacle she thought it to be.

'People always say that. My friends say I'd be beautiful were it not for the mark. They say these things to comfort me, but I don't want their pity. Maybe someone will want me for my body?' she mused. 'My body is better than my face.'

She had a neat compact figure, characteristically Chinese in its rounded bottom and ill-defined waist, its short sturdy legs and diminished breasts. I have a photo of Xiuying taken by her room-mate, posed between the library and a potted Acalypha with leaves the colour of raw steak. She wears a turquoise dress, long black socks and plastic sandals. Her head is tilted in self-conscious imitation of a Western magazine, with one hand smoothing the back of her hair.

'I thought someone wanted to marry you?' I reminded her. She had alluded to it the day before.

She paused and looked down at the floor. 'There was a man, but I refused him. He was forty and married with children. He went to America and was going to get divorced. We wrote to each other and planned that I should join him. But in the end I decided not to.' The temptation for Xiuying must have been enormous. Many Chinese would not be so particular given the chance of trading communism for Western living standards. At one time a thousand illegal immigrants were entering Hong Kong each day.

'Do girls here have boyfriends before they are married?' I asked.

'Oh no! It wasn't like that.' She took my question personally. 'If a girl sleeps with a boy before they are married he tends to lose respect for her and marries someone else. There are boys who try and talk girls into it, but I think it's better not. If on or before your wedding night a boy discovers you aren't a virgin he could call the whole thing off, leaving you to carry the disgrace.'

'What about affairs after marriage?'

'It happens, though not often.'

'Is there a punishment for adultery?'

'There is always the fear that someone will find out. If you're caught you'll be criticized and looked down on by your neighbours for the rest of your life. If you persist one or both of you may be expelled from the unit and sent to a labour camp for two or three

45

years.' Isolation was greater punishment even than shame, and most people would be too scared to get into the situation in the first place.

'Does it happen in England?' she asked.

'I would guess that well under half the married people in England had always been faithful to their partners.'

'But aren't such people cut off by society?'

'There is gossip, but it soon dies down. Adultery is so common.'

'Do you think it's right?'

'I think like you.'

But for the evidence of children there was no outward sign that sex existed in China at all: the absence of visible sexual stimuli, the formless clothes (a girl with loose hair or top button undone was not a nice girl), the non-sensual lifestyle, the prim public façade and the lack of any outward show of affection lead most visitors to presume the Chinese are repressed. One had to go to Hong Kong or Taiwan to find pornography (though there was a growing black market in China itself), or back in history to classical literature like *The Golden Lotus*, or to the 1930s when sexual apparatus was sold in the street, or to 1949 when Shanghai was home to 80,000 whores, and VD and snail's disease between them afflicted a quarter of the population, to realize that the Chinese were as physically motivated as anybody anywhere. And English friends who'd been involved with Chinese had seen that inscrutable Oriental mask dissolve into passion, into petulance, joy and rage.

So it was not wholly fair of Xiuying when she asked: 'Why is it that in the West so much emphasis is laid on sex? My friends and I are full of admiration for your way of life, your freedom, your education and your modern outlook; the only thing we don't understand about you is your attitude to sex.'

I explained in so far as I could, touching, finally, upon homosexuality to see what her reaction would be.

'I never heard of such a thing!' Xiuying exclaimed. 'The Chinese don't do that!' Even those Chinese who admitted its existence wrote it off as a bourgeois, Western conceit.

'I know that they do,' I replied. 'Look into your literature. Look at Hong Kong. It exists in every society. Because it's illegal and a punishable offence no one would admit to having such feelings and you might never learn of it.' An American homosexual living in Beijing believed China abounded in latent gays who dared not come out; convicted people were sent to prison and allegedly sometimes shot.

Xiuying was chastened: for a moment I had silenced her. Then she said: 'I have *never* discussed such things before, and would never do so among my friends.' She nevertheless found the subject one of compelling fascination, from which she returned reluctantly to the question of her marriage, the matter that worried her most of all. 'There was another man who wanted to marry me,' she confided, 'a young doctor who trained in Shanghai. I didn't love him enough so I turned him down, though I said I hoped we would remain good friends. We have done, and I'm glad. Men often become bitter towards girls who refuse them. But he wasn't strong enough to make a good husband, and our children would not have been sturdy.'

'What does a Chinese girl look for in a marriage partner?' I asked.

Her eyes twinkled. What girls used to want was Party members, but now things had changed. 'A tall handsome man with a good salary, non-drinker, non-smoker, with a university education, a similar class background, relatives abroad, a capacity for getting things done through the back door and no living parents to take care of. He must of course obey his wife,' she added facetiously.

She seemed to be considering something. 'I love my teacher.'

'Your former English teacher?'

'He's thirty-five. Do you think that's too old?'

I mentioned friends of mine in England, a couple with fifty years' difference in their ages. She gasped.

'Does he love you?' I asked.

'Yes, but he's married. He and his wife don't get on well; she's uneducated and their marriage was arranged.' I detected a slight pomposity in her tone. 'I feel sorry for her,' she said.

'But what can you do? He can't get divorced.'

Divorce was seen as socially destabilizing and as somehow immoral, a loss of face to both divorcee and Party. 'People can get divorced only when there's absolutely no chance of reconciliation. Couples are usually told by a committee to go home and work at their marriage,' she said.

Her situation was hopeless. No wonder the confusion. No wonder she threw herself into her work.

'Do you see him a lot?'

47

'I could see him every day if I wished, but I try and keep away. After a while it gets too much and I seek him out.'

Something she had said earlier made me imagine she would avoid all physical contact with a man. 'Don't you ever feel like putting your arms round him?'

'Of course, and I do. We hug and kiss, but that's all.'

'Do you wish you could sleep with him?' The impertinence of my questions left her unmoved, perhaps because of what she was, perhaps because I answered her similarly forthright queries with equal frankness. In other circumstances such directness would have been excruciatingly bad-mannered.

'Sometimes I do,' she replied. 'When I feel like that I try and concentrate on my work instead.' The Party published a booklet on the sublimation of the sexual urge: cold water, loose underclothes, vigorous exercise and plenty of Marx and Mao. Sexual energy wasn't seen as a governing force in human behaviour, but as something elastic which the individual could learn to manipulate. Romantic love was similarly discouraged as a self-indulgent bourgeois conceit; it was spontaneous, it was private, it dissipated energy that could be harnessed elsewhere. 'If I slept with him I'd be ostracized,' she said.

'Do any of your friends sleep with men?'

'A few do. But we have nowhere to go.' Her friends lived at home or in dormitories; parks were deliberately played down. It was easier in the countryside, where girls were known to be more permissive, for they could always go out to the fields. 'What happens in England if an unmarried girl gets pregnant?' In China such a girl might be exiled to a labour camp, though many became pregnant before marriage.

'She can have an abortion,' I said. 'Most girls use some form of birth control and don't get pregnant. Some choose to have their babies and bring them up on their own.'

'And they are not outcasted?' She gazed at me, open-eyed.

'Not any more.'

'It would be difficult for us to get contraceptives; people would talk.'

It seemed to me that in spite of Xiuying's claim to morality, what prevented her, and others, from sleeping with men was the risk of pregnancy, the difficulty of marrying someone else later and the fear of lifelong alienation rather than a belief that extra-marital sex was intrinsically wrong. It was shame not guilt that would be hard to bear, shame that would disgrace both herself and her family, shame from which there was no escape, no anonymous flight to another town. Shame was more potent even than law. Given such constraints many Westerners would be celibate too.

'What do you think?' Xiuying asked me. 'Should I develop my feelings for this man?' Their affair was something the Chinese called 'flowers in the mirror and the moon in water' – an illusion. Xiuying was in love with love.

'In the circumstances it might be easier to avoid him, unless you can alter your relationship to one of ordinary friendship.'

She sighed and looked away. In profile her birthmark covered her face.

'Will you write to me?'

I said I would.

'We have loved each other for two years. I have never told anyone before.'

'There was no one you could tell. You were right to keep it secret.' Her happiness and sorrow must be borne alone. Had anyone noticed that Xiuying and her teacher were spending too long in each other's company and reported them to a cadre there would have been public disgrace.

'What are your reasons for not getting married?' she asked me.

'I travel a lot, I enjoy my work and I'm not afraid of being alone. But if I found someone and believed it would work, then I might.'

I was surprised when she said, 'My best friend thinks just like you.'

'Would you consider marrying a Westerner?' I asked her.

'Oh no!' she said, shocked. 'I would only marry a Chinese.'

'But why?' I insisted. 'What would prevent you?'

'He would be unfaithful to me,' she replied without hesitation, but beneath her condemnation I sensed deeper taboos. 'Surely you wouldn't marry a Chinese? Would you?'

'I would marry a Chinese or an African as soon as I would an Englishman. What matters is attitude and compatibility.'

Chinese distaste for miscegenation stemmed from long insularity, a sense of superiority and a dislike of foreign habits, and although

49

marriage to foreigners had been officially permissible since 1979 it was still generally disapproved.

'What about Hassan and Marguerite?' I asked Xiuying. Hassan was Iraqi and Marguerite a French girl, both studying Chinese in Nanjing. Xiuying had met them when she came to the hotel to look for me. 'They come from different countries with different religions and cultures. Marguerite is more than ten years older than Hassan.'

She avoided the question. 'She is beautiful, don't you think so? I told him his wife was beautiful.'

'They aren't married.'

'Oh!' She was deeply shocked, as if knowing such things went on in the West was one thing, but confronting them another matter entirely. 'But they were sleeping in the same room!'

'They have been together for five years, and so far as I can tell have a close and loving relationship. Surely not all married couples in China are happy?'

'It's true,' she admitted. 'Many are not, and usually it's the man's fault. We often hear couples shouting, even fighting each other physically, but we leave them to get on with it for they'll have calmed down by morning. Sometimes the women are stronger than their husbands.' She smiled approvingly.

Fortunately for such people marriage in China was less a central pivot of life than it is in the West. There were comrades at work, neighbours at home, communal activity at the Cultural Palace. Husbands and wives were not expected to be happy all the time.

Leading on from her remarks about physical brutality between husband and wife, I asked about the treatment of animals. Pet dogs were exterminated in 1950 and still not allowed in towns. I had seen live ducks strung from handlebars or jammed in lidded coops. I'd seen fish and animals bound for the table skinned and hacked up alive. I'd seen horses with skin rubbed bare by their harnesses, pigs transported in sausage-shaped cages, kittens carried by a string round their necks, chickens tied in bunches and lying in the street, and children spitting at a bear in the zoo. Yet somehow it was negligence not cruelty I witnessed, a thoughtless regard of animals in the service of man.

'I have heard,' said Xiuying, 'that in your country old people keep animals because they're lonely. We keep dogs to guard our houses. We keep cats to catch rats. People in England can afford the luxury of caring for animals. The Chinese are too busy looking after each other to have time for animals as well. If we had the time we still wouldn't have the money to feed them. We look after our old people instead.'

Touché, I thought. Yet there had been instances of suicide by elderly people abandoned by their children, and sentences for the son or daughter concerned. 'I would never leave my mother and father to grow old on their own,' said Xiuying.

Xiuying was tough, headstrong and emancipated. Despite long traditions of non-individualism she remained her own woman. Her will to succeed, her search for perfection – perfect love, perfect knowledge – might be translated by her elders as a putting of herself above society as a whole. She would not marry unless she was sure. If her job was tedious she would throw herself into free-time study to the possible detriment of those around her.

She would not have found favour with the elderly seaman I met in Guangzhou, who yearned for the days when women wore gowns and lacquered their hair and looked like women and stayed at home. She would not have found favour with the man who'd had the greatest influence over the greatest number in the history of mankind: Confucius. While appreciating perhaps her respect for learning, her family loyalty and so far her virtue, he would have found her too vain, too enterprising, too opinionated, too cocooned in her ambitions for success and happiness, even for a man.

'Women and people of low birth,' said Confucius, 'are very hard to deal with. If you are friendly with them, they get out of hand and if you keep your distance they resent it.' Neither would Mao have upheld Xiuying as a selfless heroine of the new social order. As a graduate she was by definition an 'intellectual', synonymous, almost, with being counter-revolutionary. She had no ideology, no interest in politics outside its effect on her personal life. She was open to 'bourgeois' ideas from the West, averse to labour and disparaging of anything that related to the peasantry. Xiuying was a member of the New Chinese, a foretaste of the China to come. I liked and respected her. Perhaps I understood her better than most Chinese.

Six months later and home in England a letter from Xiuying brought news of her family. Xiuying herself was in love again, with a 'medical student practising in the hospital where my mother was under treatment. We attract each other with our shared interest in languages, and our ambition to polish ourselves with knowledge. Any success I have in translation will make up for the prejudice against my class background, which almost drives me mad. This is why I took the liberty in my previous letter of asking you to send some modern short stories valued both for their style and ideology . . .'

Each one of Xiuying's letters brought requests for books or magazines. I sent her books but they may have been the wrong ones. Her enthusiasm waned from 'memories of your hearty laughter ringing in my ears' (the Chinese are compulsive collectors of clichés), to 'my brother asked why the foreign sister hadn't written for so long'. Friendship was functional, and binding. Cultivating *guanxi*, or friendship ties, was a major preoccupation in a country where much was achieved through connections. Many of the contacts I made in China turned out to have some end in view, some material gain for the Chinese concerned. Yet when I mentioned this to an Englishman who'd spent twenty years in Hong Kong he replied 'Oh, but it goes both ways! The Chinese stop at nothing in their kindness and hospitality, always giving far more than they can possibly afford.' Whatever they had the Chinese gave. But Xiuying had nothing to give.

3

•••

A Walk in Kunming

7 a.m. It is dawn. Bells tinkle on unseen bicycles and the air smells of dust. Between the blocks the eastern sky gleams lilac and pink. The streetlamps are the colour of warm peaches.

Beijing Lu, the straight wide street leading north from the station to the heart of Kunming. Indistinct figures float by in the shadows or cluster round the stall of a steamed bread vendor on the corner of a side street. Cigarettes dance like fireflies in their hands. Rising vapour silvers in the dawn light and charcoal smoulders in the brazier beneath. They rub their hands, they clear their throats, they fill their mouths with soft warm bread. It is cold.

The sky lightens. The blocks absorb the pastel shades of morning clouds: salmon, mushroom and grey. Their ground-floor shops sleep shuttered behind bars, their conformity veiled by trees. In a forecourt of a building a man performs *taiji*, like an insect paying homage to the dawn. A woman goes by, three Chinese onions dangling from her hand. Masked street sweepers rest their brooms against a tree and tip baskets of refuse into pale blue paladins. An encampment of acrobats, two men and a monkey, bend over bedding, folding, tying, unwinding from sleep to another new day.

The sky reddens. Flowerbeds burn with the intensity of first light, tomato poppies, cherry-pink hollyhocks, orange marigolds dotting rust-rich earth. The sun rises in a pomegranate sky.

Half-past seven and the city is awake. Buses distended by standing commuters. Hand-painted posters of a bright technofuture. Bicycles, bicycles and yet more bicycles; face after face neither smiling nor angry nor bitter nor wondering, sacks of vegetables slung across handlebars, bright-cheeked children balancing on crossbars, strings of live chickens and carcasses of pigs. Bus queues, blue clothes and breath like mist. Twenty years ago there were fields.

Beijing Lu gives rein to the current planning urge to make things big, formal and symmetrical. Five times the width of a traditional city street, it has the scale of a British motorway. Wide is grand. Wide is beautiful. Wide will accommodate the brave new future when Kunming will be full of cars and trucks and Mitsubishi buses. The trees enhance the illusion of grandeur, the expectation of arrival. The cavernous buildings that wall the street are intentionally so: they are the image the Party wants to project, an image of itself as being solid, reliable, powerful, even dull. Traditional buildings comprising elegant latticework, paper-lined windows and carved wooden brackets convey neither unity nor strength.

Kunming is a city of two million inhabitants, capital of the southern province of Yunnan. Of all Chinese cities it is the one in which I would choose to live for at five thousand feet its climate is equable, its cultural life is comparatively diverse, its environs are attractive and many old lanes are well preserved. Of China's fifty-six minority nationalities, twenty-three of them live in Yunnan, splashing Kunming's streets with their many-coloured clothes.

Yet much has been destroyed. Pagodas are decaying; gateways, mansions and temples have gone. Since 1949 the urban boundaries have crept onwards and outwards, consuming the wheatfields, expanding the city twofold, threefold, into broad new boulevards and factory compounds, and sports grounds and housing blocks and railway depots and transport yards, their planning and detail unthinkingly transgressing the laws of *feng-shui*. People flocked to the cities for jobs and schooling and medical care and the State needed workers to fill the new factories. Beijing Lu is a product of all this. East of it and west of it lies street upon street of five- and six-storey housing blocks interlocking like parquet in a sterile equality of mass and void. Borrowed from the post-war architecture of the West, a building system then in its infancy whose shortcomings were as yet unrecognized, it filtered through the Soviet Union to transform urban China into an alien apology for Marxist ideals. Its style has nothing to do with China, either in form or context or social scale. The blocks were not built with an eye to effect but are the child of supposed necessity, absolved by the chaos out of which they were born. The philosophy of equality has brought design standards down to the lowest common denominator of aesthetic possibility, stripping mankind of humanity, reducing people to sums.

Turning west into Jin Bi Lu (Chinese directions are given in compass points) I enter a world of ochre-washed houses and olive-green shutters, of knobbly plane trees pruned like goblets and pots of pansies growing beside doors. Along the river spring willow trees sway and elderly residents greet the sun. They bend and jog and swing their legs, limbering, loosening their limbs. A young man squats on the river wall, toothbrush and toothmug one in each hand. A line of washing billows in the breeze; the air is sharp, the morning still cold.

West of and parallel to the riverside walk there are older streets still, traditional lanes of wood-panelled houses, rust-red, jungle-green, with windows of latticework, friezes carved with flowers and birds and narrow balustraded balconies. Pot plants perch on projecting planks; parrots poise on metal hoops; songbird cages hang from hooks. Through doors left ajar there are glimpses of court-yards, small and mysterious for being half-hidden, walled with panelling and paper-lined windows, garlanded with two-tone Chinese leaves, cluttered with hen coops, with sieves and baskets, studded with woks and jars. In the street rag mops are propped to dry. There is a muffled tread of cotton shoes, a rattle of bicycles from Jin Bi Lu, the splash of water, the splintering of wood as it's riven by a cleaver, the clucking of hens, the cooing of doves. Smoke furls upwards from just-lit braziers. Coopered wooden buckets jostle beside taps. Pot plants smell damply of earth and leaves. Women emerge to swill slops into gutters and to hang dripping washing on poles above windows. A man is being shaved, a bicycle repaired. Grandmothers perch on bamboo stools, shelling peas and knitting in the early morning sun.

Among the wooden houses of the former merchant and professional classes is an occasional Big House of a landowning family, concealed behind gateways and magnificent crumbling walls. Although large in size they are never anything but domestic in scale, built on the pattern of rooms around courtyards with ornate woodwork and carved stone quoins. But in thirty-five years they have become near-slums through lack of maintenance and multi-occupation, their tile roofs weed-grown, their courtyards piled high with machinery and fuel stores, their proportions destroyed by new brick walls. Their woodwork crumbles and is patched with concrete; their hallways are converted to carpentry workshops; their fragile balconies sag beneath lumber and heaps of coal. Here lies equality taken to its ultimate, equality at its most heartless and stupid, the slow sure decay of an artistic heritage of which the most unfeeling Chinaman ought to be proud. When the houses finally disintegrate – if the planners allow them to survive that long – these last surviving remnants of a thousand-year tradition will never be replaced. In less than a generation, when today's youth is middle-aged, they will exist only on visitors' snapshots, in self-conscious set pieces revamped for the tourists, in elderly memories and faded dreams.

Now mid-morning, shoppers are heading for the side lane markets where women in blue perch on low stools among heaps of green, weighing their produce on a bamboo rod with a scale and sliding pole. There are chickens and ducks and pigs and frogs. There is a man selling bracken, another with bean curd, a third skinning eels and the road is splashed with blood. At the end of the lane there are mountains of cabbages being loaded and unloaded from lorries and carts, arriving and disappearing, quilting the streets with rotting leaves. The way is jammed with bicyles and shoppers; peasant women with embroidered aprons, city women with polyester and perms. They haggle over prices; tempers fray and fly. Shoulder poles clash like rutting stags' antlers to a chorus of shouting and bicycle bells. A repeat performance takes place at four for the Chinese go shopping at least twice a day. With no fixed notion of what they will buy they choose what is cheap and fresh and good and carry it home on a length of twine.

I emerge into sunlight and Dongfeng Lu, the broad new boulevard that slices westwards through the heart of old Kunming. Layers of history overlap in a collage, lacking cohesion and orientation. There is no real centre in modern Kunming, nothing big or pivotal of eye-arresting worth. To the Maoist the city was a symbol of sin so the utmost was done to limit its scope. About as metropolitan as the High Street in Chipping Campden, its pace is unhurried, its shops provincial, its streets half-empty of cycles and cars. China never favoured the grandiose statement, or florid conceits of individual style. In the thirties and forties there was a sense of the cosmopolitan of a different kind, of shops gay with banners and stuffed with merchandise, of smartly dressed people thronging streets that have widened and temples that have gone, of monks and merchants, missionaries and mandarins, of pedlars clashing cymbals to advertise their wares, of public weddings and funerals, of traditional festivals and temple fairs, of rickshaws and beggars and opium dens, of all the diversity of stratified urban life. Now no more ceremonies vitalize the streets. Marriages and funerals are private concerns. The monks, the mandarins, the missionaries are no more.

Heading west along Dongfeng Lu beneath state-pruned plane trees, between monolithic buildings, past a tailor's, a photographer's, a minorities shop, I arrive at the Kunming department store. Grey and sober and five storeys high, it might be a hospital or housing block except for its prime commercial site on a quadrant of a roundabout and windows showing shoes in sparse display. There is the same lack of identity about all new buildings: schools look like factories look like clinics look like stations look like administrative centres, for all are constructed in a similar way.

The similarity goes further still, for every Chinese department store, be it in Kashgar or Beijing, resembles that in Kunming. There is the same despondency of too much space, the same gloom of terrazzo stairs and the same drab layout like a wartime Woolworths: glass counters, poor lighting and not much on sale. I wander about in search of hats, bashing through drifting streams of shoppers, dispersing, coalescing and forming in queues, past Spring Thunder radios, Flying Man sewing machines and White Rabbit sweets; there is more variety, certainly, than in other communist states, and plenty of what is available – so much so that whole counters are duplicated to convey an air of plenty – but every time I am looking for something it is certain to be found on the uppermost floor. And the ceilings are high and there are no lifts. And the stock has run out and will not be replaced for quite some time, and nobody knows or cares when.

The belligerence of salespeople in China is legendary. Commerce is associated with capitalism and service workers are less well paid. Being less well paid than factory workers they get their own back by sullen resentment and refusing to serve their customers. They cannot, as yet, be fired.

'I would like to see some hats,' I call to the sales assistant at the end of the counter: she is reading the paper, studiously ignoring me. Please and thank you have no role in Chinese sales vocabulary, and I am trying to abandon them. At the completion of a transaction both parties say, 'Good – good-good-good . . .', or words to that effect, implying that both have benefited but neither needs bow to the other. Nice-mannered thank-yous smack of the old feudal hierarchy, as if by thanking people you are somehow belittling them, making them lose face. Since salespeople's duty is to serve the customer they need not be pleased or thanked. After some minutes, whose intention is to show that she is not a lackey at anyone's beck and call and least of all a foreign capitalist's, she moves ponderously towards me, reaches for the nearest hat, drops it on the counter and saunters off. It is not the kind of hat I want but by now she is snubbing another customer. Chinese people are careful shoppers. They look around and they take their time for there is no guarantee of size or replacement. Finally I interrupt. 'I wanted a brown one.' It is a Soviet-style hat with fur-lined ear flaps. Millions wear them, and go on wearing them till the fur drops off with age and moth, but it is not so simple to find the right one.

She replaces the first hat, puts down a brown one and gazes into space beyond my shoulder. A 'Serve the People' slogan looms large and red upon the wall.

'It's too big. Have you got a smaller one?'

'*Mei you.*' The universal *mei you*, the most often used word in the Chinese language. It means, no, there are none.

'It needs to be a bit smaller,' I explain.

'Out of stock.' She moves off heavily, leaving me standing there.

Not every salesperson is as disenchanted as this. There are many as polite as she is rude, who despite all odds are able to maintain a friendly face and shower a visitor with smiles.

It is the end of an era. Department stores will soon be brought in line with reforms in other spheres. Managers who for thirty-five years have implemented central planning dictates over what to sell and where to buy and how much salary to pay their staff will be required to change, to hire and fire workers and make a profit on their sales.

Hatless, hungry, I turn down the back lanes looking for lunch. Since Deng's new policies came into force thousands of small businesses have opened along side streets: tailors, repairers, restaurants and shops. Even state-run restaurants have ceased their practice of closing for lunch.

Little more than a hole in the wall, a private noodle shop opens on the street. A ladder leads up to the one-room quarters of the one-child family above. It is comfortable here in the tiny room on a foot-high stool at a practical height for siphoning rice from the edge of the bowl. As the girl feeds the fire I stare out between thermos flasks at a framed evocation of old Kunming: a heap of cabbages, a horse munching leaves and a small railed park beyond. She stirs the wok while I advise: 'More ginger,' I say, 'not much oil, no dofu . . .' (dofu is bean curd) and the girl only smiles and rocks the child asleep on her back. My vegetables sizzle and steam in the wok and are ready as soon as their cooking has begun.

She pours tea in fresh bowls and we gather round the fire. Her baby has woken and is drawing on her breast while her husband looks proudly on. The streets are quiet. It is the hour of *xiu xi*, the afternoon rest, when office employees unroll bedding on their desks. In the park beyond the railings a woman is teaching her workmates *taiji*. The horse munches cabbage leaves and the baby drinks from his mother's breast.

The Jing Ying Wen Yi Cha Shi opens on a lane of rust-coloured houses. It occupies a small front room, crowded with tables and elderly men. Everything dates from the turn of the century or gives the impression of doing so: the occupants, the furniture, the porcelain and the panelled walls the colour of dried blood. I sit on a bench and nurse my tea.

Teahouses are regarded as questionable relics of feudal society, wasters of time and venues for potential counter-revolutionary debate. There were some attempts to close them in the Great Leap Forward and more serious ones in the Cultural Revolution, but they resurfaced afterwards and are once more growing in popularity.

'I'm eighty-seven,' an inmate addresses me by way of introduction. 'And he's ninety-two.' Steam rises in tongues from their porcelain cups, smoke billows from their bongs and metal-bowled pipes, each one different, each a mastery of craftsmanship. I smile in approval. Age in China is a matter for respect, even veneration.

'And how old are you?'

'Thirty-six.' Or thirty-seven by Chinese calculation, which considers a child a year old at birth.

'Ah!' They nod in sympathy. A meagre age.

It is hard to sit by oneself in a teashop. Though the old men have their personal seats and personal friends, in a sense we are all one gathering. I am accepted quietly, neither stared at nor ignored. The men fill their pipes and spit on the floor. One group plays shuttle cards. A couple plays chess.

A woman steps in with a steaming kettle, a ruddy-cheeked peasant face with short-cropped hair. She fills and refills our flower-fronted cups and the tea unfurls like cabbage leaves. For two pence one can drink all day.

It is half-past one and story time. The sun is high and the shadows dense, drowning the carving on the housefronts. A man in his seventies with thinning hair and hollow cheeks mounts a platform in the corner of the teahouse and lowers himself on to a stool. Conversation stops. The cards are put away. All eyes rest on the raconteur, heir to a line of peripatetic story-tellers who kept Chinese history alive. He recounts the day's episode in the ongoing saga of a Ming dynasty emperor, enacting his tale with expressions and gestures in exaggerated operatic style. His eyes roll, his jaw drops, the sinews on his neck are drawn taut as violin strings. He opens and closes and reopens his fan. He thumps the bench with his fist. He stands up, sits down, performs with conviction and never forgets a line.

It cannot be a new story, but the teahouse is packed and the old men are clearly enthralled. The kettles stand idle on the table tops; the tea grows bitter in the lidded cups.

At the conclusion of the episode the story-teller leaves and a dozen old men leave after him. The rest sit on, bring out tobacco pouches, deal out cards. There is a clatter of teacups, a slumber of voices, a slap of playing cards and a gurgle of water as they draw on their bongs.

The Chinese improve with age. There is a dignity, a mellowness, in their gentle ways. In the West we tend to want everything too soon, and gradually we lose what we most indulge: our youth, our looks, our vitality, our ability to attract those we wish to impress. In an Oriental partnership there is, in theory, a build-up of love and understanding which continues expanding to a zenith in old age, an honourable state of wisdom and calm. As Confucius said, 'At fifteen I set my heart upon learning. At thirty I had planted my feet firm upon the ground. At forty I no longer suffered from perplexities. At fifty I knew what were the biddings of heaven. At sixty I heard them with docile ear. At seventy, I could follow the dictates of my own heart; for what I desired no longer overstepped the boundaries of right.'

Across the heads of the pavement overspill I watch the activity in the street beyond. Laminated layers of Chinese history – Imperialist, Nationalist, Maoist, Pragmatist – parade before my eyes. Bicycles glide by, a therapeutic relaxation in their stately pace. One has a sofa strapped to the saddle-rack, a peasant bringing it to the city to sell. A procession of children carrying brooms, proud in the red neckties of the Communist Party's Young Pioneers, passes on its way to perform good works. Old ladies hobble, vulnerable as ninepins, their feet mere stumps and bound in bandages, squeezed into shoes scarcely four inches long. A parrot swings on a copper perch. A woman passes bearing baskets on a shoulder pole, her hair in rollers. A girl squats on the kerbstone with a bowl between her knees, dipping chopsticks in noodles with the clacking regularity of a knitting machine. Two doorways down a man washes rocks, a jagged trio of limestone crags studded with miniature trees and temples and set in a shallow bowl, a landscape encapsulated in a foot-high stone. On the corner of the street the orchid sellers set out their plants. Small boys kick a shuttlecock, keeping it aloft with their knees. A washing machine judders its programme on the pavement and drains itself into the road.

From a bench in the teahouse an oldish man rises and crosses the street. He takes up a broom and sweeps the pavement in slow careful strokes. His hair is cut close to his scalp. His clothes are heavy, ragged and brown. Then, bending, he enters a chest-high shelter of canvas and cardboard built against the façade of the opposite house. I awake with a start; that shack is his home. But I want to be sure.

'Does that man live there?' I ask the old men. One speaks some English.

'He does.'

'Who is he?'

'He's the son of a Qing dynasty minister.'

He can't be!

But it's true. In a sudden flash of disillusion, China's history and politics become real to me. In spite of Xiuying's family background until this moment the revolution has been words in other people's books. The Qing dynasty was a dreamland rather than an epoch persisting in my grandmother's youth. That the rich were now poor, or elsewhere, or dead, and former peasants in positions of high authority was outside my experience; that the streets I now walked had been a stage for a life so remote from the present was the stuff of theatre since I'd not been there. Until now.

'Why does he live in that shack?'

There was no shame or reticence about recounting his story. 'His father was a minister in the province of Hebei. They fled to Kunming in the Japanese occupation of the late 1930s and lost the rest of their fortune after 1949. Because he comes from outside he isn't entitled to a resident's card, and without a card he cannot get work. He subsists by selling herbal medicines in the street.'

There's more to it than this, but the old men don't say. Many Kunming residents come from different provinces but they have cards – and jobs and homes. Thirty-five years on, a wealthy class background is still a stigma. Without registration not only can he not work, but he has no right to either housing or ration coupons, to his rightful allocation of cotton or grain.

'What happened to his family?'

'His parents are dead. He had a wife, but she left him and married someone else.'

I turn back to the shack. There are pots and baskets piled against the window of the house behind. A stack of firewood blocks the front door. On the pavement stands a table and stool.

'Do the people not mind who live in that house?'

Apparently they don't. 'They have a back door as well.'

The Qing dynasty minister's son re-emerges from his lean-to and greets a passing friend. There is something in his bearing that validates the story: his large northern frame, his upright carriage and the trace of past authority in his movements and speech.

Once more the teahouse changes gear. A new character enters, a middle-aged woman with a pile of papers over her arm. Most men buy one, a single, cream-coloured, folded sheet, a pattern of horizontal and vertical characters in which photographs are few, and small, and blurred. They peruse the print, pronouncing words clearly for their friends to share; though most city people can read a little, few, understandably, can do so fast. I ask them what it says, for my own *China Daily*, the English-language paper, contains articles, I imagine, of a different substance entirely.

'There's some news about the programme for National Women's Day. There's a thing about a restaurant being asked to reform since its kitchen isn't clean. This half-page is an episode of a story. That bit is jokes. Here there is sports news and the rest is local events.' This sounds more relevant than the Marxist theory voiced by the papers a decade before, but there is still no comment on religion, environment, foreign news or the arts. It is the 'internal' papers with restricted circulations that hold real information, the accounts of corruption, poverty, brutality, most of which leaks out via word of mouth or 'little road news'.

Leaving the teahouse I enter an alley and walk along winding, mud-brick lanes, between low whitewashed houses and sloping tiles. Thin white chickens peck in the paving cracks and a boy cleans his face in a white enamel bowl. A woman turns melon seeds on mats to dry, to salt and roast and sell. It is as if the city has been whisked away and I've landed in a village in China's feudal past. There are barrows and bushes and the faces are of peasants: there are shoulder poles and mud-floored yards and stacks of drying wood.

At the junction of two alleys I meet Qi Fushen, an elderly pensioner with toothbrush hair and a face that crinkles like old leather when he laughs. As a member of the local neighbourhood committee he is partly responsible for its triumph of cleanliness, the litterless lanes and newly whitewashed walls, the creation of small gardens, even a straw-thatched shelter at a junction of paths where old men gather to play cards. Set in the walls are landscape paintings, and blackboards chalked with careful characters inciting the neighbourhood to respect the elderly and nurture good morals in the young. Yet though the lanes are neat and orderly the houses themselves are crumbling and crowded, with no running water or loos. The neighbourhood committee, controlling about forty thousand residents, comes under the wing of a district committee, the equivalent of an English city borough. This in turn is responsible to the municipal committee, which supervises factories, rural counties and 'communes'. The neighbourhood committee is subdivided into street committees whose work is more local, and courtyard committees of perhaps a dozen households. Half the residents in Qi

Fushen's care are factory workers. A quarter are children and students; one-eighth are retired. Among the houses are schools, a clinic, workshops, co-operatives and shops.

'What else do you do?' I asked him.

'Whatever is needed,' is his reply. 'We carry out health campaigns, promote family planning, encourage political study and the equal treatment of women. We care for the old and sick. We help school leavers set up co-operatives. We mediate in disputes and give moral advice. In China we believe prevention to be preferable to punishment,' says Qi Fushen.

In theory such committees are communism at its best, helping, caring, assuring the modicum of needs for all (or almost all), displacing corrupt officialdom by a system of fair play, creating an environment that helps to generate a positive social commitment. In practice they represent control at its most suffocating, prying, harassing, spying on visitors, searching homes for signs of poor hygiene and illegal migrants from the countryside, accepting bribes for the awarding of privilege and keeping mum. So complete is the network of local control that everyone is his neighbour's warder, or as the Chinese refer to it, 'policemen with small feet'.

We have reached the limit of the whitewashed lanes and arrived in a street of green-shuttered shops. Produce is stacked in tiers upon the shelves and heaped in sacks put out in the street and pegged on sagging strings. Sunlight dances on rows of green bottles and on glass-fronted cupboards and screw-top jars.

Beside one I pause; there are posters on its outside wall. The rose-petal colours of their glue-wrinkled paper animate walls throughout urban China. In their fluid, hand-crafted, ink-black calligraphy they are works of art, but illusive in their incomprehensibility. The more I see of them, the more significant I imagine their message to be.

'What does that one say?' I ask Qi Fushen.

'It's an advertisement for tomatoes.'

I cannot believe that this is all. 'And the one next to it?'

Qi Fushen wrinkles his nose and studies the cursive characters. 'That one is for a private school that opened recently. It tells you what subjects it is offering.'

'What about the pink one?'

'The pink one is for a dance being held in the theatre this evening.'

I find this information quite riveting, and say so.

'No,' says Qi Fushen. 'Not interesting.'

I leave him and continue through narrow lanes, past the Confucius temple, dusty now, its memorial tablets to Confucian disciples pillaged and destroyed, to Green Lake Park. In the parks the Chinese have come into their inheritance; they are well maintained and very well used. Green Lake Park is a place of willows and placid pools, their water cloudy like jade. A water-filled park is cooling, calming in a city buff with dust. In summer the pools disappear beneath lotus leaves, but in spring the willow trees weep in waterfalls, dipping their twigs in the water's edge. I walk between lakes along willow-lined causeways, over angular bridges, to a pattern book of chinoiserie in their midst: a courtyard of venerable bonsai trees, and pavilions and galleries with Chinese-red columns and upswept roofs of glazed green tiles, and geometric latticework, and moon gates and dragons and pitted grey stones. Through a bamboo gateway there are glades of cherry trees in a froth of pink bloom; old men play chess beneath their boughs, balancing on benches in the blousy, petal-floating afternoon.

Kunming in spring sunshine is the most seductive of all Chinese towns. The sky is blue; young leaves unfurl in the delicate pastels of melon and grape; pink and white blossom clouds over walls. Arriving from cities asleep in a pall of winter gloom, where beauty has withdrawn to bare-branched trees and the gentle greys of smoke and cloud, for me Kunming contains the magic of a world reborn.

Leaving the park by its southern gate and heading back towards the hotel I find the way enlivened by people and activity, by eruptions of entrepreneurial skill. It is difficult to walk many yards in Kunming without being distracted by something – perhaps a street of tailors at work along the pavement, perhaps a painted shopfront patterned by hand-drawn characters, perhaps a branch of crimson camellias against a sea-green lattice wall, perhaps a group of schoolgirls playing shuttlecock or hopscotch or Chinese jumprope; perhaps a dofu workshop where aproned matrons row their arms in steaming barrels and hurl buckets of liquid in a vibrating sling; perhaps a private library where for a penny a child may perch and peruse a picturebook; perhaps an old man telling fortunes by employing a finch which hops from its cage and selects a numbered stick, a relic from the days when cities abounded in bone manipulators, physiognomy readers, palmists and astrologers; perhaps a Dai woman in long coloured sarong or a Sani with head-dress of braid.

Most basic operations are still performed by hand. I watch a woman bonding packages by folding the polythene over a saw blade and running it slowly through a candle flame. I watch men lifting bricks with a tool resembling sugar tongs, four at a time. I watch dentists feeling into gold-filled mouths with fingers stained by nicotine. I watch a group of youths making cotton-padded quilts in a wasteland of half-demolished walls. I watch men and women shovelling sand and unloading sacks and hauling heavy hand-carts and heaving iron barrows and sweating under poles. Even manufacturing co-operatives are only semi-mechanized, each shed crammed with blue-clothed workers and oily black machines.

Street stalls and private enterprise have re-emerged since Deng came to power, revitalizing lanes with a sudden explosion of doctors, dentists, chiropodists and wart removers, with fortune tellers, shoe repairers, clothing merchants and noodle stands, with roast-chestnut sellers, umbrella menders, baked sweet-potato vendors and peripatetic melon-seed men. Many of the hawkers cycle miles from the countryside and sit or squat on the ground all day to sell a few peanuts and make a few pence. Their presence seems natural in a country like China yet for a decade all street stalls were banned.

On a broad piece of pavement I encounter a crowd being engaged in sales talk by a pair of Tibetans, men redolent of high plateau lands, living by their wits. I can feel the mountains in their faraway eyes and the snow-bright sun in their skin baked brown. My glance travels down past their yakskin coats, past the knives at their belts, past the knee-high boots to the array of spare parts at their feet. There are heads, there are legs, there are feet, there are trunks, once belonging to monkeys, to antelopes and bears. While one man keeps the crowd amused the other shatters leg bones with an axe. Hardly is my camera out of my bag when there's a shout from a third man posted on watch. The bone-crusher looks up with menace in his eyes. He speaks in Tibetan but there's no mistaking the meaning of his words. 'If you take that picture,' he warns with a snarl, 'it will be your leg next.' He brings down his axe with unnecessary venom and shards of tibia splinter into the crowd.

Past Changchun Lu and Wucheng Lu, rounding the hospital of traditional medicine and the small railed park where I had my lunch, I find myself back in the vicinity of the teahouse, in the bird-market street, my favourite street of all. It generates a wholeness, so rare a quality in a Chinese street, a sense of enclosure and of all being well. Under a tunnel of plane trees the bird men gather, displaying bamboo cages with tapered feet, and ceramic feeders and knobbly perches and sacks of grain and chirruping crickets kept as company for their song. Flecks of sunshine filter through the leaves to spatter the shade with lemon-drop light. Old men drink tea on pavement stools, trousers rolled up to air ivory-smooth shins. Flower girls knit among the pinks and madders of cut camellias and the sun stabs like fire at a blood-red rose. Here is the epitome of a city as it should be, combining the essence of the countryside with civilized urban life. Work, social and family activity are plaited in a matrix of market stalls and homes. Each of the senses is mobilized, in the powder-puff softness of owl chicks for sale, in the chorus of bird song, the scent of azaleas, the taste of fresh tea and the strong colour harmonies of blue and green. Green leaves, blue clothes; green houses, blue sky.

Turning the corner by the orchid men I am back at the teahouse where a pride of bird fanciers has gathered on the pavement and hooked their cages over bamboo beams. Bird raising is an ancient Chinese custom once confined to the bourgeoisie but latterly favoured by elderly ex-workers who have the time to indulge it, to carry their bird in its swinging cage as they walk to the teahouse or park. Struggling to stay upright the bird gets all the exercise it needs while its owner gets company and fresh air.

The low sun slants between the rust-red houses, and glitters in the dust and dances in the steam, and glances off polished cycle wheels in a catherine-wheel sparkle of spokes. In this painterly light, in the animated babble of chatter and bells, the birds give voice to an evening song.

'The uncovered cage hanging in the centre is the teacher bird,' a man explains. 'It's worth well over a hundred yuan for it has a beautiful and unusual voice. The other birds are its students.' Two dozen cages hang in a circle, each covered with a cloth except for an opening facing the teacher. 'The owner of each bird pays one jiao a day to the proprietor of the teacher bird who slowly recovers what he paid. They're all the same sort – we call them *hua mei*, painted brow birds – but the teacher's song is not normal to their kind. It's been trained to imitate different bird calls, even the sounds made by animals or man.'

I retrace my steps along Dongfeng Lu, its broad sheet of tarmac transformed into gold by the melting sun, to a large open square at its eastern end. Squares were not a traditional feature of Chinese towns and by day it feels raw and new. But as the sun goes down, tracing lamp-post shadows on the paving stones, it becomes a venue for people flying kites. Those floppy paper dragonflies, butterflies and flying cranes are long familiar on Western walls, but soaring in the China sky is where they ought to be, swooping and dipping among evening swallows as the sun sinks down in the East Wind Road.

In the brief half-hour between sunset and dusk people spill out on pavements and lights go on and China still seems an ancient place. The evening streets are thronged with strollers, tobacco sellers and rice-cake stalls. The daytime vendors have packed and gone, swaying down the streets with their cumbersome poles, trundling off with hand-carts, cycling off to distant countryside homes. Turning back south I focus on a state-run restaurant for if I don't eat soon everywhere will be closed. I peer between the characters red upon the glass but instead of food there's a weekly, obligatory, political study group. A cadre reads from a pocket book while the cooks and waitresses slump at tables in various attitudes of infinite tedium. They lean on an elbow, they yawn, they sigh, they gaze through the window at passers-by.

Near the hotel is another mass restaurant, this time open and bursting at the seams. I force my way through to see what they have; those who don't, remain for ever at the back. I queue for a ticket and queue once again while the soup is being made. We are sprayed and buffeted like boats in a storm by people pushing in and others pushing out with overflowing soup bowls, while harassed waitresses steer a zigzag course with wobbling stacks of plates. The place seethes with men and noise and light and chewed-up bones and dirty crocks and terrazzo table-tops covered with slops – its customers like it hot and bright to complement their homes which are not. They smoke, they spit, they slurp, they shout, they apply themselves to the food in hand with a preoccupation peculiarly

Chinese. I enjoy such places when in the mood: they are lively, they are fun; they're a true taste of China.

By the time the soup comes there is nowhere to sit. I extract two chopsticks from the box on the wall (the Party is trying to phase them out and replace them with knives and forks) and stand between tables fishing out compost and gulping down broth from the side of the bowl. Tendrils float like seaweed in a rockpool: lily flowers, Jews' ears, pea leaves and mushroom, transporting me back to childhood beaches and chemical gardens in isinglass.

A row breaks out at the end of the hall. The queues grow long, snake out in the street and no one gets any food. A florid man with a small moustache and a vest showing pink through his thin white shirt is drunk and insulting an employee. People shout, people push. The waitresses shrill and the florid man sways. I grab a stool in the momentary lull and sit nursing my bag since the floor is too filthy, and is always too filthy, to put it down. Having queued once again I savour my way through a hundred-year egg, sliced on a bed of fresh coriander and served with ginger and hot soy sauce.

Chinese tables are normally round so that all may have access to every dish. There is an optimum table size and the largest seats twelve; thus, eating in restaurants, several couples or groups may share. The men sharing mine are smoking while they eat and a cigarette dangles above my plate. While the row continues they moan about the service, shout rudely at a waitress and gobble their food. They pick up their bowls and bend their heads and purse their lips and suck up their rice. Once the bowl is half-empty they employ their chopsticks in the manner of workmen shovelling gravel. They spit out their bones on the tablecloth, wipe their hands on its edge, lean on their elbows and let out loud burps. They blow their noses between finger and thumb and wipe their hands on the legs of their stools. It's not they who are rude but I; who not knowing the rules pick up salt with my hands, put fingers in my mouth and drown my food in soy sauce.

Back outside I wander. The streets are emptying. The blocks are chequered with squares of light and people are moving in curtainless rooms. I see a man at a table examining a chain; behind him there are cooking pots stacked on a gramophone, a sheet concealing a sleeping space, a goldfish bowl and bicycle. In the adjoining room another man smoothes a pink flowered sheet on a bed. In a third a woman sits sewing by the light of a fluorescent table lamp.

Re-entering the world of wood-panelled houses I merge with the darkness in the labyrinth of lanes. Interiors that in daytime were secreted from view are now illumined by the paraffin-soft glow of forty-watt bulbs. It is I who am invisible now. I slacken my pace and peep through lattice and doorways still ajar, pause to sniff cooking smells of spice and rice wine and listen to an *erhu*, a two-stringed instrument, that tells me, most emphatically, what country I am in. What by day was precise and impersonal is transmuted into a half-defined dreamworld of Oriental smells and sounds. People are teeming in medieval interiors between belongings wedged and stacked and slung in every conceivable nook and space. Baskets, birdcages, bags and cooking pots dangle from ceiling hooks. Firewood and bedding are folded into gaps above wardrobe tops. Camphorwood chests are piled like pyramids. Bamboo ladders pierce the upper floors. Pet cats strain on strings tied to table legs. Mirrors and calendars decorate the walls.

By half-past ten Kunming is quiet. Bicycles pass, lampless in the night. Shadowy figures detach themselves from walls and move through pools of pale, leaf-sieved light. Even in the main streets sounds are muted: bicycle mechanisms, voices, footfalls, a tinkling bell. The stars are shining, different stars which Chinese astronomers group in constellations of Chinese imagining. Through the butter-yellow rectangle of an open doorway women hang noodles over racks to dry. A grapefruit moon hangs poised between branches. I walk undisturbed in the middle of the road. The streets are empty. The city sleeps.

4

Day out at Black Dragon Pool

'Do you mind if I talk to you for a little while?'

'Shh!' I said. The old men had turned and were regarding us sternly. One of them snapped at the boy who'd approached and stood before me, a youth about half my age and half my size, dressed like a wood nymph all in green. It was early afternoon at the teahouse in Kunming: story time.

Requests for help with English were frequent in the cities, and normally I welcomed them. Several of my friendships started this way, for there were many Chinese who shrank in fear or even distaste when approached spontaneously by a foreigner.

I imagined the young man had gone away but at the end of story time he reappeared, repeating his line: 'Excuse me, do you mind talking to me for a little while?' As the Chinese were normally so wary about meetings, preferring formal introductions and the gradual assimilation of new friendship ties to their formation at whim, this must, I thought, be a determined young man. He sat down at my table and sipped his tea. Then, instead of posing the ritual questions in order to evaluate my personality and play for time, he plunged straight into business and brought out a notebook. Could I tell him what digraph meant? I couldn't. I doubted that it was a proper word.

'It must be! It was in a book.'

According to the look on the young man's face I wasn't much more helpful in explaining the difference between to learn and to study or to know and to recognize, so I started asking questions of him instead. It was all the same to Cheng Weimin, so long as he practised, and I corrected his English. Was he studying the language at college?

His face remained impassive, a receptive face, somehow serious and playful at the same time. 'I am a night-shift worker at the Kunming Number 4 Machine Tool Plant.'

71

'How do you come to be working there?'

'We live there; our unit has its own accommodation. My father still works and my mother retired three years ago at fifty-five. They allocated her place to me.'

'How much do you earn?' This was a customary question; people frequently asked it of me.

'Thirty-five yuan.' A little over £10 a month, not much more than I was spending, for want of edible alternatives, on cake. I'd met service workers who earned even less (and others who earned more than ten times as much), but at least it was more than he would have been earning had he been born before Liberation. Coming from a poor peasant background he would have been working longer hours, mostly to pay off family debts.

There was an eight-point scale of workers' wages with a differential similar to that of Western factory employees. Weimin earned the lowest wage, yet he didn't look poor. His clothes were clean, his manners unimpeachable. Chinese poverty was very deceptive.

'And your parents?'

'My father earns 80 yuan. My mother gets a pension of 40 yuan, three-quarters of her former wage. But she helps voluntarily in the nursery school.'

'I thought men and women received equal pay?' While the position of women had improved enormously from the days when rural landworkers earned one-sixth of their husbands' wage, I was coming to the conclusion that women in the eighties were still unequal, were still believed better at traditionally 'female' occupations such as sewing and fine work, repetitive jobs that were less well paid. Many millions were employed in unskilled work, in housewives' collectives (the equivalent of Western sweated labour) and in work that could be taken home. Men still resented women earning equal pay though it had been in force for thirty years, and though women held their own in jobs which in the West were still the preserve of men. 'Women hold up half the sky,' said Mao Zedong, and they held up half the shovels too, probably a good deal more. They did menial jobs alongside men and were frequently allocated the harder tasks, mixing concrete, building boats, pulling carts and toting night soil on shoulder poles. On a building site it was the women who laboured while the men laid bricks.

In Weimin's mother's case the answer sounded logical enough:

'My father earned more because he'd worked there longer.' It was the same with doctors, with teachers, with cadres (though not with peasants); the older you were the more you earned, a question of age commanding respect, the just reward for longer experience and years of hard work. But it was equally plausible that Weimin's father earned more because he'd been given a more responsible job. Male workers climbed the pay scale faster and earned, on average, half as much again as their wives. Weimin's parents were a case in point; women were the new exploited class, China's new proletariat. Though the Party saw employment outside the home as the key to female emancipation, women *had* to work, and work for less, or they would not eat.

'Do you get holidays now?' I asked.

'We work six days a week with Wednesdays off' – this staggering of workdays reduced the Sunday pressure on shops – 'though some of my colleagues work continuously and then take days off when they need them or in a block. Most units still have no annual holiday, only single days off on national festivals – Youth Day, Workers' Day, Women's Day, PLA Day . . .' Xiuying was fortunate working at a university, to have time off.

'Say you had wanted to do some other kind of job,' I suggested half-heartedly. 'Would you have been able to?'

'It would have been difficult.' He meant impossible. Only a handful of privileged people had any choice in their future career.

'What if, for instance, you wished to be a doctor?'

'I would have had to show a particular aptitude in that field at school, and then pass the medical college exams. Standards are very high.'

'Do you actually like your job?' He seemed too intelligent, too alert, too fragile, to be working at Kunming Number 4 Machine Tool Plant.

The kettle came round and replenished our tea. Weimin sipped gingerly, sieving the coarse leaves through his teeth. A giggle of girls went past in the street and turned to stare. Weimin ignored them. 'I don't mind it for a few years. Though monotonous it's secure, but I shouldn't like to have to spend the rest of my life there.' A factory job carried no risk of political estrangement. Rent was cheap, education free and Weimin could not be sacked. As yet. Soon after our meeting Deng introduced his economic reforms. The mid-1980s

73

would see the collapse of job security as factory after factory became independent of state control and introduced a system of more pay for better work and reforms based on supply and demand. The shattering of China's iron rice bowl was the second blow to supporters of Mao, the second denial of a basic Marxist creed. Already in 1981 the State had ceased to be the sole employer; private individuals could set up in business, hire helpers and trainees. The result was eloquent in every city street.

I well knew the scenario of Weimin's plant for I had seen it all before. The socialist answer to capitalist exploitation – to make life easy and the work pace slow – was as depressing a picture, though in a different way, as an overworked nineteenth-century textile mill. There would be large draughty sheds with equipment lying idle, workers sitting talking, rubbish strewn about the floor and a total lack of safety regulations. Redundant people; redundant machinery; redundant slogans in red upon the walls. The Party might pride itself that people had jobs (though up to one-fifth of urban citizens were unemployed), but much of the day, even much of the year, was taken up by smoking and resting, reading the paper, bathing and shopping, political study, meal breaks and tea. Deng Xiaoping believed in enterprise, believed consumption was the principal motivating force of mankind, believed it would be possible to triple production in almost any state factory and in a very short time through management based on supply and demand. He was up against the remnant Maoists who still upheld genuine worker control and feared loss of central and personal power and price increases and maybe sheer hard work. "Why are people not working?' I would ask out of habit when I visited a factory, for I knew the reply: 'They don't have any work. They have fulfilled their quotas.' This might mean materials had been exhausted, or machines were not running, or insufficient workers had turned up on the job; or it might be true.

It was a similar picture in many state-run establishments: over-employment; underproduction. Walk down a street and there are men washing railings with bowls of soapy water. Enter a modern luxury hotel and there are dozens of people emptying empty ashtrays, dusting spotless tables, making work for themselves so as not to look idle. Go to a college and teachers may outnumber the people being taught. Go to a bank and half the employees will be reading the paper, studying English or chatting to their friends, and the others pushing papers, a study in slow motion. Once during orthodox opening hours I found a whole bank closed. 'There's nobody here!' said the caretaker with relish. 'Come back tomorrow.' It transpired next day they'd been to see a film.

In a private co-operative, in startling contrast, the air would be vibrant with energy and drive. Everyone would be working, touting for custom, fighting against time. In a state-run enterprise two were employed where one would do, and they seemed to be sharing their salaries too.

'Can you really live on 35 yuan a month?' I asked Weimin.

'My parents help me out. They bought my bicycle when I was still at school.' Only one in six Chinese had a bicycle. 'They have always treated my brother, my sister and myself the same, going without themselves that we should have books and clothes.'

I was bombarding Weimin with questions. People sometimes got irritated when foreigners addressed them as dispensers of information rather than human beings, but since Weimin was treating me in a similar manner he was unlikely to object: we were merchants trading knowledge.

'What you would really like to do,' I put to him, 'is go to university and read English, isn't it?' Weimin had English fever. Like millions of his urban compatriots he saw English as the most potent tool available for making out and getting on. While in itself it opened no doors it was still a key allowing him contact with the world outside and a renunciation of the status quo. Wherever I went I found young people swotting up their English in readers and listening to cassette tapes. Television university had reopened and Radio Beijing broadcast three English classes a day. The commitment to language learning was later brought home to me on an icy December evening in Beijing. Snow was falling on the open rooftop of the Foreign Languages Bookstore where two hundred people had paid one jiao and gathered in the dusk to practise their English. Never had I seen such dedication as this. 'What chance do you have?' I asked Weimin.

'At the moment none at all. When I left school five years ago my grades were too low to sit for university. Since then I've been learning English on my own. Every night when I finish my shift I study from midnight till two in the morning – it's quieter then –

from books and foreign radio. But it's hard to improve when there's no one to practise with.'

Weimin's ambition was to be an English teacher. Yet the teachers I'd met all longed to change jobs for that most glamorous and sought-after and probably downright tedious position as interpreter in the tourist trade. It held the same mystique as the job of air hostess when I was a child, offering opportunity to those who did not know.

At this point the old men intervened. They wanted to know who Weimin was, what unit he came from and why he was talking for so long to a foreigner. With memories of Cultural Revolution atrocities still fresh in their minds many Chinese remained wary of too much being said to people like me. Those who associated with foreigners could be victimized in the event of a future political swing.

Weimin's replies were vague. I could tell this inquisition annoyed him, yet his manner was respectful in deference to age. He later explained that he set great store by courtesy. Young people nowadays were forgetting their manners, Weimin said primly, especially girls. Give them a uniform and they threw their weight around.

It was time for Weimin to start his four o'clock shift. Would I like to meet again next day? I would, I said. He would bring a spare bicycle and we could go where I chose.

Arriving ten minutes past the appointed time I found him waiting, smaller than ever, about to give up and go home. It was a mark of those manners so important to Weimin to be on time. China was punctual: buses and trains left dead on schedule, people turned up when they said they were going to, and usually early. Nobody ever let me down. Weimin, recovering, shook my hand and introduced me to Ma, a lanky fellow in spectacles, as tall as Weimin was short. He smiled uneasily, turned away and shuffled his feet. Then he mounted his bicycle and rode off home.

'He's a bit shy,' Weimin explained unnecessarily, 'but he wanted to meet you all the same.'

I swung my right leg over the wheel – a practice uncouth and un-Chinese that caused much amusement to passers-by – and wobbled off into the stream. I kept my eyes on Weimin's green back for my machine was unfamiliar (no lights, no gears), the bicycles were numerous and I didn't know the rules. As it happened there weren't any. Whoever made most noise had right of way. People turning left veered diagonally across the oncoming stream with nary a signal nor glance to their rear.

And after a while it began to be fun. I was lifted out of the world of the tripper and given the illusion that I belonged. The cycle was sound, its metalwork polished, gold-lettered black. Everyone rode at a stately pace and motorized traffic was rare. There were babies in wicker seats strapped to the crossbars, men with furniture poised on their heads, whole families balanced on a single frame. Later, when night fell, my eyes became tuned to the even consistency of trusting dark, for since nothing had lights no one was dazzled and it was easy to see.

Bicycles were possessions of passion and pride. If a rider so much as dented another's mudguard a storm would erupt in which the culprit would laugh alongside the audience, making it hard for the victim to shout without making himself look a fool. With the cost involved, and long waiting lists for coupons to purchase, the theft of a bicycle was a common crime. Few Chinese had been in a car, and what vehicles there were were communally owned. But private ownership was coming and would come: more noise, more pollution, more accidents . . . and greater rifts between rich and poor. As with television, which almost a decade before very few people had had, the change would be fast, the effects unforeseen.

Adrift on our bicycles we turned off down back lanes to the destination of my choice. We paid our two pence and descended three flights of concrete steps into the bowels of the hillside beneath the zoo. I had read about the Beijing bomb shelters, a network of tunnels built by 'volunteer' labour in the Cultural Revolution when the fear of both America and the Soviet Union was at its most paranoid. Every unit, every shop, had its own private entrance. Every city had its shelter, dug by hand with picks and barrows after working hours, consuming materials in short supply. Several had now been converted for use as storerooms, dormitories and shopping arcades in the knowledge that were nuclear war to break out they would not be sufficient to withstand the blast – nor indeed to survive a conventional war.

Passing three sets of blast doors we found ourselves in a looking-glass land of whitewashed tunnels, gently curving, gently sloping, disappearing into mysterious distances and echoing with unseen footfalls. The aspects of bomb shelters that most intrigued me – the electricity generator and air filtering systems, the waste disposal unit and food supply, the broadcasting apparatus and deepwater wells, the dormitories, the classrooms, the clinics, the loos – were not to be seen, if they still existed behind the bolted doors of a herringbone of side tunnels, but they were portrayed on a notice board. The picture was so calm, so ordered, so spacious: mosquito nets on comfortable beds, children absorbed in arithmetic, laundered nurses administering to patients, potted plants and goldfish bowls and placid smiling faces. It was typical, in its way, of the Party lie, of pulling the wool over people's eyes, as if to say: 'If a nuclear bomb drops we'll go underground and our lives will be just as they are today.'

Yet beside these spurious images there were photographs portraying the reality of war: devastated cities, radiation burns, missile bases and dropping-out hair. Weimin, beside me, the top of his head not quite reaching my shoulder, looked concerned, though not afraid. The reality of those photographs belonged to other lands than his.

'Does the possibility of nuclear war not alarm you?'

'Of course,' he replied. But I had the feeling he was being polite, saying what he thought I expected him to say. Though a bomb exploded in north-west China in 1964 has since led to outbreaks of cancer and deformity and poisoned pastureland in oases on the Silk Road, and though there have recently been demonstrations about nuclear tests, I never met a Chinese in favour of disarmament, or who felt real fear about nuclear attack. Either their personal lives were more immediate or the facts were being concealed.

We emerged into daylight, Weimin springing up the steps like an antelope and me thumping after him, and retrieved our cycles from the bicycle park. Then Weimin hurried home to start his shift.

On the following Wednesday, Weimin and Ma's day off, the three of us set out for Black Dragon Pool. We cycled north along the edge of a spur, through a suburb of chimney stacks and walled factory compounds above a plain green and level with unripe wheat.

Weimin was in a good mood. While the spider-legged Ma rode on ahead, Weimin pointed to the distant hills rimming the edge of the Yunnanese plateau, bare and eroded from the cutting of trees. Since

Liberation there had been nationwide tree planting, mobilizing schoolchildren, workers and the unemployed, though much timber had since been cut for fuel. 'Our unit planted pine trees on those hills,' Weimin recalled. 'The State provided the seedling trees and our whole unit – thousands of workers – spent three days planting them. It was good, we enjoyed it. We got paid as usual and had fresh air and exercise. It was much more fun than being in the factory, sitting in front of the same machine with the noise and smell of oil. Awful!' Weimin screwed up his nose and laughed. He looked more boyish than ever this morning, in a short-sleeved shirt and hand-knitted waistcoat. Weimin wasn't one to let a mere dull job spoil his enjoyment of life.

'What do you think about while you're operating your machine?'
'I try to think of other things. I think about music, and films and sport. I like sport. Every morning I go jogging for half an hour.' Grinding uphill, having difficulty talking and keeping pace, made me feel ancient. Never having known a day's illness in his life it was beyond Weimin that another should feel frail. 'This morning I got up at half-past five and went for a run. My mother got up with me, to clean the flat for you.' His parents had invited me to lunch.

We turned off right along a winding lane where I was reminded of spring in Punjab: the narrow earth bunds between the unripe wheat fields, the wild spring flowers and scented rape, the eucalyptus trees divested of their lower branches and the buffaloes with long curving horns. We passed through villages of mud-brick walls and low tiled roofs with upturned ridge ends, and straw stacks and wood piles and a shagginess of byres. The lane curved on, a satin ribbon in the sun.

Black Dragon Pool, a Daoist temple in a wooded valley at the foot of the hills, was now a public monument. We paid to get in. We kept close together so as not to be parted in the crowd of tourists come, like us, for a day out at the pool. Nobody wanted to take the lead so we hovered politely at every divergence of paths. We admired the peach blossom and the fish in the pool, exclaimed at the size of the Song dynasty cypress trees and complained of the noise that other people made. Reluctant to show discourtesy I saw much less of the temple complex than I would had I been on my own. For Weimin and Ma it was a background to their outing; they knew nothing of its history, of the Daoist philosophy responsible for its being.

79

The temple was built in the fifteenth century, a haven for the monks among rustling trees, far from the maelstrom of common life. But during the Cultural Revolution its halls were ransacked, its priests disbanded in a frenzy of pillage that swept the nation, and though the buildings themselves had been partly restored (to their original garishness, some Westerners might claim, of egg-yolk roof tiles and deep red columns and latticework, and multi-coloured patterns on supporting frames) they were empty shells inhabited by ghosts, made public and rid of their feudal past.

It was still just possible to picture the temple as it must have been, a series of shrine halls dedicated to different gods and immortals, where grey-robed monks practised sword play and *qigong* (deep controlled breathing to revitalize the system) and searched for elixirs on the mountainsides, nourishing their vitality through abstention from a life of sensual goals in their quest for the secret of eternal life. Now converted as a pleasure ground it was the kind of place I instinctively shied away from, devoid of context or meaningful use, the skeleton of a memory I could not share. As a functioning temple it was part of its culture, moving with history, interacting with change and time. Now, packaged and preserved, its past and future had been frozen in the present; its tranquillity destroyed by paths and railings, by concrete and graffiti, by litter and spittoons. One shrine hall was a tearoom, another a shop selling reproduction scrolls. Repair work was sloppy, the painting crude, instigated by cadres and performed by workers with no expertise. The courtyards, once havens for contemplation, were cluttered with tables and stools. Black Dragon Pool had been divested of spirit: even the hills had lost their soul.

I recollected then a monument more poignant for being of my own discovery, unmentioned in guide books, mantled in bushes, sunken among the weed-tumbled grave mounds of a cemetery near Guilin. Gazing out at the distant crags was an ancient processional way, of brooding figures and mythical beasts, silent sentinels of time-weathered stone. China is full of places like this, all the more haunting since apparently no one knows they are there.

Like flocks of sparrows the Chinese trippers flitted and squawked and chattered in the galleries at Black Dragon Pool, and perched in rows in the shade of the eaves and pecked at their tiffin in aluminium trays and disported themselves on the grass. No one came to worship for the shrines were bare. No images sheltered in silk-hung niches, no oil lamps flickered in darkened halls. Black Dragon Pool was a park for the people, degraded by ticket booths and loud bus queues.

'Where do these people all come from?' I asked Weimin.

'Some have come on an organized visit with their unit. Others may have travelled from elsewhere in the province, though it would be hard for them to afford the fare. Those like us have their day off today.' We watched the arrival of a Japanese tour group, the women in silk, their faces powdered, their husbands' spare cameras slung over their shoulders. The men came after them, small and dapper, dutifully clicking the courtyards and shrine halls, clustering po-faced behind their guide.

The Chinese were indulging a similar passion, not on the temple but on family and friends. Almost every group had a camera with flash (which some used in full sunlight) and would take it in turns to pose for a shot, then move a few yards and pose again, standing like statues facing the camera, or in the avant-garde style of the street professional, with one hand on a rail. Once the film was exposed the group would descend on a man with a bucket who developed it in minutes and hung the wet negatives on a branch to dry. The youngsters squealed and exclaimed with joy: they were made so happy by such small things.

The taking of photographs was a private matter between families and friends. To people who were poor it was natural that when having their photograph taken for others to see they should wish to look their best. Seeing foreigners taking pictures of old streets, old buildings and old people in old clothes offended some Chinese, especially those who disliked us anyway and did not want us to have any part of them.

Considering that people *were* still so poor, and that film price in China was twelve times higher in relation to earnings than it was in England, the amateur photographic enthusiasm was astonishing. But the camera was the latest Chinese toy, symbolic of the growing affluence, a game that everyone who could must play. It was also a reassurance, it seemed to me, to those portrayed in the smiling groups, that life after all held moments of joy. It was a prop to the ego, for so long crushed by oppressive rule in surroundings devoid of personal reflection: it was proof of individual being.

In a holiday setting like Black Dragon Pool to take photographs was almost compulsory.

'I hope you've brought your camera,' said Weimin.

I apologized meekly about the black and white film, which was all the Chinese could afford. Colour was status, which black and white was not.

'What would be the best place to take our photographs?' he mused, half to himself.

Ma, who until now had not said a word, suggested the temple buildings as a background. Weimin fancied the Song dynasty cypress trees whose girth was twelve feet round. My own suggestion of some Liquidambar foliage was generally thought senseless.

'There are too many people around that tree,' objected Weimin, not liking the idea of total strangers trespassing the borders of his personal portrait. When we passed through a portal he and Ma were both in favour, but I thought otherwise.

'When I take portraits I take portraits,' I explained. 'If I'm photographing a building I would rather not have people obscuring it. The two would compete.'

'Oh, good!' exclaimed Weimin, instantly seeing the logic of that and thrilled to bits at acquiring new knowledge of Western habits and taste. I was allowed to take their pictures against a background of leaves, as I wanted to do all along.

We retired to the tearoom to gulp scalding green tea from handleless cups. Whereas I had often encountered such cups, delicate porcelain bowls with lids, for Weimin and Ma they were new. I was startled again by how sheltered they were, how rarely they did anything out of the ordinary, how little they knew of the city their home. After three weeks in Kunming I knew my way round it better than they, and we were mutually surprised, they at my familiarity, I at their ignorance. Weimin and Ma's conception of the city was of a matrix of neighbourhoods and unit compounds punctuated by landmarks: main streets, cinemas, coffee shops, sports grounds, department stores and bus stops. They had never wandered the whitewashed lanes, bought vegetables in the markets, eaten barbecued dofu or potato cakes at street stalls. I knew university graduates who were afraid to ride a bicycle. Weimin at twenty-two had the emotional maturity of a lad of fifteen. Until his marriage or even long after he would have no real decision to make because everything in life would be laid down.

Weimin's family lived on the industrial outskirts of Kunming in a fourth-floor flat of a newly built block within the grounds of the Kunming Number 4 Machine Tool Plant. I knew what it would look like before we got there; in city after city I'd felt the sterile sameness that alienated people both from nature and each other. I'd walked streets bleak with telegraph poles and padlocked doors and high brick walls where people kept their eyes fixed straight ahead.

Most blocks seemed unfinished. Walls needed rendering; streets cried out for trees. Dust filmed the windows and felted the gutters and clouded the air. Ground-floor flats never looked like homes. Every surface seemed hostile: the discoloured grey of concrete walls, the wound-raw orange of Kunming bricks and the harsh cold blue of the sky. Block after block, the scene was unrelieved by the animating movement of cats or clouds or wind-blown leaves.

Revolutionary totalitarianism, hideous new buildings purporting to be modern, replaced the traditional diversity, the elegance and harmony of the Chinese town. Qualified architects had been pushed aside and design work assigned to the cadres in charge. Paper-backed lattice had gone to monolithic concrete; winding lanes to straight wide streets. It was claimed the old buildings would be hard to convert, that replacement with high-rise blocks of flats was justifiable on the grounds of land scarcity and because people couldn't travel long distances to work. But as recent Western housing schemes demonstrate, it would have been possible to build at high densities in Chinese-style terraces at similar cost, providing each dwelling with a yard or patio instead of the squares of unused and unusable indefensible space. The only advantage of the blocks was speed – facility of planning, ease of construction – and time was what China did not have. With decades of lost time to be made up the Party's response was to bolster the ailing economy. The influence of environment on the residents' well-being was forgotten in the surge to house the homeless (in blocks with no gardens or markets or cycle parks or space to play), and with shoddy workmanship and inferior materials even new projects seemed old. There were cities where revolutionary activists had already demolished every last trace of China's architectural heritage. A similar strategy was planned for Kunming, to restore a few monuments for the benefit of tourists but to flatten old neighbourhoods and erect modern blocks and to widen the streets for the traffic not yet there.

Weimin was immensely proud of his home. It had been allocated to the Chengs six months before, their having priority due to the time Mr Cheng had worked in the factory. To Weimin the flat was new and palatial: to me it was sterile, and in a supremely ugly part of Kunming.

I thought to myself, but I kept it quiet, that people were brainwashed into liking their blocks because blocks were Party policy and they had no choice. Were Weimin to intimate a preference for an old house to a poky flat on the fifth or sixth floor of a walk-up block looking down on nothing but tarmac, he would risk being criticized for his feudal mentality. His pride was a rebuff to my disdain. And Weimin knew something that I at the time did not: that the average urban Chinese flat was only half the size of a Russian one (which in itself was small enough), that each urban citizen had on average three and a half square metres of space, that one-third of urban citizens had a 'housing problem', and that one-seventh of those were not housed at all, but might sleep on a desk, or like the son of the Qing dynasty minister, in a shack on the street.

And thus I began to understand and accept. While the blocks were not all they might have been they were not so much worse than blocks in the West, and in terms of new housing they were all there was. They supplied running water and sometimes gas and bathrooms, which the older properties did not. They were easier to heat, easier to clean, lighter and more secure. They represented a new social pattern, a gradual move towards the comforts of the West. It was easy to judge them with Western eyes, to compare and discard; harder to see them as the Chinese did, as harbingers of better things to come.

We entered the block and climbed a narrow concrete stairwell stacked with lumber and surplus stores. Weimin and Ma heaved their bicycles up after them, mumbling darkly about thieves. Weimin's mother, hearing thumps, was waiting by the door, a matronly lady half-hidden by her apron, soft-skinned, large-hearted, her grey hair cropped short. Mr Cheng had gone to market to buy vegetables for our lunch and his younger son and daughter were still at school.

There was nothing homely about the flat, no thought of decor or craftsmanship, no warmth of colour or texture or line. It was rare to see something old and beautiful in the People's Republic except in fossilized state on stage or at a 'beauty spot' like Black Dragon Pool: the artistic heritage had been virtually extinguished by militant Red Guards. What mattered now was status and propriety, the seating of visitors so no one should lose face. Weimin led us to his bedroom, spare and conformist, everything clinically neat and clean. The walls were painted – the first paint I had come across outside a state building – in convalescent green. There were the usual hard chairs, plain cupboards and stools, and maps on the walls and a bed the boys shared. By Chinese standards the room was large, with the furniture at right angles, flat against the wall – except the television, which tyrannized the middle of the floor.

Weimin pressed me to sit down. 'What kind of music would you like to hear?' he asked politely.

'Anything Chinese would be nice,' I replied.

'Chinese?' he echoed, startled. 'I don't have anything *Chinese*. I like Western music, popular music, country music and blues. What is blues?' I explained. 'I don't like Chinese music. It makes so much noise. And I *hate* Chinese opera. Only the older ones like that kind of thing. Young people aren't interested.'

To counteract the lure of Western culture, the new Chinese faith in the superiority of foreign things, the Party painted an unfavourable picture of our crime and unemployment, strikes, racial conflict and greed. But when the British pop group Wham! gave a concert in Beijing in the spring of 1985, the first such visit, people queued all night, paid three days' wages for the privilege of a ticket and packed the workers' gym. It was seen by correspondents as a diplomatic move, a show of goodwill after the signing of the agreement about the future of Hong Kong. A year before at the time of my visit to Weimin's house such a concert could not have been staged.

'How do you get hold of Western music?' I asked Weimin. In the Cultural Revolution people had been sentenced to fifteen years' labour for owning Western records. Even now only classical music was thought to convey a suitable tone; anything abstract, or atonal, or pertaining towards rock, was still officially eschewed.

'I record the songs I like from the BBC or the Voice of America.'

'Are you allowed to do that?'

'*No!* Many people do though. It's forbidden to even listen to Vietnamese radio. But since we cannot buy the music we want to listen to, we have no choice but to record it.' Weimin had a Shanghai-made cassette recorder costing £30 and a couple of dozen tapes, each costing the equivalent of two or three days' wages. For one who earned only £10 a month he was a fortunate young man: I had been to several Chinese homes so poor they hadn't even mugs from which to drink tea.

I wondered how the Chengs survived on so little. With two children at school and Weimin's mother on a pension their combined monthly income was 155 yuan, roughly £10 apiece. Having paid the rent, a nominal sum of under a pound, and perhaps £6 per person for food, there was little left over for furniture and books and cinema and bus fares and clothes and coal. Each item of furniture, each article of clothing or electrical equipment was a major achievement, a representation of months, or even years, of selfless frugality and going without.

Out of interest I compared the Chengs' finances with another and larger family I knew, who had given up working in a factory to open a noodle house. From a former joint income of £60 a month supporting a family of nine (four workers, one retired, one mentally subnormal and three school-age children) they had increased their funds to £100. Two adults still worked in a factory and the rest in the noodle house, paying £2 for rent, £5 in tax, £6 to a pension fund and £13 for the wages of a boy to help out. They worked longer and harder but claimed they were happier by far.

Thirty years of national austerity had been imposed on the Chinese by wages held so low that a combined family income was barely sufficient for basic necessities, and by the cost of luxuries being kept so high that almost no one was able to afford them. At times I was staggered by how cheap things were – eight lettuces for a penny, or to send a book three thousand miles only three and a half pence, hardly sufficient to cover the wages of the three people it took to stick on the stamp. It cost no more to buy a new book than to reserve one from the library at home. Yet other things were expensive: a short woollen coat cost £20, a sheet £5, a washing machine more than £80 . . . Qualified professionals such as teachers and doctors earned roughly the same as factory workers, which amounted to the equivalent of something rather less than the

English dole. Inflation was rising, a shock to those accustomed to stable prices. There had been two wage increases since 1976 and salaries had gone up ten per cent, too little to compensate for rising prices on the open market, too little to cope with people's rising expectations. No longer were standards judged by comparison to those in force in the 1940s. People compared themselves now with their better-off neighbours, with Western lifestyles as seen on TV, and with what they believed they deserved. Everyone wanted the up-to-date products, new fashions in clothes, high-quality equipment, televisions, motorbikes – and to achieve them they were taking on spare-time jobs. It was as if, I told Weimin, this spending was a reflex to decades of scarcity and Maoist austerity, and to a fear of returning to leftist rule.

'Exactly,' he replied. 'You have understood us perfectly.'

Compared to other accommodation this new block was certainly an improvement in size. Opening off a hallway it had three rooms to the usual one or two, a tiny kitchen with a balcony for storage, and an inside loo, with communal showers elsewhere. The more usual arrangement was to enter through the kitchen, cramped and blackened, directly to the living and sleeping room, often no more than ten foot square. No plants, no view. Corridors between the furniture; a desk, a bed, a table, some stools . . .

The Chengs were fortunate in other ways too. Living within their unit they wasted no time travelling to work, and they shared their day off. I later made friends with another worker's family, who rose at five and stood for an hour on the bus to work. Li had a job in a biscuit factory and his wife was a cadre in a printing shop, obliged to spend her evenings doing political and administrative studies at night school. Li did the housework when he got back at seven and cooked food for his wife who collapsed into bed on return at nine. Their three-year-old son lived with his grandparents in the countryside and met his mother and father on their respective days off while they caught up with washing and going to the shops. Because their free days didn't coincide the three could only be together as a family on the seven national holidays each year. What they did have was independence and a workable marriage. Many of their friends shared their parents' homes which put a strain on their relationships in addition to the hardships of the system and their work. For all the appearance of smiling faces, life in China was a continuous strain.

The smiles were a front, a belief that a cheerful countenance sowed the seeds for a happier state of mind and thus a better life for those around.

Mr Cheng had returned with the vegetables, which he and Weimin's mother had spread on the floor of the adjoining room to string and chop and shell. With his blue and white striped T-shirt and brush-bristle haircut Weimin's father reminded me of something from a comic strip, more diminutive even than his elder son, but exuding strength from his Popeye arms and springing about like a horse.

'He's never been ill in his life,' Weimin boasted. 'He goes running and swimming and gathering fungi on walks in the mountains. He never gets angry or shouts at his children as most fathers do.'

It was five o'clock before lunch was served. The vegetables had been picked that morning, gathered, as always, while young and sweet. Fish and poultry, often sold live, would have been fresh too but vegetables had been bought on my behalf. 'I'm like you,' Weimin had confided when I'd warned him I didn't eat meat. 'I don't eat pork either. Only dog.' Few Chinese could understand why a healthy human being should not eat meat.

'In England,' I told Weimin, 'most vegetables are grown until they reach full size, when they are tough and have lost their taste. It may be a day or so before they reach the shops and more days before they are sold. People sometimes leave them a week or more at home, and then boil the remaining vitamins out of them.' The table was so crowded with vegetables that we held our rice bowls cupped in our hands. There were young broad beans and mangetout peas, steamed cabbage and chard, a salad of scallions, a soup of radish greens, and peppers and lettuce root and beansprouts and dofu and peanuts fried in oil. Some of the vegetables I had never seen: a good Chinese market might have more than sixty kinds. 'Chinese vegetables are the best I've ever tasted,' I complimented Weimin.

'Eat! Take more!' cajoled Mrs Cheng, selecting titbits with her chopsticks and dropping them in my bowl. The abrupt commands no longer seemed crude. 'Don't stand on ceremony; take what you like.' Having noted my favourites she moved those dishes to the side of my bowl. The only courtesy required of me was to eat and praise the food. A guest should eat twice as much as his hosts.

Glancing up from the table I caught sight of my reflection in a mirror on the wall. It reminded me sharply of the difference between us, one so easy to forget when all one saw was Chinese. But what happened next was a yet more forcible reminder of the barrier, a barrier near impossible to overcome.

'We will now go back and make a recording,' announced Weimin when we'd eaten our fill. This was what he'd been waiting for, the chance to make a language tape from which he could practise colloquial English. He switched on the machine and I shifted nervously in my chair.

'First question,' he said. 'Could you tell us something about your family?'

By now I knew a good deal about Weimin's family, but after all our hours of conversation I realized I had told him nothing about mine. So I swallowed and said: 'There are five of us, like you. My parents are divorced and live a hundred miles apart. My two younger brothers both live with their girlfriends. We all live independently in different parts of England. I live alone.'

There was a horrible silence. It would be hard to imagine a family further removed from the supportive Chinese one of which Weimin's was a classic example. When Weimin came to he decided to change the subject.

'What hopes do young people in England have for the future?'

I had often been asked questions with the general gist: we Chinese do/think/say such and such this way – how do Westerners do it?, to which there was no answer because we all have our own ways of doing things. Unlike Xiuying, who, as an individual, was prepared to accept me as one too, Weimin seemed inclined to take my views as the unanimous Voice of the West. They would thus be doubly disconcerting. 'What I feel or believe isn't necessarily the same as other Westerners,' I warned him, 'for we are taught to think for ourselves. I try and base my decisions on my own experience rather than the collective attitude of society.' Weimin nodded his head but looked rather puzzled. 'As to the future, I don't believe we dwell on it the way you do. People may be absorbed in material gain, or trying to fight that instinct and discover their own souls. When the present is adequate there's perhaps less need to pin hopes upon tomorrow so people tend to concentrate on today instead. Some believe Western society is collapsing, morally, socially, economi- cally – I am one of those. Some fear loneliness or alienation. Some lack motivation or direction. Some campaign for change. The majority are terrified by the threat of nuclear war. Unlike yourselves we have much to lose, perhaps less, in material terms, to gain.'

So long as I kept talking I noticed no one looked at me. It was rude in China to watch people while they spoke. 'We Chinese are clearer about where we are going,' Weimin told me. 'Everyone believes that conditions will improve, that we will live in greater comfort. It is for this that we look to and admire the West, for your freedom and opportunity to do the things you enjoy.'

I almost asked Weimin if he was happy, then remembered in time it was not primarily happiness he sought but wealth, and wealth was assumed to presuppose contentment. As long as things were materially better than they were before life would be bearable. Never had I come across a race of people so directly and unashamedly materialistic in their values.

Weimin's sights were fixed on the West. His culture was borrowed Western, though his attitudes were Chinese. A good Confucian, he was courteous to his elders, virtuous in his behaviour. An English lad of similar age might have found him a prig, conservative, emasculated and immature. In terms of independence he was the equivalent of a Westerner of about fifteen. Yet in terms of stability, of acceptance of his place in family and society, he was far advanced. In China there was no adolescence, no cult of rebellious youth. Weimin passed his boyhood growing into the man he would become. Any move he made towards self-expression had been curbed in childhood, compensated for by that special kind of closeness the Chinese had with the young. He grew up feeling safe and cared for, loved but not glorified, persuaded but not punished. The Chinese world was a network of others; the goal of society harmonious life.

I did not fit. Weimin may well have been shocked by my attitudes, my undoubted transgression of social convention as he knew it to be. When I asked him to a meal at a restaurant he declined on the grounds of a government ruling forbidding Chinese to take gifts from a foreigner. Accepting presents made the Chinese lose face.

I left at seven. Weimin's father slunk downstairs to check that the coast was clear. Though in theory not forbidden to invite foreigners to the unit there were those who could make things unpleasant for the Chengs. He gave the all-clear and I crept out alone. I waited for my bus in the unlit street. Next day I left for Dali, and I never heard from Weimin again.

5

Foreigners in China

More than anywhere in China I wanted to visit the province of Yunnan. And more than anywhere in Yunnan I wanted to go to Dali. Set among fields between snow-capped mountains and a deep blue lake, capital of the ancient kingdom of Nanchao, built of marble and home of the picturesque Bai minority, Dali had an aura of fairytale. Being twelve hours from Kunming and nearer to Burma, I thought order and conformity might have dissipated so far from the centre of control in Beijing.

Dali was closed to foreigners. I plotted and schemed about ways of getting there. But luck was with me for the very day I entered Yunnan it opened its doors to the outside world. I went to the Public Security Bureau (police station) to have Dali stamped on my alien's permit before people changed their minds.

Then I met Rosy. Rosy was an English girl who lived in a henhouse in the backwoods near Ottawa and made a living painting flying pigs on long johns. 'Where are you travelling to?' Rosy enquired. 'Dali,' I replied. 'I think I'll come with you,' said Rosy.

Over the next three weeks we went everywhere together. We travelled west across the Yunnanese plateau and in the evening turned north through a watercolour landscape of cool green wheat and grey and white houses, salmon-coloured mountains and pale spring flowers. The blue lake shimmered under a periwinkle sky. We came to rest in a town of tiled houses with ornate gateways and marble quoins set close about courtyards and threaded by narrow cobbled lanes. We washed in water ladled from a wok with a wooden scoop. We ate in a garden surrounded by pot plants, rhododendron and azalea carried down from the mountains, camellia and peony, bamboo and fern. We slept in a traditional Chinese building, carved and galleried beneath an upswept roof.

We spent our days wandering. Since everything seemed wonderful, we had no need of destinations. We ambled through the countryside, past orchards underplanted with lettuce and peas, past seedbeds mulched with a thatch of straw, past pools fertilized by rotting weeds, past people picking beans as though gathering flowers, past fields newly harvested where lines of peasants were breaking the earth with picks and hoes, past verges speckled with fumitory and daisies, with trefoil and medick and yellow rockrose. We rested by the lakeside watching people loading vegetables on to big blue boats, or fishing with circular Chinese nets or floating in the distance under square-finned sails. We found a Bai market in a nearby town in a cobbled square presided over by two large trees, where the colours of the costumes were almost Bolivian, primary and singing in the clarified air. We were taken under wing at a festival by ranks of grannies shaking handbells and clappers and intoning texts, while in front of the temple young men were swirling with a dragon in the dust. We took part in a pilgrimage where paper offerings were burnt in pyres, where lines of old ladies clad in tunics and headscarves and embroidered shoes and belt ends, bowed and chanted and banged their bells and cooked their lunch on portable stoves. We drank tea in a courtyard of men playing chess in the sun slanting down over whitewashed walls through a filigree of wistaria casting patterns on the stones. We searched for flowers on the short spring hillside, found iris and azalea and banks of purple primula, and women cutting branches and men in fibre capes. We lunched in a monastery just below the snowline, in an earth-floored hut where ferns and mosses clung to the interstices of the inside walls and the bed was a pile of straw. We followed a funeral, trumpets and cymbals and paper wreaths, a solemness of elders in long blue gowns, the coffin on a bier, the family in unbleached cotton capes, the men bent low on knee-high sticks, the women chanting, sniffling, wailing, winding up the mountain to the burial place. We sat silent beside the pagodas at dusk as a shadowy stillness enfolded the fields, as the moon rose pale behind bare-branched trees and wind chimes tinkled on a breath of air.

In Dali I fell in love with China. Smiling people waved from windows and invited us in for cups of tea. We visited factories, sat in on classes at the local schools, talked to doctors of traditional medicine, inspected gardens, spent evenings with families, were presented with calligraphy and everywhere were received with welcoming smiles, provided with stools and pressed to stay.

Nowhere else had people seemed so sane. After thirty-five years of isolation they were bursting with curiosity and benevolence, for the foreigners they knew before that time were not traders but missionaries; foreigners who cared.

In some ways Dali was not as remote as I had hoped. Its present was no match for its splendid past. The native Bais were under the constraint of a dubious Han administration (the Hans are the majority Chinese race, comprising more than nine-tenths of the population). Modern buildings destroyed the street frontage; temples had been lost and mud walls were dotted with circles of whitewash on which Mao Zedong Thoughts had once proclaimed: 'Store food against famine!' or 'Prepare to fight!' or 'Chairman Mao is the sun in our hearts!' In other respects it was endearingly old-fashioned. Cloth shoes were still lined with layers of old rags glued together in a wad. Paper cut-outs adorned the windows of houses where a marriage had recently been held. Shops opened, or stayed closed, as they pleased. People kept dogs and cats as pets. Triple horse carts were the local transport and field work was done by hand. Old jade was on sale in the Sunday market, and bamboo paper and coloured glass beads and home-made rope and pickle jars and baskets and primitive threshing tools. Girls of the nearby Yi minority sold bundles of firewood and ponies chomped chaff up a dusty alley where the charcoal vendors squatted on their haunches up against a wall. Both Yis and Bais wore traditional clothes and wove their plaits around their heads and carried heavy loads in Himalayan style in openwork baskets on their backs.

Every village had its *feng-shui* practitioner who advised on dwelling sites, illness and burial though his identity was still more or less kept secret. The villagers consulted him in place of a doctor, believing that illness was possession by a spirit which the *feng-shui* man could exorcise. They gathered at temples on festival days. They told each other local fairytales. They bought their coffins before they died and slept in their proximity. They worshipped their ancestors and offered them food. They decried cremation and buried their dead in old hillside gravelands according to the dictates of the *feng-shui* man. They swept their graves at Qing Ming festival, cleared them of weeds and adorned them with paper streamers and flowers, and made offerings of food to the spirits of the dead.

More and more travellers were arriving in Dali and those already there stayed on. Dali exerted its charm on everyone; it was cheap and tranquil and the air was clean. Even in the fortnight we stayed in Dali we perceived the change, the effects of its opening to foreigners: the locals grew less timid, less curious of our ways, and the children were learning to shout hello. Everything depended on the travellers' attitudes. While many were friendly, tales of obtuse and insensitive behaviour were beginning to circulate round the town: of three Germans rebuffing a local teacher, of Australians expecting preferential treatment and accusing the hotel of being capitalist, of yet others taking photographs of beggars and loos. Word travelled fast. In three months, I believed, the innocence, the friendliness and the simplicity of Dali would be gone.

What happened surpassed my worst fears. Two years later some friends went there to find the guest-house extended and four times the price, and the town overrun with 'foreign friends'. In their estimation there were five hundred visitors at any one time, including overseas and Hong Kong Chinese: when I was in Dali there had only been twelve. Local Bai villagers now accosted the outsiders, selling earrings and bracelets and belts. A dozen new cafés had opened up with trendy names like Peace Café and Coca-Cola Café, serving hamburgers, pancakes and French fries.

Foreigners now went to Dali for the food. They went to Dali to meet other foreigners, to sit in the sunshine and write postcards home. They went to Dali because everything was easy: menus were in English, bicycles were on hire and there were organized tours, tourist maps and boat rides on the lake. The quiet little town had become a resort; its inhabitants no longer greeted the foreigners or invited them into their homes.

Nowhere else had I objected so much to the presence of other travellers. Elsewhere in China I had been the only Westerner, or if others were around the cities had absorbed them. But in Dali a mere ten or twelve seemed too many. Foreigners were everywhere it seemed even then, ranging down the main street with their long jeaned legs, their ever-ready cameras trying out angles or concealed in shoulder bags with holes for the lens, laying on the charm for the quaint minorities while ignoring the ordinary Chinese, buying up craftwork and shipping it home to sell at huge profit, slipping off illegally for the Burmese border – and being caught and fined. The

Yi girls particularly watched every foreigner with fear and apprehension, ready to dart into the nearest doorway at the first suggestion of a telephoto lens.

The trouble with some travellers was their negative feeling about Chinese bureaucracy and the Chinese themselves, a divisive attitude of us and them. Thrown with other Westerners in hotel dormitories I was drawn into conspiracies about black-market dealers and how to pay bills in renminbi, discussions about itineraries and visa extensions and tales about the curious Chinese. Many travellers complained of the hours spent queuing or waiting for beds 'to be found'. They bemoaned the deviousness of the Chinese mind, its refusal to give a straight reply; were the smiles real, or were they a cover-up for a deeper hostility, or obedience to the Party as it wooed its Western friends, or respect for our wealth and lifestyle in the hope that it symbolized prosperity to come? They whinged about hygiene, about spit and staring and litter on floors. They grumbled about officialdom, expense and exhaustion though often the fault was theirs; their stay was too short, their programme too long and they rarely left the well-grooved run. Travel for some was an ego trip, a vying to get better deals, or to travel further or longer or more dangerously than others of their kind on the minimum possible sum.

Sometimes complaints were justified. When some money was stolen from a traveller's rucksack the hotel manager disappeared, only to return once the traveller had gone. When a French girl's camera was stolen on a bus Public Security was unsympathetic. Not only did they refuse to give her a statement to show her insurance firm (which might have been official reluctance to admit that such things happened in China) but they implied that the camera might not have been stolen and that she had sold it illegally but needed to prove otherwise at customs. To whom could one turn when hotels didn't care, when the China International Travel Service (CITS) was uncooperative and Public Security put the blame on ourselves?

Few visitors were wholly positive about China. Westerners felt alienated, frustrated, disillusioned. They tended to pick on exceptional incidents to support their preconceived notions of the continent and saw little they were not already disposed to believe. Even an overseas Chinese who had lived on the mainland for fifteen years still found it strange, still couldn't fathom the Chinese mind. People arrived in China searching for the dreamworld of the willow-pattern plates but found instead an outer Moscow suburb. Some felt themselves victims of political lies. Many got ill. Everyone was hassled by stubborn bureaucracy and a few were even glad to get out.

And few made an effort to speak Chinese. Spoken Chinese was not so difficult to learn, though it was made to seem so by those who wanted an excuse not to try. They shouted in English or pointed at phrase books, humiliating those who couldn't understand. I once asked a worker at CITS if he felt like exploding when foreigners were rude but he replied that if one was kind and polite even the most obnoxious Westerner could be brought to heel.

Several months later, travelling in the north, I was complimented by a hotel clerk on my Chinese. 'Quite a lot of foreigners pass through here,' the girl observed, 'but most of them don't speak any at all.' The brunt of this remark fell not upon me for speaking limited Chinese, but on those who did not. It dawned on me then that the Chinese *expected* us to speak their language. People often addressed me in Mandarin, China's national language, without pausing to ask if I understood, and at first, when I didn't, their expressions would sometimes register annoyance, as if to ask why was I travelling without a guide if I couldn't be bothered to learn Chinese? They seemed to interpret our ignorance as insult, a lack of respect to their superior status.

Therein lay the core of the conflict, a clash between peoples who each considered themselves superior, the Chinese on the grounds of history and size and social structure, ourselves because of our former empire and recent technological advance. For however fashionable it was in the West to consider all humans equal there remained an inherited underlying conviction that the white race was most equal of all. It was inadvertently voiced when I mentioned to fellow travellers that the Chinese held themselves superior and their reply came pat: 'They don't, do they?' Yet a recent survey found the Chinese to be the most intelligent people on earth, with the Japanese second. Memorizing difficult characters as children and studying diligently in later years was thought to stretch their minds.

Chinese and foreigners were expected to maintain a discreet distance. It did not do to become too familiar or speak the language too well. I once met a French girl who spoke Chinese fluently and worked as an interpreter in Beijing (for which she was paid two hundred times as much as the Chinese doing the same job). With her capacity for the language she behaved as one of the locals, chatting colloquially to everyone around her and laughing – rather too loudly for some. People responded with fairly well-concealed astonishment. Foreigners were different and ought to remain so; they were invading Chinese territory by adopting their slang. Chinese and foreigners ought not to marry, for such contact was defilement of the race as a whole.

In most cities and villages many Chinese avoided 'foreign friends'. Bus conductors would hand out a ticket for an average sum without asking where we wanted to go. Sales assistants' faces clouded at our approach. Occasionally people pushed past in queues, as if, as foreigners, we did not exist in the frame of humanity to which they belonged. If we asked for directions a person or group might turn silently away, afraid they might not understand the question, often too nervous to try. They were shy and apprehensive about our behaviour and afraid of political rebuke.

Most Chinese saw us, as most Westerners saw them, not as people with feelings the same as their own but as units pertaining to a different species with habits as revolting – we drank unboiled water, we blew our noses into handkerchiefs, we sweated and smelt – as we found theirs. Our foreignness defined our personality and was a greater wall between us than our inability to speak their tongue. We remained outsiders even if we stayed for twenty years, even if we married a local Chinese. We all looked alike in Chinese eyes and I was often mistaken for someone else (though the only time I remember thinking how uncanny was the resemblance between a Chinese on a bus and another on a train the day before, it was actually the same man). Later in the north-west, seeing foreigners for the first time after a fortnight, I learnt to see myself as the Chinese saw me. The group of Europeans seemed big and hairy and untidily dressed, with unattractive voices and manners quite gauche.

We were still the invaders, seldom accepted (for all the kind smiles), and invisible barriers kept us apart. For a hundred years no foreigner came under the jurisdiction of Chinese law; we could rape, kill, steal, bring in opium, and remain for ever with neither visa nor passport. The Chinese had historical memories. Foreign devils they called us then and some of them still did now. Watching a game of mahjong in Guangzhou I had heard someone say: 'A foreign devil has come to spy on us.' 'Be careful what you say,' said another. 'It doesn't matter,' replied the first, 'they never speak Cantonese.'

It was this mutually antagonistic perception of good manners that frequently prevented a deeper dialogue. People stared. Children shouted a litany in the streets: '*Waiguoren! Waiguoren!* Here comes a foreigner!' Replies to requests often seemed rude. 'Excuse me, where can I buy flour?' 'No.' Or, 'Excuse me, which bus goes to the Temple of Great Goodwill?' 'No.' Yet when a query demanded a yes or no answer the reply would often be, 'I'm not too clear,' or, 'Complicated.' Sometimes a question would elicit the reply, 'Moment,' and the disappearance of the official for up to an hour.

Rude though the Chinese sometimes seemed in their dealings with Westerners (and even more so in their relations with Africans, whom some called black dogs and believed lived in trees) they could be equally uncivil among themselves. As I was enjoying a bowl of noodles at a street stall my meal was interrupted by the arrival of two arrogant young men. 'There's nowhere to sit!' they exclaimed in loud voices. 'How can we eat when there are no proper arrangements to sit down?' Anxious for custom the woman, a peasant, rearranged her clientele to allow the young men the best bit of bench. They sniffed ostentatiously. 'What sort of food is this?' From one city to the next the street fare varied, for the vendors had developed dishes of their own. In this instance dinner was noodle soup to which one added coriander, spring onions and pickled carrot for a total outlay of eight pence. 'We don't know if it's any good, do we?' sneered the young men. 'Well, we'll see. We'll try it once and find out. If it's to our liking we might come back tomorrow. Otherwise we won't.'

But in many ways travelling in China was easy. Considering its politics there were some in authority who were friendly and helpful to foreigners; it may have been duty or hospitality, or it may have been sympathy for our helpless plight. And outside of bureaucracy most Chinese seemed genuinely friendly, respectful and courteous, going out of their way to direct or assist a foreigner in need. So far as

I know I was never followed, though surveillance was the very structure of society, acting like radar, supplying information to the Public Security Ministry. None of my letters appeared to have been opened. With a little of the language my requests were far more frequently met, and calling people comrade almost always elicited a courteous response, though few Chinese used it themselves. And as a woman on her own I was safer in China than in almost any country in the world.

On a beach near Sanya on Hainan Island I had parked myself on the soft white sand half a mile from humanity and begun to read. But a figure came sprinting along the beach, a nimble man in a bright blue vest. He slowed his pace and veered round towards me. He sat down facing me clasping his knees, a foot away, defying the boundaries of my personal space. He considered me, bird-like, his head on one side. He peered round the side of me, first to the left, then to the right, as if it were an awful way round to the back. I swallowed, felt naked, hoped he'd get bored and continue with his run. I read my book. He peered over my shoulder. I put the book down and gazed at the tourists, small black specks on the distant sand. He decided on action. In front of my feet he dug a hole, perfectly straight and perfectly round, scooping out sand and patting it down in a rim round the edge. When he could no longer reach with his hands he sat on the edge and dug with his toes. When he began on the second hole I got up and walked away.

It took some time to get used to the fact that there was neither threat nor danger in a situation such as this. The man had observed me with passive objectivity and seemed to want nothing but comradeliness. Had he been rude, had there been sexual innuendoes, I could have removed myself sooner than I did. As it was I owed pleasantness in return.

One thing I enjoyed about staying in Sanya was that the foreigners at the guest-house were not rapid-transit travellers but teachers and students living in China. Most spoke Chinese. Their outlook was broader, they felt some commitment to the country that was temporarily their home. 'We like it here,' said a couple who had taught in China for four years. 'The people are so nice. We like the respect we earn as foreigners, the politeness so lacking at home.'

Staying at the guest-house was an Englishman in his fifties married to a Canadian ex-missionary. They had lived in China for thirty-seven years, through Liberation, through the Cultural Revolution, and were presently teaching in Beijing. I asked if they had ever been harassed.

'During the Cultural Revolution I believed strongly in the ideals of one of the opposing Red Guard factions, and therefore felt I should act. So I fought alongside the group I supported.' What he did not add, but what someone told me later, was that he had been imprisoned for three years for his actions and on release had been barely recognizable.

David Crooke (this is his real name) and his wife deliberately sought out the newest and youngest foreign guests who would not know his identity or ask him questions about the Cultural Revolution. Everyone's reaction was the same: 'Gosh! You've lived in China for *thirty-seven* years? I expect you've seen a few changes in that time. It must have been fascinating!', and the Crookes were somewhat sick of it. When they left to go home almost everyone got up and formed a line – two dozen foreign experts and students at Chinese universities – to shake their hands and say goodbye. In no other country would a couple be revered merely for having been there for thirty-seven years. This alone, in China, was a claim to fame.

It was seen by most travellers as a feat of endurance to remain in China for more than three months. Yet the majority of tourists remained less than three weeks. Before Liberation the Nationalist Government had channelled its tourists in manageable groups to pre-empt unwholesome reportage in the West: the communists merely took over their ploy. International friendship, as the Party saw it, meant controlled groups of tourists spending their money in luxury hotels and Friendship Stores. It did not mean travellers wandering at will through villages and back lanes, striking up acquaintanceships and spreading bourgeois contagion, though the Party put up with them for the dollars they brought in. A Chinese would patronize the best hotel that he could afford, not automatically occupy the cheapest dormitory. International friendship was China's fear of being left behind. It was a plea for foreign currency, foreign technology and foreign markets. Thus the order of privilege conferred upon visitors gave Western tourists the top priority and Japanese second, then overseas Chinese, with Hong Kong compatriots last.

The heroes' reception for wealthy tour groups who were bannered and clapped, sung to and danced for had recently faded, but the attitude remained: buildings were tidied, people were briefed and some visitors thought they had found the ultimate in co-operative socialist organization. Shown examples not of the country as it was but as the Party wished it to be, they were cocooned from reality by coaches and comfort and the group itself. China would remain the reclusive enigma it had been for the previous thirty-five years, impenetrable and somewhat dubious. Even could such visitors make any headway into the soul of this vast continent, they might not want to. China was explained to them by numbers; so many million people producing so many million tractors, growing so many million tons of grain and planting so many million trees. The visits to communes, to hospitals, to schools, represented ideal situations rather than actual ones; they were rehearsed vignettes of doubtful perfection seen in statistical focus against a blurred background of common life. The visits to factories and Friendship Stores were a means of extracting the maximum foreign currency from the sale of souvenirs; the usual craftwork in long glass cases, the usual assistants with long glass faces, the same in every town. It shocked a few of the tour group visitors (as it did some Chinese) that people should be travelling in China on their own, dossing down in sleazy dormitories, free within limits to wander where they chose, penetrating the country by cheap public transport to its extreme north, south and west. But it impressed them no end.

By comparison with Western diplomats and journalists who lived in foreigners' enclaves in Beijing, whose movements were watched, whose visitors were censored, who ate in special restaurants, were cured in special hospitals, were guided and chaperoned and virtually unable to have an ordinary friendship with an ordinary Chinese, independent travellers were relatively free. Within the areas that were open I was never prevented from going where I wanted or talking to anyone I pleased. Though I always kept my notebook with me and usually wrote in privacy, and though the Party could have checked had it chosen to, no one seemed concerned.

New places like Dali were opening all the time, but the majority of the countryside remained unexplored. Knowing that China's most fascinating sights were still out of bounds – romantic ruins (and others not so romantic), unrestored monasteries clinging to mountainsides, hunter-gatherer peoples living deep in the forests or nomads wandering the plateaux of Tibet – I often felt annoyed. Even the ranges of mountains near Dali, home of the royal blue Himalayan poppy, were out of range to travellers like me.

There was generally good reason for places being closed. Unsuitable sights for the tourist gaze included unsettled border zones, villages lacking hotels and food and the backward regions where poverty was explicit in unpaved streets and ragged clothes, where feudal perversions were obvious even to the untrained eye and where the desolate ruins of misplaced destruction in the Cultural Revolution had not as yet been cleared away, or tidied, or restored. The Chinese authorities are now growing resigned to the fact that most visitors want to see not the socialist present but the relics of the past, and that if they want foreign currency they will have to comply. So they are rebuilding pagodas and opening new towns. Sometimes they move a monument to somewhere more convenient, or build a composite relic of reusable fragments from several different sites.

Tourists in China are expected to deal in foreign exchange certificates (FEC) and in theory are neither supposed to need, nor have on them, renminbi. But because of a widespread and flourishing black market, Western travellers, not rich by their own standards but infinitely wealthier than 99 per cent of mainland Chinese, are able to purchase everything but beds at cheaper rates than the natives themselves.

Between January and December 1984 the rate went up from 130 to 170 per hundred FEC, and was to rise even higher before dropping back down late in 1985 when the government cut back on goods from abroad. Passers-by would stand and stare as wads of notes were counted out quite openly, outside hotels, in bookstores and bus stands and principal shopping streets.

So much for those cadres who used their position to gain privilege. Many foreigners exploited the system too, telling lie upon lie to maintain prestige and save a few pence. They purchased fake Taiwan student cards which gave them concessions on the railways and a reduction in rates at hotels. We laughed at the tale about the bona fide student being refused a concession and being told by the rail clerk, 'That's not a proper student card, they all have these other ones,' but it wasn't so amusing for the person concerned. Were the Party not so shameless about milking foreign visitors, if it allowed them to decide which hotels they would stay in and pay the same as a native Chinese, they'd be less hell-bent on beating them at their game.

While I was in Dali a German called Johan was selling renminbi at half the current black-market rate to fellow travellers who had failed to buy sufficient in Guangzhou or Guilin where the dealers hung out, thus making twenty per cent profit for himself. He said he just happened to have a bit spare. I bumped into Johan on several occasions, leaving the country with copious currency, coming back in with copious luggage, of Japanese radios and cassette recorders for sale to the locals at a profit of two or three hundred per cent. Being older than most travellers and more courteous to officials, nobody seemed to suspect him.

Since the days of Confucius the Chinese had paid homage to visitors from the West, concealing their latent distrust with courtesy, treating them deferentially as honoured guests. They strove to generate a good impression and felt insulted when their overtures were shunned. Though they charged us more, preferential treatment for foreigners by officialdom was still in force. Disembarking from a bus in a town in Guangxi the other passengers fought and clamoured for rooms from the only clerk at the only hotel while I was asked inside to wait in the warm. I sipped tea on the bed while the service girl dealt with the people outside, barking out questions at each successive face. 'Name? Unit? How many people? How many nights? Coming from? Going to?' When someone didn't understand, speaking a regional dialect rather than Mandarin, she lost her temper and screamed. Then, turning to me, all smiles and concern, she apologized for the delay and hoped sincerely I wasn't too tired.

At another hotel where foreigners were few and the staff therefore charming, after five days of travel I needed a bath. The bathroom was occupied so the service girl bashed on the door. 'Eh! Come on! Hurry up out of there! A foreign guest wants to use the bathroom!' But on a later occasion when a local was asked to move her belongings along the bench so that I could use the shower room too, there was an angry retort. I had often wondered what the Chinese felt about being treated as inferiors in their native land, barred from the trade fairs, barred from the luxury tourist hotels, barred from Friendship Stores and the foreign books sections of Chinese shops, and imagined that many resented this rule. The girl in the shower room was in a bad mood. She may also have felt an antipathy towards foreigners, founded on inheritance, colonial abuse and recent anti-capitalist propaganda (in view of which the general friendliness was remarkable) for she snapped hysterically, 'Why should I move? Don't foreigners and Chinese have equal rights? Why do we have to give preference to foreigners?', much as a Westerner might have done if ordered to make way for a Chinese. At this the service girl lost her temper too, and cursing shrilly she slammed the door, leaving the bather and me alone with our silence in the steam.

Anti-Japanese feeling was still widespread too. Once, in a post office, an English-speaking clerk would only deal with a Japanese traveller through me. 'What does *he* want?' he asked crossly. 'He would like to send a carpet to Japan,' I replied. 'Ask him where he bought it.' 'In the bazaar,' the Japanese replied. 'What kind of money did he pay for it with?' 'Renminbi.' 'It is against the rules!' screeched the clerk, victorious; 'he has to pay in FEC.' The Japanese quickly gathered his wits. 'FEC,' he muttered to the clerk. 'I paid for it in FEC.' 'Where is the receipt? He has to present the receipt!' The Japanese pleaded ignorance. The man from whom he had bought the carpet was a peasant and probably illiterate. 'What is the value of his carpet?' asked the clerk. 'One hundred and eighty yuan.' 'It is against the regulations to send any parcel worth over a hundred yuan unless it is paid for in FEC.' He seized the package, carefully sewn in unbleached cotton (the kind used for mourning) according to the rules, and dumped it on the scales. It weighed fourteen kilograms. 'It is not allowed,' announced the clerk with relish, 'to send a parcel weighing over ten kilos to Japan.'

There was another kind of foreigner in China, one never treated as honoured guest but tolerated, patronized and disdained. These foreigners accounted for sixty million of China's population and occupied over half its area, the inhospitable parts that agriculturally China could do without but because of their valuable mineral resources and China's paranoia about its neighbours, it was extremely loath to rescind.

The majority Hans wrote and spoke of their 56 minority nationalities as of a problem, all one problem, to which one might apply a single solution with similar result. In reality they were peoples from terrains as disparate as snow-covered plateaux and tropical rain-forest, as desert oases and Mongolian grassland; peoples at different stages of 'civilization' from hunter-gatherer to the modern-minded Hans; peoples with different means of survival and different racial origins. The way the Party went on one would think it was only through its leniency that the minorities were able to survive at all. Yet it imposed severe strictures during the Cultural Revolution, prohibiting migration of nomadic peoples, enforcing grain-growing on unsuitable land to ensure supplies for urban Hans, restricting languages and the use of different scripts, banning religion and destroying its temples and abolishing traditional ways. Though policies had become more moderate, condescending attitudes still pertained. The Bais around Dali were gentle and manageable and the Hans could indulge their chauvinism without comeback, 'allowing' the Bais their traditional costumes and obsolete gods, their quaint superstitions and curious ways. When we asked the Hans about the Bais they could tell us nothing at all. Some Bai men had rejected their traditional culture too, seeing advancement as lying in the adoption of Han mores, viewing their customs like the Hans, as symbols of ignorance and backwardness.

Tibet was the most extreme example of brutal Chinese expansionism. Presenting a threat it demanded control. Nearly two and a half thousand monasteries were reduced to ten. Only one in fifty lamas remained. Wheat had been sown on barley land, denying Tibetans their staple food. A few of the temples were being restored, but much activity was fool-tourist sham.

It put me off going, but I did visit Kumbum, a Tibetan lamasery of the Yellow Cap sect on the Qinghai plateau which was formerly Tibet. Kumbum was spared the ravages of Red Guards for its defence had been strong, though many older lamas had been subjected to labour reform. One of six surviving lamaseries, it was the focus of pilgrimage for visiting Tibetans from Amdo and beyond, spectacularly dressed, spectacularly unwashed, with the weather-beaten beauty and untamed hair of prides of shy lions. By day they shuffled round the sacred halls in their long yak coats with sleeves to their knees like elephants' trunks and frequently naked beneath. They prostrated themselves and turned their prayer wheels and spooned butter into lamps and offered silk scarves before the thrones in the scripture hall. At night they slept out on the gravelly forecourt with no more than their coats in the snow.

The Hans looked on in disgust. They stood and stared, unsmiling, unfriendly, at what to them seemed like neolithic cavemen wearing animal hides over skin like old leather, seeing nothing, I imagined, but the dirt and wildness and feudal ornaments they wore in their hair, feeling none of the romance they held for me. All the Tibetans could do was pretend to ignore them and carry on eating their tsampa with their fingers, though in response to me they would tug each other's coats crying 'Look! Quick, look!' and gaze with the innocent wonder of a child.

As part of its move to show tolerance to the minorities, the authorities of Dali had arranged a competition of song, dance and comic entertainment, the first of its kind, to be held at the cinema in between shows. The hotel overflowed with musical troupes from away in the mountains, with buffalo masks and woodwind rehearsals and Yi girls exotic as tropical butterflies in red and black and kingfisher green.

Each evening they performed to an audience of villagers. The Hans themselves displayed little interest and kept away. By cultivating the minorities' heritage, patting it, potting it, putting it on stage, I feared they were trying to tame their traditions, to embalm them for tourists as had happened elsewhere. Taking music and dance from the villages and fields might be to freeze their evolution, to turn spontaneity into work. But this was the first time, and there was a freshness and innocence that more polished presentations would have sacrificed. Luscious Bai girls with narrow waists and rounded bottoms and rosy faces tanned by the sun, sang and danced in traditional folk rhythms to music belonging to forest and hillside, played on flutes and chanters, erhus and drums.

I was drawn most of all by the Yis. Nothing I saw or experienced in China moved me, transported me, totally possessed me as did their dance. I longed to go to their villages in the mountains; I asked and asked but no one would tell me where they were except that being a foreigner I could not go. Yet the magic of their performance was not its music; the singing was harsh, atonal and shrill and the accompanying instrument, a right-angled pipe with a gourd at the end, only played two notes. It was not the dance; the swirling and stamping was neither difficult nor intricate. Nor was it the accomplishment; sometimes a girl would stand for a while, her movements forgotten, as unabashed as if still in the fields. But the rhythms and sounds and movements were all one. They belonged to a world of earth and air and seemed to emanate from an ancient knowledge of a deeper harmony between man and his origins the contemporary world had lost. For a moment I wondered if the purpose of music was to link people back to their inner souls. For a moment I touched on the meaning of life, but it ran through my fingers again and was gone.

6

Slowly to Sichuan

Nineteen eighty-four was the year of the rat. Rat stamps were issued and letters appeared in the papers saying why all this fuss about rats when they were carriers of plague (which persisted till the sixties) and consumers of grain and outnumbered Chinese people by several to one?

Street market hawkers sold rat traps and poison, and displayed stuffed rats to demonstrate their worth. But Rosy and I had a friend in Dali who had his own way of catching the rats that scurried in his roof and kept him awake at night. 'I read about it in the newspaper,' he told us. 'First I catch a rat in an ordinary trap. I tie up its feet so it can't run away, then I stuff a dried pea in its anus. Having sewn up the opening I set the rat free. It feels so much pain, the article says, that it will bite and kill twenty more rats.'

'That's cruel!' we cried. 'Don't do it again!'

'My wife doesn't like it either,' he confided. 'She says it's disgusting.'

Being so close to the countryside we could see our food being grown. Sometimes we saw night soil heaped in the fields or spread to dry in a threshing yard, or being ladled liquid on to growing crops, and sometimes there were shreds of soft pink paper stuck to vegetables on sale.

Although night soil collectors were in theory regarded as socialist heroes, championed by folk tales, serenaded by song, it was hard to find out what they actually did. I wanted to know how the night soil was processed, whether it was dried or kept in wet pits. When I asked Yao, my botanist friend, he snickered in embarrassment and looked away. And once when I followed a night soil collector in a city hotel I was cut off by two men and shooed away. Then one day in Dali Rosy and I saw two elderly 'gentlemen of the nights' perfume', as they were euphemistically called, in faded clothes and old peaked caps, galloping down the main street leaving a stench of sewers in their wake. Their muscles were braced to take the weight of the brimming wooden buckets at the end of their poles (which doubled as ladles) and ensure that none was spilt.

We set off after them at an energetic trot, thinking them unlikely to be going very far. But these old men never slackened their pace. They shifted their poles from one side to the other and swung off down a stony track that ran beside the old town wall and veered off across the fields. Fifty yards in the rear we panted, sweating, in the morning sun through fields of wheat and bean. We charged through a village and out the other side, to the astonishment of villagers drawing water from a well. Back out in the fields and already miles from Dali the old men stopped for a smoke. We sauntered on ahead but they soon overtook us, springing along on their stringy bow legs, glancing back from time to time to see if we still followed them.

Four miles from Dali by the third village well, our gentlemen parted ways. We followed the more ragged one, twisting and turning along dusty alleys between whitewashed walls until he dropped his pails and fled.

Defeated yet again I asked a schoolboy, and this time received a credible reply. Since night soil could be sold (five jiao for two buckets), people built loos wherever they could. There were loos along bus routes and well-travelled field paths; loos hung over pools to stimulate pondweed which in turn fed the fish. Our hotel facilities were placed near the entrance so passers-by could leave offerings too.

Our gentlemen were peasants buying compost for their fields. Having taken it home they would pour it in a pit, to which water would be added, and weeds and other refuse, and to hasten the breakdown the pit would be covered with earth. But according to season time might be short and the night soil spread neat, not a commendable practice, the schoolboy agreed, but there was nothing the Party could do. Vegetables could be fertilized three times during their growing season, which was why Chinese greens were so carefully washed. Not always quite carefully enough, unfortunately, as Rosy and I were soon to find out.

I had already had dealings with the Chinese diet and would do so again. One evening in Sichuan the only food available was a cauldron of red liquid bubbling on a fire like an alchemist's brew. I dropped in beansprouts and brought them out dripping, like a mass of fleas and water snails on pondweed fished from a pool. The smell should have warned me: those clinging 'snails' were whole Sichuan peppercorns, hotter by far than anything in India or anywhere else in the world. I swallowed a few mouthfuls, aware of nothing but searing heat. My eyes watered, my nose streamed, my head was on fire, and though starving I could eat no more. Not only that, but a kind of madness overcame me. I ran from the noodle shop and thrust my head beneath the nearest tap. I stood in the street and gulped down lungfuls of cool sweet air. I fanned my sweating face with my hand and panted in gasps to put out the fire. I scratched my palms and tore at my feet for I thought the irritation would drive me insane. Never in my life had I eaten anything with such spectacular effect.

Although traditional cuisine was rightly fabled and healthy ingredients were usually on sale, it was hard to find wholesome cooked meals. It was not just the pork fat, present in everything from noodles and dried milk to biscuits and cakes and combined with sugar as a substitute for jam, but the dearth of winter vegetables, the expense of fruit, the monosodium glutamate added, like salt, to every meal, and above all the lack of fibre. Ask a Chinese what his favourite food is and he will probably say rice. Boiled white rice. A friend of a friend, after twenty years in China, was cut open so that a ball of white rice that had lodged in his gut could be taken out. Something of the kind was happening in mine, so when I met a bank clerk who spoke some English I asked what he could recommend. Without replying he went to his desk and brought out four phials sealed up with wax, each containing numerous little red pills. 'Take a whole phial,' the clerk advised. I did as I was bid, swallowing pills in handfuls, 137 of them, and by morning I was cured.

According to Western scientists 200 million Chinese still live in a state of near-starvation. People are always thinking about food and feeling lethargic because of its lack. Ninety per cent of the Chinese diet is still made up of grain. Yet the compensating benefits are being eroded by campaigns encouraging people to eat more meat, promoting the consumption of dairy food and condoning the rise of Western fads: fast food, French wine, processed products and Coca-Cola. Already there were problems of child obesity, spoilt children being indulged with sweets and cake.

*

March was designated 'politeness month'. On the assumption that people would perform more 'spontaneous' good deeds if they had to, children, students, doctors, workers and the PLA were mobilized during March to clean the streets, help old ladies, carry out repair works and give medical treatment at wholesale prices in return for public praise.

On the Sunday morning of the weekly market, doctors from Dali's PLA hospital set up shop in front of the department store. It was our last day in Dali, and we were already nostalgic. In a nearby alleyway the Catholic church was holding its first service for thirty years. Peasants pouring in to market were pausing to watch the PLA'S performance, the clipping of hair, the massaging of joints, and eventually the practice of acupuncture that Rosy and I had come to see.

A woman presented her young deaf daughter and held her down, screaming, as the doctor stuck a needle in the skin beside her ear. One man had neck pain and another had a headache, a condition which the local Bai women cured by sticking broad beans on each side of their heads. Rosy by this time had a headache too, and with that Western proclivity for wanting to experiment with everything that's going, she placed herself in the doctor's chair.

The crowd increased. Rosy looked apprehensive; she had trained as a nurse and was frightened of pain. But the doctor looked kindly, the sort of woman one would want for a mother, we told her through a friend.

Gold needles pricked the joints between the thumb and forefinger of Rosy's hands, only for a second, and the treatment was done. Rosy said it hurt. Then she felt dizzy. She put her head between her knees and passed right out. The doctors lifted her, smirking at the weight, and laid her on a bench. Everyone was laughing in the ambivalent way the Chinese had, when it was impossible to tell whether they laughed through amusement or embarrassment or guilt. I was laughing too, and I recognize now that the roots of my laughter were not dissimilar from theirs. Although it had its funny side there was something that concealed my embarrassment for Rosy, something that worried for her and kept me in control, and something that pretended nothing was wrong so the doctor should not lose face. In a land where it was undignified to show sorrow or shock or anger or shame at inappropriate times laughter was multi-functional, the only acceptable emotional vent.

Rosy lay on the bench, her face the colour of an unripe quince. When she regained consciousness they helped her up and gave her a lurid green drink. As her own colour returned she noticed the crowd and smiled a bit sheepishly, embarrassed by her reaction to mere needlepricks. But at least, she said, her headache had gone. People kept apologizing, though it was no one's fault. A PLA reporter from the *People's Daily* had photographed the episode and was sending his pictures to the paper to print.

We left that evening, and spent the night in a Chinese-only hotel in Xiaguan where, too tired to go out, we dined in the canteen off reheated rice and garlic greens.

It was a pleasant ten-hour ride across the Yunnanese plateau. Red-brown hill slopes were strewn with patches of gold-green wheat. For a while we drove through a flowered land of Monet-conceived pastels, of sea-green beans and primrose rape, ice-pink cherry trees and celadon wheat and foaming banks of lilac vetch. Then we entered a valley, dark-slope-forested, where fragile willows clouded the river banks and rice of a vivid electric hue furred the valley floor. The most startling sight of all was a wheat-covered plain spotted with villages hardly more than a stone's throw apart, a landscape more crowded than anything I'd ever seen, more crowded than the Yangtze deltalands where two thousand people occupied every square mile. In true Chinese tradition of intensive and sustainable cultivation each family had no more than an acre to farm.

Back in Kunming at the Kun Hu Hotel Rosy fled to the loo. While I went in search of the oranges she craved she retired to bed up five flights of stairs. By the time I returned Rosy's face had resumed her sickly pale green of the previous day. She'd been running to the loo ever since I left, until, too weak to get back to our room twenty yards away, she'd collapsed on the wet concrete floor and wept. She recounted how one of the service girls had opened the door, had stared at her quite devoid of expression and had shut it again without a word. Somehow Rosy had got herself back, but she had outrun her energy and lost all control of her bowels.

Against her will I went for a doctor. It was past eleven and the city was asleep; I could hear the sound of my boots on the road. I asked directions of everyone I met and arrived at a hospital nearby.

Explaining why I'd come I was led to a young Dr Han from Shanghai. He would willingly escort me to the Kun Hu Hotel, he explained in the shout which some Chinese used when speaking a language not their own, but he needed permission to go. This was not just New China regulations, but Old China caution and etiquette. Given a tricky situation a Chinese would pass it on to his superiors. He would watch which way the wind blew and never stick his neck out – I was to experience this infuriating but understandable habit many times. We sought out the cadres, two stolid ladies who refused to grant the permission we required. I smiled as sweetly as was possible under the circumstances and after further discussion they grudgingly allowed Dr Han to come with me to Rosy's bedside, 'Just to check her condition,' they said.

Getting out of Dr Han's own unit was one thing; gaining admittance to someone else's, and in the middle of the night, another one entirely. In spite of his white coat and stethoscope, his open face and pleasant speech, the man on the door of the Kun Hu Hotel would not let him in without another long wrangle. Dr Han had no certificate to justify his presence and the hotel had locked up for the night. Yet it seemed to me there was more behind the man's reluctance than a dutiful guarding of territory from intruders, for he was of peasant stock and the doctor an intellectual from Shanghai. The classes were as mutually distrustful and exclusive as ever they had been. Dr Han was even contemplating marriage to a Chinese American he'd never seen in order to escape the rigours of communism, though I didn't know that then.

The hotel lift was still out of action and we had to trail – for the fourth time in my case – up those five flights of stairs. Rosy was barely conscious by this time; Dr Han took one look at her and told her she'd have to be admitted to the hospital. 'Can you walk there?' he asked.

Rosy teetered down the corridor clutching my arm, but collapsed on the floor as we drew level with the loo. Dr Han looked nervous; his voice rose a tone. We carried Rosy back and the doctor went down to ring for the ambulance, and wake the hotel staff to operate the lift.

Half an hour later we set off again. Rosy clung to my shoulder, dragging her feet, but we'd not gone ten yards before she passed right out for the second time. With difficulty we manoeuvred her into the lift where an armchair was waiting. No one offered us any assistance, neither staff standing watching nor guests glued to television on the hotel landing. Down in the foyer we carried her, unconscious, in the heavy armchair, and again no help was offered by anyone.

At the time I was angry: I had not been in China long enough to know. I often saw people in need of assistance, ill or lost or standing in buses when healthy young people were occupying seats, and no one would offer support. As I walked down a street a month before a man had jerked his bicycle back from a cycle stand and a fierce metal spike had gashed my calf. I shrieked and bent down to nurse my leg, bleeding and swollen and still scarred two years afterwards, while the culprit mounted and rode off without a word. And I once met a traveller who had seen a man lying in a Beijing shopping street, and two hours later he'd still been there. Rosy and I had ourselves helped a peasant whose cart had tipped up at a Kunming crossroads, chasing kohl rabi while the crowd that had gathered dispersed in disdain. The puller of the hand-cart did not acknowledge us, and I sensed his unease, his shame and puzzlement, for it was considered unlucky to involve oneself in a stranger's misfortunes which could then be transferred to you. Assisting strangers brought fear of reprisal; by helping someone you damaged their prestige and caused them to lose face.

Whereas in the West we see people as equals with similar claims on our concern, the Chinese were responsible, not to society but to a formal friend and kinship network, beyond which they seemed indifferent, even brutal in their ways. Although Mao called for mutual aid, the degree of concern within the group left little love for those outside. Just as Indians didn't 'see' beggars, perhaps the Chinese, with all their hardship and compromise, simply failed to register a stranger's distress.

'Diarrhoea can be very dangerous,' announced Dr Han in his trumpeting voice when we'd loaded Rosy into the van. 'It can kill you,' he said.

Fortunately Rosy was too far gone to be aware of anything anyone said. We helped her into the entrance hall where a group of doctors examined her, interspersing their questions with demands for payment: seven jiao for registration, five yuan for the ambulance, before her treatment could begin. Still in the entrance hall, through which staff and patients and their relatives were passing and gathering round to see what was happening, Rosy was asked to undress. I objected, but Rosy complied; the doctors wanted a swab. So I stood in the doorway and held off the spectators and glared at the porter who'd already slipped past and was advancing eagerly for a close-up view of a Western woman's anatomy. Forty years previously no Chinese doctor would have taken the liberty of examining a woman, for which purpose small statuettes were made.

Arriving feet first in a state of semi-coma, Rosy had bypassed all the procedures that I had followed seeking treatment for bronchitis a month earlier, and would have to suffer many times more. On arrival at a hospital you queue for registration, queue to see a doctor who as often as not is 'unable' to see you, in which case you queue for an urgent treatment note. You queue again for the doctor who advises some tests, queue in the room where blood samples are taken, and again for an X-ray, and yet again for an injection (having queued several times to pay for them first); then you queue for the doctor who examines the results and writes a prescription out. You queue at the pharmacy which presents you with a bill, queue at the cashier and queue for the last time to collect your remedies, pills and powders wrapped in small square packages, with instructions in characters on the front.

Rosy knew none of this. She was moved to an anteroom containing two battered bedsteads at careless angles, and attached to a drip. Her room-mate was a man apparently dead and likewise plumbed with tubes. Besides prescribing vitamins for almost every ailment they knew, Chinese doctors had a penchant for treating intravenously, whether the problem was typhoid or pain in a tooth.

Twenty minutes later, having ascertained that Rosy was suffering from a virulent strain of dysentery, they decided to move her to the infectious diseases ward. I was under obligation to stay and nurse her; if I wanted to go out, I, like Dr Han, would have to seek permission from the cadres. But I would not have left, even were I asked to. Rosy spoke no Chinese and the hospital staff (besides Dr Han who was about to go off duty) no English. She was frightened enough as it was.

Our ward was much like the wards of other hospitals I had trespassed into to see what they were like. It was a six-bed ward containing nothing but the bedsteads and six small cabinets, only it seemed more desolate because we were going to have to stay there. There was no light or bell to call for assistance, and the single nurse on night duty was stationed at a desk twenty yards down the corridor, from which she administered to half a dozen wards. There was a rusty bowl for washing in, but neither flannel nor soap nor towel. Under pressure I was granted a small cake of soap, since I was a foreign friend they said, and would be needing to wash my hands very thoroughly each time Rosy used the bedpan and I cleaned it out. I even had to ask for the provision of the bedpan, and for rags to protect the bedding from soiling, and for something to drink from (it came, eventually – a dirty bottle; we were told that we ought to have brought our own) and for a thermos of water, and for various other things one would have thought a hospital would have worked out for itself.

Rosy's consultant in the infectious diseases ward, fortuitously empty but for ourselves, was a middle-aged woman wearing heavy black-framed spectacles. 'That doctor is dull,' Dr Han confided when she'd passed out of earshot, whereupon Rosy hit the roof. Dr Han changed tack and was forced to pretend he had meant it as a joke, when in truth he was annoyed about not being permitted to treat Rosy himself. Together the doctors took Rosy's pulse, her temperature and blood pressure, and pricked her little finger for samples of blood, but as they had forgotten to remove the thermometer in the meantime she jumped, and bit it in half.

They turned to me. 'That'll be six jiao,' they said, and I had to pay up at once. A new thermometer was procured and the doctors, one on each side of Rosy's bed, held a heated discussion over whether they should chance it to her teeth again or put it under her arm instead. Within minutes they had broken two cardinal rules, by belittling a fellow member of the hospital staff and having a public row.

We passed a lonely and sleepless night. There was something desperate about that ward with its empty beds and discoloured walls and naked light bulb and grubby concrete floor, silent but for Rosy rolling and groaning, unable to find a comfortable place. I was in and out emptying bedpan after bedpan, and scrubbing my hands in a concrete tank – the habitat of two large cockroaches – and massaging Rosy's buttocks and thighs, and pouring water and smoothing sheets and administering pills at regular intervals. With somewhat less regularity the night nurse appeared in mask and gown, tapping the drip to regulate its speed, ignoring our requests for sleeping pills. '*Please* give her some painkiller or sleeping pills,' I repeatedly pleaded. 'She cannot sleep'. 'She can,' replied the nurse, shocked at this display of weakness, her face set firm as she returned to her station down the corridor. Even women in labour made little outward show of pain.

By six in the morning we were both exhausted and finally on the point of sleep. For everyone else it was time to get up. From the wards along the corridor an army of patients came crashing up and down with their flapping shoes and washing bowls, slamming doors and turning on taps and peering in through our open door. Then came doctors, and questions, and tests: Dr Han had been so worried he hadn't slept all night.

Since we needed to remain in the hospital ward, so the doctors said, I returned to the hotel to check out of our room. Two hours later I checked back in again, Rosy having had a row with the people in charge at the hospital. What they were demanding was far more than any Chinese would have paid, whether their unit had a medical insurance scheme or not, and more than Rosy could afford (the Chinese paid only manufacturing costs, which was balanced by a mark-up on luxury goods).

'Don't the Chinese want to give a good impression to foreign visitors?' Rosy asked Dr Han.

'No,' he replied. 'The only reason they allow you in is because they want your money.'

Our former room at the Kun Hu Hotel, supposedly cleaned and ready for new customers, abounded in traces of the night before. 'Would it be possible,' I asked Dr Han, 'for you to request the hotel to change the bedding and wash the floor, and to let us have the room to ourselves?' If I asked myself, my plea would be ignored: too many foreigners had passed through the doors of the Kun Hu Hotel and its staff despised us. After the friendly Dali guest-house, not thus exposed to independent travellers over the previous five years, the Kun Hu was depressing in the extreme. I had forgotten how awful the Chinese could be.

'I can't do that,' sighed Dr Han. 'For one thing the Kun Hu is not my unit, so I have no authority over anyone there. For another it is not up to you to worry about anyone catching the disease. In China each man is responsible for himself. If the hotel knew you had something infectious they would not let you stay there at all.'

I cleaned the room myself. In so doing I remembered the oranges and tea eggs (eggs hard-boiled in tea) I had put in the drawer and forgotten to remove on checking out. They had gone.

'Do you know what happened to the eggs and oranges I left in our room?' I asked the service girls, mopping the floor of the loo. They laughed in a manner intentionally humiliating. Then one of them led me down the corridor to where our oranges lay buried in dust and waste paper in a rubbish bin. My boots were there too, I saw with surprise; it said little for the legendary Chinese custom of returning used biros and empty packets that foreigners left behind. We'd had our fill of the Kun Hu Hotel.

In the evening Rosy came home. For someone who just twelve hours before had looked about to die, she'd made a miraculous recovery and the doctors evidently knew their job. Although tending to overprescribe, Chinese doctors would discuss an illness with the patient concerned and would offer them alternatives or combinations of Chinese and Western medicines. Far from behaving like gods in little empires their quotient of arrogance was roughly equivalent to the service personnel in the Kun Hu Hotel. I had seen better hospitals even in Kunming, where all was fresh and clean and white, the equipment up-to-date and the staff underworked. I had seen far worse, though not in Kunming, where patients suffered unattended on benches and nursing relatives slept in deckchairs and corridors became wards for the overspill and the entire complex stank of stale pee.

The Kun Hu Hotel was packed that night, with people sleeping on sets of chairs and on tables in the lobby once television closed down. Johan the con man was camping on a staircase. With no hope of sleep I washed my clothes and sluiced myself down in the washroom on the eighth floor, wedging the door shut with the handle of a mop. For an eight-storey hotel built in the sixties the washing facilities were minimal in the extreme.

Over the next two days instead of travelling on to Sichuan we spent half the time in bed. I ate almost nothing, hoping to stave off the ominous rumblings. Rosy was better, but by the third day I was bad enough to spend the morning in hospital tied to a drip. By lunchtime I was free, and we set off south-west to recuperate at

Shilin. Villages of red mud clustered in the hollows of rounded hills, and maize cobs hung yellow in tall green trees. The further we went the nicer it became, until we descried the forest of rock spires in the folds of the hills, sharp grey spines like porcupine quills, vertically fissured by percolating rain. Set among fields of wispy wheat it all seemed real, much more than the playground for day-return tour groups I had imagined the Stone Forest would be. We stayed for two days, resting in the heat when the visitors came, walking at dawn and again at dusk when the air was cool and the pathways quiet between scented green flowers and tumbling white roses, through caves and gorges and shady hollows spread with tiers of leaves upon leaves. The pure, pungent, pine-scented wind put strength back inside us and we returned, replenished, to Kunming.

Rosy was now cured. Short of time and worrying about long johns she left for Xian, leaving me to travel on slowly to Sichuan. After a couple more days I caught the evening train to E Mei, a twenty-hour journey in a hard-seat coach.

A little boy bounced on the opposite bench, half the night and all next day, while his mother stood tiredly in the aisle. All you could see was his ruddy face beneath a rabbit-eared hat, the tips of his fingers poking from the ends of arms sticking sideways in ten wadded layers and an expanse of genitalia through back-slit pants. This was not the proverbial Chinese angel, a child taught above all to be quiet, submissive and well behaved, but the recent product of the one-child rule, an egocentric spoilt brat. He cared neither for his mother nor anyone else; his behaviour expressed the unshakable belief that the world existed just to satisfy his needs. He sensed somehow that he could sing and shout and jump up and down and annoy other passengers and that because he was a child, a dying breed, no one would complain.

There were practical reasons for spoiling a son. Before Liberation parents pampered their boys in the belief that they'd care for them when they grew old and venerate their spirits once they had gone, a kind of savings account or insurance bond. Sons continued the family line while daughters were a burden, eating its rice and then leaving the clan for another man's home. To have no sons in old China was to have failed. To decline to have children, or as many as it took to achieve a son, was to dishonour one's parents, the greatest transgression of the Confucian code. In contemporary society the old logic survives in diluted form, and most peasants still yearn for a boy.

Male or female, the newfound race of single children know their power and use it to the full; they are doted on with all the affection previously spread over four or five. If they want to see they push others aside and the grown-ups just smile and coo. They tend to fuss over food, bully their elders and refuse to obey their commands.

Everyone's hope now lay in the young. Children might succeed where their parents had failed, might benefit from the freedoms that they were denied. Ambition was handed down the generations and heaped lavishly on the only daughter or son. Everyone needed to offload their affection and in the absence of religion and a family clan, in a country like China where one daren't trust one's neighbour what safer beneficiary than a child? Denied their gods, people turned to children as surrogate deities, especially since the death of the god-like patriarch Mao Zedong. Where once there were images of gods and altars there were now bonny toddlers, red-lipped, pink-skinned and wobbling with fat, riding pandas and goldfish on posters along walls.

The one-child campaign was launched by Deng in 1980 with the aim of reducing population growth to nil by the year 2000. If it succeeds there'll be food for everyone, but if it fails, warns the Party, millions will go hungry and die.

Without government interference China's population could reach four billion in a hundred years. It has already doubled since 1949, having previously been checked by floods and famines, female infanticide, contagious disease and civil war. But though production has improved, grain yields per person haven't increased in two thousand years; a quarter of the world is being sustained on one-fifteenth of its arable land, one-tenth of a hectare each.

Penalties for giving birth to more than one child vary from place to place. Minority peoples are now exempt and in many rural areas the peasants can have two. Stricter controls are kept in towns where deviant couples lose their places on the housing list, have their wages reduced, lose pensions and other benefits or are made to pay fines. Generally everything is made so unpleasant for non-conformists that almost everyone eventually complies.

Will the one-child policy survive? There may be fewer mouths to feed but the kinship structure of brothers and sisters and cousins and uncles is being upturned. China will become a different place, socially, culturally and emotionally, with each couple caring for two sets of parents and four sets of grandparents while scarcely being able to look after themselves. The generation gap will widen as spoilt children rebel. Already there are signs of the policy's relaxation as people are exempted from the rule. In twenty or thirty years, say the Party, it will once again be permissible to have two.

Many young city couples saw the logic of the policy and were able, almost, to accept – especially if their baby was a boy. With their higher expectations, their minimal living space, their lack of funds and new security in old age most couples I met didn't want more than two children, even had large families still been allowed. The chief Chinese gripes were nearly always the same, not lack of children so much as poor living conditions and insufficient funds. But a few spoke out. Talking in Kunming to a railway employee in her morning break she asked if I had a child. She herself had three. 'Naughty!' I chided her, and everyone laughed. 'One child good, two not so good, three very bad!' 'No, no!' she shrieked. 'Three children *good*!'

The opposite attitude was far less unusual than one would expect of a country like China. Women were beginning to question their roles and a growing percentage of young intellectuals valued their freedom above having families and didn't want children at all. I had met such a girl in Nanning. Married to a man who taught at university, Sun Lin herself worked in films. Sullen but attractive, with ivory skin and wavy hair, Sun Lin complained that her baby had aged her, that she now looked more than her thirty years. It was her husband who'd insisted they have a child. Her ambitions were suffering from her tiredness and half her salary went to pay the fees of their private nurse. State-run nurseries were large and crowded and children received no individual care. They were not good enough for Sun Lin.

Pressure from the West was greater on the issue of the one-child rule than on any of China's other policies with the possible exception of Tibet. What the West most deplored was the degree of coercion the campaign involved. Individuals were pressurized even by their colleagues, who earned larger bonuses if the unit as a whole signed the one-child pledge. Women were brainwashed day after day till they 'agreed' to sign a paper for a tubal ligation or the abortion of their unborn child. The Party denied such things were enforced but evidence was widespread, from first-hand witnesses, from books and on film. During the 'high tide' periods of the one-child campaign millions of women were compulsorily sterilized or forcibly operated on to terminate their pregnancies, by Caesarian if the baby's birth was near or injection if the embryo was still small. It was useless to oppose a current campaign; anyone who did would be exposed and attacked as an enemy of the State.

On the train my illness got worse. Through a haze of discomfort, through the raucous screams of the bouncing boy, between the roar and confusion of a hundred tunnels, I gazed out upon gorges, upon broad slow rivers and gentler hillsides, and then upon Sichuan – the romantic Szechwan of my schoolday geography – a fertile land of grey-green wheat under rain-full clouds. It was a feminine land-scape, sensual in its softness. Farmsteads were scattered in bamboo groves, invisible over the sea of wheat and waist-high rape but for their broad thatched roofs. After the masculine dryness of the eroded Yunnanese plateau lands it seemed so safe; I wanted to leap from the train and run my arms through the fern-fine foliage and bury my face in its damp earth scent, and walk barefoot on the short grass field bunds and feel the silken air upon my skin.

Alighting at the small half-timbered town of E Mei, the base for the ascent of the holy Buddhist mountain of E Mei Shan, I checked in at the hotel, went to the hospital to get some medicine and retired to bed. It was the third of April.

On the fourth of April 1984, the day of the opening of George Orwell's book, I was still in bed, looking out upon clouds and a large heap of coal that obscured the hotel courtyard from my view. From time to time a worker passed the window, dressed in baggy revolutionary blue. At noon and five-thirty came a clattering behind the coal heap as a crowd of people queued for the canteen, handed in grain coupons, scooped rice from a tub, collected bean curd from a counter and gathered on benches in the whitewashed hall. Unable to face food I lay reading stories from the Cultural Revolution concerning loyal young heroines with courage and pigtails giving their all to the socialist cause. They had correct class backgrounds, perfect ideologies and they always triumphed in the end.

April the fourth 1984. Much of Orwell's vision of London could have been China in the Cultural Revolution. Posters of Big Brother were plastered on every wall. There was ceaseless talk about pig-iron production and over-fulfilment of the ninth three-year plan. Though laws had been abolished people knew what would earn them a sentence in labour camp. The renegade backslider ('capitalist roader' in Maoist terminology) who had once been a leading Party figure and was currently slandered in hate campaigns might have been Deng. Any enemy of the Party was absolute evil while the Party itself was absolute good. Every word of Big Brother was infallible truth, a soothing elixir, a focus for all the love, fear, reverence and gratitude that had formerly been dissipated on family and God. Perpetual war and deprivation kept people constantly struggling for survival with no energy left over for dissent-provoking thought. Brainwashing techniques involved a drowning of consciousness in self-hypnotic chanting, constant confessionals and a lack of free time, a transformation of sexuality to political fervour, an altering not just of opinion but of instinct, of human nature itself. Those who thought were suspect in a regime where orthodoxy was synonymous with not thinking and not needing to. Personal feelings were of no account; political fervour was truth. Children spied on and denounced their parents. Executions were a public spectacle. Loudspeakers dominated people's lives. Rations were insufficient for the common man, yet high officials lived in privilege. Old things were destroyed and history rewritten according to the current Party line. Statistics were botched to show figures always healthier than the previous year; stronger, happier, better educated people; more houses, more grain, more cotton, less crime. 'But, thought Winston, life bore no resemblance to the ideals the Party was trying to achieve.' He might have been thinking of China.

Nothing was private, even now. One grew accustomed to communal life, to bathing in company, to loos without doors. The hotel wash-house was a row of taps above a slab beyond the coal heap. Needing to bathe I approached the shower room, which being open for only two hours every evening was loud with splashing and thick with steam. Urged on by the man on guard outside by encouraging gestures of soaping and scrubbing I opened the door and peered inside. Half-obscured by steam, half a dozen women were flannelling their heat-pink, almost hairless bodies. There was little variation in their size or shape; I rarely saw anyone either fat or thin. A woman over seventy was as firm of flesh and smooth of skin and as lithe of movement as a girl of seventeen.

No one in the communal shower room in E Mei was disturbed or embarrassed by the presence of a foreigner; the Chinese were less self-conscious than ourselves. I remember a foreigner returning unwashed from a communal shower room where two girls were soaping and sponging each other with an intimacy she felt only lovers should share. Strangers on buses and trains often touched me, taking hold of my garments to check their sufficiency, holding my hand to help me down steps, stroking my arm to test the white skin. Men touched me too, but in a brotherly way in which I felt no lust. Perhaps I was wrong; the Chinese were such masters at concealing what they felt.

Next day I attacked the holy Buddhist mountain of E Mei Shan, but I'd eaten nothing for days and my strength was gone. The path shot up in steep stone steps through a mountainside patterned with a tapestry of leaves: orange, copper, silver and crimson like old stained glass with the sun showing through. Birds sang suddenly from invisible treetops; white irises starred the shadowed ground. I spent the night in a purple-painted monastery standing on stilts among deep green trees, but a worsening of illness sent me scudding back down, jelly-legged, to E Mei at dawn. My only thought was to reach Chengdu where there were better doctors and proper hospitals and an end to my debility.

Chengdu was noise and monochrome flatness, the antithesis of E Mei Shan. Horns hummed, machinery whined: the skyline was punctured by cranes. Yet diving down lanes in the older neighbourhood I found tree-lined streets reminiscent of Warwickshire; half-timbered houses with gabled roofs and a low-eaved homeliness of wattle and daub. Clothes hung from poles. People sat shelling peas by Paulownia trees in plump lilac bud, and pushed babies in bamboo prams.

Almost as soon as I entered the door I was seen to a room and three doctors converged with comforting smiles. Within minutes the dysentery was correctly diagnosed and in four or five days I was cured.

7

Walls within Walls

Fifty miles from Changsha I telephoned Jan to let her know I'd soon be there. Jan was a Londoner, almost thirty, whom I'd met on holiday in Yunnan. She had been in China three months, teaching English to teachers at an institute in Changsha.

'I'm fed up,' said Jan. 'All the excitement has worn off, leaving nine more months of tedium and red tape. There's a leak in my bathroom, a mildewy wall and a cupboard I keep telling them I want removed. Since I came back from holiday four days ago I've been living on cream crackers – I just can't face the canteen.'

'I thought you liked it,' I said.

'At first I did,' she replied. 'The Chinese seem so friendly and courteous, but it's just their habit, not necessarily sincere. Their laughter often hides some other emotion but I never know which, that's the trouble with me. The Chinese don't react as we do, don't show their feelings. It disturbs me,' she said.

Jan was not alone in reacting the way she did. I heard similar tales of woe from almost every new 'expert' I came across. To be flung, often alone and unable to speak or understand Chinese, into a year's assignation with unit life, even with the privileges foreigners were awarded, could be crushing and exasperating to anyone used to the freedoms of the West. The luckier experts, of which Jan would be one, would pull through their depression to discover the language was not so impossible, that they were starting to adapt to ways not their own.

Rebecca and Paul, American experts of eight months' standing, were less fortunate than Jan. They had thrown themselves into their new experience, dressing like the Chinese, eating their food, adopting their habits and exchanging confidences in their bid for acceptance. But they gradually discovered that nothing they said was ever kept private, and that their attempts to accommodate the Chinese lifestyle, far from flattering their students, merely bewildered them.

They slackened their efforts and ultimately dropped them, returning to being Americans, to Western diet and dungarees. Rebecca stopped trying to learn Chinese and withdrew into knitting sweaters for Paul.

'They don't trust us,' she said resentfully, pausing in the middle of a row. Her curly hair was haloed round her head, an Indonesian textile adorned the wall behind her, and a contemporary novel lay open on the floor. 'They dislike us because we have more than them, yet they envy us at the same time. They don't trust each other because of their system, but they trust the foreigners even less.' The Chinese were wary of saying too much. Foreigners had got them into deep water at times, deep enough in which to drown.

Although Rebecca and Paul had tried to fit in they had adopted the wrong clothes, either feudal peasant fabric-fastened shirts or the baggy worker blues which were forced upon people in the Cultural Revolution and consequently despised. Chinese students, as I discovered from Xiuying, neither wanted nor expected us to look or be like them. They would rather we conformed to the image they had of us, rather put us on a pedestal to be admired and imitated and even ridiculed, to be living examples of the Western culture they cultivated, envied, cherished and abhorred. Traditionally we were either masters or barbarians. Our looks were still bizarre to them, our behaviour inexplicable. We never were friends.

However bad things seemed for Jan and other experts, they were infinitely worse for the other two thousand residents in her unit, the difference being that the Chinese didn't complain. In their eyes Jan lived in unimaginable splendour in her large bed-sittingroom in the unit guest-house, the only building with any semblance of homeliness, with a venerable pine tree in a garden at the front. It was a unit within a unit, with its own walled compound and its own venerable gatekeeper asleep inside his hut. Below Jan's window was a circular fishpool with a mossy water-worn rock in the centre, gazed at for hours by entranced Chinese visitors and ignored by Westerners (Jan and me). A fountain played from the mossy rock, so that even when it wasn't raining you believed it was.

Jan was asleep, slumped over her desk. She looked so vulnerable, a small blonde English girl with startling green eyes, alone in a community of two thousand Chinese. Around her were the trappings of Western comfort, some of which I hadn't seen for several months: carpets, an electric fire and air conditioner, a TV, cassette player and short-wave radio, cupboards, armchairs and pictures on the walls.

Over the week of my stay I came to understand a little of what it was to be an expert in China. Unlike Rebecca and Paul, Jan had no retreat into the safe familiarity of her own cultural background, for there was no one there to substantiate it. But perhaps she had less need to escape. Over the months she was patient. She allowed her friendships to happen naturally, waited for the Chinese to come to her, and gradually she made real friends. She wore her own clothes, English clothes which suited her. She remained her own woman. Without trying, she succeeded.

Discoloured walls and a wet bathroom floor were not the only hardships Jan had to overcome. She had to learn to teach in the way the Chinese were accustomed to learn, not in a creative, interpretative, boundary-stretching way but dispensing information, explaining every figure of speech, every construction, every cliché and colloquialism for her students to memorize. She had to be prepared to spend much of her own time in private tuition to students who materialized in her room at all hours. She had to rely on her inner resources, for with few outside stimuli the world might grow narrow and her brain get dull. She had to tolerate the kind intentions, the admonitions to take rest when it was the last thing she required, and the lengthy formal rituals. She had to adhere to the unit rules and come to terms with the (literal) red tape that was wound and knotted around everything she did. She had to accept that her wish to be integrated in unit life was beyond the comprehension of her superiors the cadres. She had to expect to be criticized, and compared unfavourably with those who'd come before. When she misunderstood what was said to her it was: 'Oh *Margaret* would have understood, she spoke very pretty Chinese.' When she showed no inclination to sprint round the running track four times before breakfast she was told how sporty Lesley had been. '*Lesley* took first prize in running at the sports meeting.'

These odds having been overcome a camaraderie evolved between Jan and her students, a two-way process in which they guided her through China and its language, while she was teaching them about England and ours. The students became real, each with their quirks, but loyal and thoughtful and determined to improve. What may have retarded their friendship at first was Jan's status in China, a privilege equivalent to a senior cadre. She had moments of guilt about her large furnished room; about her salary that was ten times what most Chinese earned and yet all of which she spent; about her access to the places of general privilege to foreigners; about her exemption from exercise and political seminars; and the respect and courtesy due her as a guest. The sum of these benefits was power she might easily and unknowingly have abused. But she'd come to China not as a communist but to see the world and live in a society few foreigners had known. Most foreign experts came for these reasons: if they were less well catered for they wouldn't come at all.

Jan believed that I too might benefit from a spell as an expert, to see inside the machinery of Chinese unit life. She realized, however, that in some ways her perspective was as limited as mine. 'My life is too exclusively "unit",' she put it, 'too exclusively intellectual and by definition, sheltered. The workers are easier to talk to than intellectuals, and the peasants even more so. It's a typical 1984 plebs/outer-inner Party duality.'

Compelling though aspects of Jan's life clearly were, I would not have changed places, though I greatly enjoyed being there as her guest. I felt closer to China than I did in hotels, cycling to the city to buy vegetables in the markets and exchange grain coupons for noodles in the stores, then returning to prepare our dinner or lunch – with many splendid things to two women sentenced to mass restaurants and canteens – and to meet Jan's students and listen to their tales.

Our most frequent caller was Xiao Wu. Xiao Wu means 'small fifth'; in other words he was the fifth son born of his father or the uncles on his father's side. Traditional family names like Third Daughter or First Aunt still endured in some circles, but the more usual terms for both family and friends were Lao (old), and Xiao (young or small), suggesting a rough familiarity and affection.

A shy, softly spoken man in his mid-twenties with an earnest, fringe-swept face, Xiao Wu was slipping past the currently ordained marrying age. The cadres were dropping hints, his family in Lanzhou were fussing and fretting, and Xiao Wu was apparently being forced into a corner from which his chances of escape were rapidly diminishing. In desperation he turned to Jan and me. There was no one else he could have approached, for until an official engagement was announced such things were secret, even from room-mates; while fiancées were tenable, girlfriends were taboo, and the onus was on students to report each other's crimes. Xiao Wu seemed to think that as older Westerners Jan and I had a ready-made solution to his problem up our sleeves. People would confess all manner of things just because I was foreign. My very foreignness meant I could safely be told things that couldn't be trusted to a fellow Chinese. Many had secrets they longed to share.

Xiao Wu had been in love with a former classmate, who on graduation was transferred to Beijing. Eventually he got leave and followed her there, but his girlfriend was no longer interested in him. Seeing Xiao Wu wasn't getting very far on his own account, his cadres approached a woman in his class to act as a go-between, to select a girl for Xiao Wu to wed. Photographs were exchanged, and Xiao Wu found the girl quite pretty, he said. She was less so, however, when he saw her in the flesh, and although he'd been seeing her for over five months and considered her his girlfriend, he didn't especially like her. The problem was that the longer it continued the harder it became to break it off. He had come to know and respect her family, and worst of all he had 'put so many people to so much trouble'. Xiao Wu believed the girl had fallen in love with him.

Meanwhile Jan had heard from the go-between that the girl didn't much like Xiao Wu either, though, like him, she thought *he* fancied her. She was equally afraid of backing down in case of not finding another man. Chinese girls who declined a man were criticized for being '*tai tiao-le*', too choosy, implying that this man was as much as she deserved and who did she think she was to consider she merited something more? Their ages were right, their jobs were right – she taught in a middle school and spoke some English – and they had the same class background (the wrong one, as it happened).

I asked Xiao Wu what it was he didn't like about the girl. He never referred to her by name; it was a mark, I felt, of his half-hearted affection.

He was hesitant about saying more – he had betrayed her enough already – and but for his conviction that we could help he might have kept silent. 'She is too opinionated,' he whispered apologetically. 'The girl has a mind of her own.' This was severe criticism: it was flattering, on the other hand, to call a girl 'unassuming'. Xiao Wu was afraid she might not obey him.

Even the go-between was having her doubts, although, as in their case, it was a bit late now. 'She's too masculine,' she told Jan, adding irrelevantly: 'You can tell by her name – it means "steel".' Steel was a boy's name; her parents had evidently hoped for a boy.

What Xiao Wu really wanted was to escape to Lanzhou, home to his parents and away from his forthcoming marriage. But the cadre in charge of Xiao Wu's life both liked and respected him and wanted him to stay. This cadre was responsible for Xiao Wu's future; Xiao Wu had very little choice of his own.

Just how many Chinese people married partners they didn't like? And how many more came to grief later on? Xiao Wu had only to look around at the marriages of the other, older students in his class; what he saw would not console him. Out of Jan's group of five, only one was happily married, and that was the go-between. The only other woman was put upon by a chauvinistic man. Though she worked full-time, he expected her to do all the household chores too. Sometimes he beat her, just to keep her down. Teacher Yuan was a sad bald man whose wife had been married before. She'd been forcibly divorced in the Cultural Revolution due to allegations of her husband's 'bad character' and 'incorrect class background'. She was then coerced into marrying Yuan, whom she used as a scapegoat for the wrong that had been done her. When their child grew up, she said, she would leave him. Lao Wang was more ebullient. But he and his wife seldom spoke to each other, and they slept in separate rooms. When Lao Wang's wife attempted suicide everyone blamed it on the Cultural Revolution. No one mentioned tension, depression or her marriage. No one mentioned the flirtatious relationship Lao Wang had had with Lesley, Jan's sporty predecessor, half Lao Wang's age. It had been a silly, obvious fancy. Lesley needed a father; Lao Wang needed attention.

One lunchtime Xiao Wu came to invite Jan and me to meet the girl's family. Her father collected roots; Xiao Wu told me I'd be interested and should take my camera. What he really wanted was for Jan and me to size the girl up and tell him what to do.

The collection of roots was apparently one of the finest in the land. There were roots displayed throughout the flat – a large one in a block some miles from the unit – but they came to a head in the living room. There were roots on shelves, on tables, on the floor, on the walls, on stands, on top of the wardrobe, on top of each other. Beyond, on the balcony, were more roots lurking among potted chrysanthemums. Roots of all sizes and forms and contortions, roots with a purpose – a stool, a chair, a standard lamp – and roots that had none, but impersonated a bird or animal instead. There was a crowing cock, a standing lion, a leaping gazelle, a Bactrian camel and a monkey swinging on a branch.

Sitting on a sofa covered with a locally tie-dyed cloth which I mistakenly admired, I realized that this was the first home I'd seen that expressed the taste of its occupants. There was Ming porcelain on the shelves, bought at knock-down price from a confiscated cache after the Cultural Revolution. The furniture was traditional: simple, solid and dark.

I was less at ease with the company. Xiao Wu stood in a corner and shuffled his feet. The girl perched nervously on the edge of the bed, her legs firmly crossed, her eyes cast down upon the floor. Every other minute her mother leapt up to pour more tea into our red clay bowls and offer us a peanut. Her father, the passion behind the roots and the only member of the family towards whom I felt any latent affinity, was out. At some point in the proceedings (Xiao Wu was pointing out a root we hadn't registered), we heard ominous tearing sounds from behind the bed, and I was presented with a length of the tie-dyed calico I had complimented them on. Jan had warned me of the danger of saying I liked things, for people then felt obliged to part with them. So I said I couldn't possibly accept the cloth, much as I admired it, for there wasn't any room in my bags. At the end of an hour, the prescribed duration of informal visits, we got up to leave.

'What did you think of the girl?' Xiao Wu asked as soon as he reasonably could, wrapping his question in general conversation in the hope we wouldn't notice the real purpose for our visit to the house of roots.

Neither Jan nor I had taken to her. She had managed to convey an air of dominion without ever opening her mouth. Her face was plain and her manner unattractive. Of course we couldn't tell him so, but I did suggest that it was no good marrying when so full of doubts. And he seemed relieved.

On my return to Jan's unit six months later she and I gave a lecture to the institute on student life in England, the first of three lectures Jan had to give as part of her contract. She had left it rather late – in a month she was due to fly to England. But by this time she'd decided to return to China for a second year. To leave just when she was beginning to make friends, coming to terms with unit life and communicating in Chinese seemed ludicrous, and there was nothing to hold her at home.

We chalked the details on to a blackboard as late as we dared hoping no one would notice, and Lao Wang rewrote it in Chinese characters – a bit superfluously, for if a student was unable to decipher written English there would not be much point attending our talk.

Even so the place was packed. We could hear the students giving a slow handclap as we crossed the bare earth to the teaching block, and the sad bald teacher came out to head off our escape. As a measure of our enthusiasm, at 7.30 when our talk was due to start I was preparing cabbage curry and Jan was reading a book.

Fortunately I hadn't seen the lecture hall before. It was an intimidating place with rows of seats stepped up on tiers to the back row ten foot above the stage, brimming with washed faces and neatly combed hair. Those without a seat were squatting on the floor, standing in the aisles and crushing in at the doors. Still more were invisible out in the corridor, hoping at least to be able to hear. Jan set out to explain about Oxbridge, about university funding and degrees. We then began our dialogue, talking (or rather shouting, since the back of the hall was so far away) in a conversational manner that would be new to most of our audience. We interrupted each other, disagreed occasionally and kept up a commentary on grants, accommodation and social life, emphasizing especially the aspect that differed between our cultures – the Western students' personal responsibility to attend lectures, work hard and manage their own funds. The onus was on most Western students to think for themselves, whereas in China initiative would be instantly quelled by an incarnation of negative bureaucracy disguised by a blandly congenial mien. We discussed the phenomena of getting into debt, of drinking, of drug abuse and the forming of pair bonds in a manner Jan said she would never have dared had she been on her own. We explained how much more comfortable life was for students in the West with their private rooms or bedsits, spare time at weekends, more money to spend, and greater opportunities for extra-curricular activity.

I knew how tough conditions were for these young Chinese, for I'd met many students and they'd told me so themselves. They had very little money (grants only covered education and board so parents had to supply the rest), and were often reduced to living on plain boiled rice. They had little free time or privacy to study, and even if their families lived nearby they only went home once a week. Paying a visit to Xiao Wu a few hours previously (the problem of the girl was still unresolved), I'd been appalled by the circumstances in which they had to live. Opening off an unswept, unlit passage, half-blocked by brooms and bicycles and belongings, was the ground-floor room about fifteen foot by ten that Xiao Wu shared with three other young men. With its cement-rendered walls and concrete floor it was more like a prison cell than the study-bedroom it was intended to be. Bars striped the window, and an identical block loomed large and dismal across a patch of bare earth ten paces away. It was cold and dark; no one had heating, and the forty-watt bulb hung bare. Cold communal showers were splashing down the corridor, chilling you just with the thought of them. Loos were outside in a separate block.

Each student had a framed bed draped with an off-white mosquito net, the only form of privacy he had. On top he kept his things in padlocked trunks; underneath his shoes and enamel washing bowl. He also had a desk and chair which blocked the alley between the beds and was littered with papers and books. Articles of clothing, worn, wet, or needing washing, hung on poles and hangers like a jumble sale. Sausages in slim envelopes were suspended on strings. Small frayed towels were draped over bed frames. An electric cooking ring for use on Sundays, and pots and bowls and boxes and books, were disposed about the floor. There was no bright colour or decoration of any kind.

Although Jan and I had experienced both worlds, our audience objected to this comparison of cultures that placed England in a favourable light. Much as the Chinese continually asked foreigners what they thought of China, its conditions, its scenery, its people, its food, we were not supposed to criticize unless our comments were

Mixing flour and water in a noodle-making workshop. The dough is then rolled out mechanically in long sheets, chopped into noodles and dried.

A group of factory workers in a private enterprise noodle shop open to the street. They drink beer out of bowls and tea from patterned enamel mugs. Their women are at home.

Front window of an up-market snake restaurant in Guangzhou, beyond the pocket of most Chinese. The snakes have been trapped in the wild and will be skinned and chopped up live to be made into dozens of different dishes.

State-run dofu-making workshop in a side lane in Kunming. Many Chinese welcome the interest of foreigners in their work, and will invite someone in who is watching from a doorway. Here the process is almost complete; the dofu will be cut into blocks and sold out of buckets.

Below left: Having a perm in Dali. Most Chinese hairdressers use this system and most urban women have short permed hair.

Below right: Old-style Chinese with cloth-fastened jacket, cotton shoes and hand-made pipe, but with a new-style watch. He is the only fat Chinese I met, and a typical extrovert, in a land where expression of individual personality is frowned upon.

A bride processes to the house of the groom near Sanya, on Hainan Island. One of her girlfriends carries her dowry in a cardboard box. Her suit is grey, her headdress multi-coloured and the umbrella bright pink. I was invited to join the wedding feast, which consisted of endless toasts and glasses of spirits and a succession of dishes, some savoury, some sweet, based on the local favourite, pork fat.

The interior of a private family home in Dali, unusual in its spaciousness and the scrolls of calligraphy on the walls. Most town houses have only printed posters and calendars and are crowded, yet spartan.

Above left: New China: a traffic island in the centre of Xiamen.
Above right: A Suzhou teahouse. This was once the home of a wealthy family and the window is paper-backed lattice. Tea glasses are replenished from the thermos of hot water and the old men may sit for half the day.

Hanging out laundered quilt covers on a hotel terrace.

A private enterprise village shop. He sells biscuits and sweets and cigarettes and alcohol but mostly sits in his open shopfront watching the passersby.

A rural market held every three days. In the foreground is a library where picture books may be borrowed to read on the spot at a penny a go. Stools are provided.

Rice harvest near Guilin. The threshing machine was made by a local carpenter. There's a stand of jute in the background on the right. Cotton sunhats are replacing straw; patterned nylon shirts and plastic sandals are taking over from traditional styles.

Compulsory Saturday sweeping of a campus by groups of students. Buildings may be in a poor state of repair but fallen leaves must not litter the earth.

Members of the Wu family (see Chapter 11). *Top left and right:* third generation Wus, sons of Zhang's brother-in-law *(left)*. *Bottom left:* Zhang's mother-in-law with a neighbour's child. *Bottom right:* neighbouring grandmother minding the children of her daughter-in-law, at work in the fields.

preceded by a padding of praise. When someone said, 'We are still very backward,' or 'Mistakes have been made in the past,' they were not being self-critical but modest and courteous in front of strangers and loyal to the Party in expressing its current line. So when our dialogue was over and I had torn up paper for students to put questions without the embarrassment of asking in English in that crowded hall, and the questions came, forty-five of them in all, we were not meant to give direct replies but gentle platitudes that would not offend. I had not quite got the hang of this, and was still inclined to say what I thought. More than half the questions we had not time to answer, for the sad bald teacher started hustling us out with the excuse that the porter was about to lock up. In reality it was because things were getting a bit hot and the students were finding out too much about alternative ways of life. I would have liked to answer the question about God, whether God could forgive all the sins of mankind, because the concept of sin was alien in China, and God was superfluous since the Party provided for all the people's needs. None of the students believed in God, we were told emphatically by the sad bald teacher when we asked next day. Though the freedom to practise any religion was granted in the Chinese constitution, it was only permitted to propagate atheism. But some of the students *did* believe, according to a survey, and of the rest some believed in communism, some in science and technology, some in fate or destiny, some in the individual and some in nothing that they could define. I would have liked to answer the question about sex ('When do British students hear the call of nature?'), because it was a subject in which young Chinese got no guidance, or at least only guidance of a spurious kind. I was surprised such a question was asked at all. I was also surprised that two girls in the front should ask if it was safe for women to go out unescorted in England, but Jan assured me later that in some Chinese cities girls wouldn't even ride their bicycles alone after darkness fell in fear of mugging or rape, and if friends went out a boy would cycle each girl home. This applied to Jan too, though the unit was five miles from the centre of town: even when she was cycling once in daylight a rider had reached out and grabbed her breast.

That there were some Maoist extremists present in the audience was suggested by a question formed in angry, angular capitals: 'You tell us this money and that money! Money is important in your homeland isn't it? Why?' Next day we asked the sad bald teacher, who folded the paper and put it in his pocket muttering, 'This student must be criticized!' But we assured him that we weren't offended, that all we wanted was to understand. In this instance the attitude was fairly clear, and the teacher had verified our own interpretation: here was a true son of the communist motherland, one of those Chinese, in a minority now, who equated money with capitalist greed, who studied in order to serve the people and believed that beyond the needs of basic survival money was not the object. Until recently this philosophy had been enforced on every-one: when people couldn't make purchases because things were rationed or in short supply or simply not available, money had taken on a different perspective. What had counted then was not money but power.

Some questions were predictable, on curricula, language learning (someone asked if we learnt Chinese as a second language) and the institution of the Student Union. Many more enquired about feel-ings or attitudes, about falling in love, political debate, or how we spent our evenings and weekends, or what we first did on getting up in the mornings and whether we studied hard, and what we felt about our parents and our motherland, and if we believed that living separate from families was better than with them, and whether we could speak Chinese, and what we thought about Hong Kong, and whether we felt satisfied in China? And would we sing them a song please?

Part of the answer to many of these questions, and I believe it was as incomprehensible to these students as it was to Weimin, was that people differed and that colleges varied from place to place. Cer-tainly no one could understand how it was that neither Jan nor I missed our families or our homes, and a ripple of consternation fluttered through the hall. Hardly a week went by when someone didn't confide in Jan to tell her how much they missed home. 'Not missing our families doesn't mean we don't love them,' we ex-plained to the students, 'but we're adults and our lives are indepen-dent of theirs.' 'How old are you?' they wanted to know, and 'What work do your husbands do?'

Throughout our talk I'd been conscious of the sea of pleasant attentive faces, many of them smiling, none indicating the bewilder-ment or antagonism some had clearly felt. Though by this time I was starting to decipher people's feelings through subtleties of expression, at a distance they succeeded in concealing what they thought. It was impossible to discern the leftists among them, and impossible to gauge our degree of support. Even when I chided them for turning their backs on their Chinese heritage their expressions remained blank. We could not tell if we were heard at the back, or if they understood the way we spoke. We could not tell if our talk was enjoyed, except that one slip of paper received towards the end was a plea for us to stop: 'Many questions aren't interesting, please don't answer them for we want to leave!' But next day people told us that the clapping was the loudest they had ever heard.

Were we satisfied in China? I wondered how I'd feel if compelled to remain there, and it came to me then that much as I enjoyed being in China as a traveller, moving round with more freedom than our audience would ever know, it would be torture to live there on Chinese terms. I saw Marxism as a steamroller flattening everything to the lowest common denominator of intelligence, initiative and aesthetic taste, invalidating options by its assumption that communism was the only way. Though in sympathy with much of its theory in principle, in practice it was a system I feared. I would resent its authority and standardization. I would resent being forbidden any choice in my work, my right to live where I pleased, my right to read what I chose, my right to speak my mind, my rights to love, to travel, to be alone or in company, to stay single without child. I would resent being forbidden my self.

There would have been many in that hall who felt outraged by my placing of individual liberty above communal good, and by my vision of myself as central in my world. But there would have been others, I guessed, who like Xiuying felt exactly the same, who had distanced themselves from both Confucius and Mao, who privately longed for the kind of life I am fortunate enough to be able to lead.

But if I were compelled to remain in China, what then? Probably I would lie low, break the rules when I was sure I could get away with it, take exercise to keep my spirits up and retreat into long hours of study. Millions of Chinese respond exactly like this.

The generation of students sitting before us were comparatively lucky, accepted on merit at a time when the whole educational system was broadening, able to go on to do Masters and and Ph Ds, assured at least of an adequate training. Anyone who studied in the years that I did, the late 1960s, would be very poorly qualified, if at all. During those same years when I was at art school China was going through a holocaust. Universities were closed, lecturers imprisoned, or tortured, or worse: scholarship depended on the students' ability to propound Mao Zedong thought and for thirteen years no one got a degree. Workers, peasants and soldiers were enrolled without examinations, and education was combined with manual work. I don't suppose I once thought of China while I was a student; I don't suppose I had any idea what was happening there.

'What is your impression of our unit? Dirt? Poverty?' asked several students. While Jan passed on to less volatile things, I determined to discover what a unit did consist of, and how it functioned, and on what the system was based. A Chinese unit is the kind of place you can move around in day after day without noticing anything because its planning is so bland: at the end of a year Jan still didn't know the full range of its services, and had never been shown around. Other foreign experts were similarly ignorant, and even Chinese who had lived on a campus for several years had scant conception of the function of the buildings within its walls.

Precisely at nine the following morning Xiao Wu arrived at the entrance of Jan's guest-house to show me round, not exactly ecstatic about the nature of our mission, but eager to get in more English practice and have another frank chat about the girl. He was to continue agonizing for another year, Jan told me in a letter, but in the end he managed a transfer to Lanzhou. Yet once home with his parents he began to miss the girl and they were married in the spring of 1986.

We proceeded to the main gate to begin our tour. The red star on its arch and the propaganda boards flanking it – displaying exemplary photographs of people on parade and modern wonders of Chinese science and technology – had been my first sight of the unit eight months before. Being a stranger then I had half-expected someone to challenge me, but no one did.

It was not so much dirt and poverty that impressed me (I had been in China long enough not to notice) but shabbiness and bad planning. The campus wore an air of having happened too quickly, of having been built without feeling, for people with no souls. Most depressing of all was not something I could label as ugliness, but the absence of any imagination or care. If environment casts its mould on human nature then these surroundings would nurture citizens who were units of a unit, encompassed by invisible walls. And all the unit compounds I ever saw in China, irrespective of region, of climate, of function, were similar to Jan's. It was a blueprint for Chinese urban life.

The main axis of the compound led not, as one would think, to a hub of activity or monument to Marxist–Leninist achievement, but smack into the unit garage. Buildings flanked the roadway in blank effrontery, buildings whose function one could only guess at, buildings in ubiquitous unit style inherited from the West and spaced according to engineering sightlines. Any structure of significance – the canteen, the library, the sports pavilion – was reached along a devious self-trodden pathway and sited in the outer reaches of the compound. Road surfaces were cracked, manholes gaped open: trees offered no solace.

Though its principal function was education, the unit provided for most of the needs of its two thousand inhabitants – thirteen hundred students and seven hundred supporting workers – as a self-contained component of society. Once allocated to a unit you lived there, worked there, and if you didn't reach retirement age you died there too. If you were sick you were treated in the unit clinic, by its doctors, nurses, acupuncturists and dentists. If you were single you ate in the canteen. If you had children they attended the nursery and school. If your wiring system or your plumbing went wrong it would be mended (eventually) by the maintenance staff. If you went on a visit you travelled with your workmates in a unit bus. There were sports facilities, a running track, a cinema, a library, meeting rooms, workshops, barbers, tailors, telephones, a bath-house and storage sheds. There was a daily market by the unit gate where cotton-clad peasants sold the produce from their plots. There were state-run stores in the street behind, supplying storable food and household goods. In theory you need almost never leave the place. The hour-long journey to the centre of town took on the aspect of a big day out; a trip to a department store to buy a pen would be talked about for days before. Like being in prison or in hospital you became institutionalized, and everything beyond the gate seemed unpredictable and unsafe.

Each component part of a unit was almost a unit within itself. The unit garage had lockable gates (emblazoned with red stars and precautionary signs) and a man to guard them. Its central courtyard served as a car park for the buses, cars and a fleet of green trucks; when empty it doubled as a basketball pitch. It had a workshop and offices, accommodation for its drivers, administrators and mechanics and storage tanks for petrol and oil. Hence the absence of public petrol stations and public most other things; most units contained their own.

There was something impressive about the fierce independence of the Chinese unit. But it also implied a degree of distrust, a clannishness or jealousy of outsiders who might otherwise be sharing facilities, and the stranglehold of units over individuals. No one had any personal say, and privilege rested on the whims of the cadres and the Party Secretary, its political commissar, chosen not by vote but higher authority. Though presenting a united front to the world, each unit was riven by internal strife.

At the time of my first visit a new block of flats was being built on the compound for teachers with families. Everybody wanted one, for besides being new the flats had three rooms instead of one or two, and the stoves in the kitchen were heated by gas. Conversation among the teachers revolved around who was in current favour and who would get what flat, if they got one at all. Nobody wanted to live on the ground floor, for it was cold and dark and noisy and public and easily broken into. Nobody wanted a top-floor flat because of the stairs. Flats on the first or second floors were ideal, not too high, not too dark, safe from thieves and warmed by the dwellings above and below. Whatever the outcome there'd be pride and envy, humiliation and prestige.

Jan's group of students fussed endlessly over this new block of flats. They were still complaining on my return in December when the block was finished and the families had moved in, because cooking on gas cost eleven yuan a month, compared to the three they used to spend on coal – a considerable difference when a whole month's rent was only four jiao.

As we toured the campus Xiao Wu described a normal college day. Each day was the same, both here, and in every school and college throughout the country, like a holiday camp but without any fun. Bugle calls and energetic music roused the students at half-past six for their morning run (things not being as stringent as they used to be the majority who slept on weren't penalized). After a cold wash and breakfast of rice gruel or noodles the students revised until classes at eight. There was a twenty-minute break for exercise at ten, half-heartedly attended it seemed to me (it was ten o'clock and we were passing at the time) by less than a tenth of the student force. 'Yi, er, san, si . . .' shrilled a woman's voice over the public address system, and the students flailed their arms and legs like insects immobilized on their backs. 'One, two, three, four . . .' but no one was bothering to keep in time unless they spotted a teacher spying from the side.

Between 10.20 and twelve a further two lessons preceded the siren for lunch. The students collected their basins from the window-sills and ran to the canteen before the better food ran out. After the midday siesta, a traditional practice which was shortly due to be curtailed, classes resumed until five. There was then a second stampede for the unit canteen, a building resembling a temporary station ticket hall where coupons were exchanged via a row of small guichets for portions of protein and solid blocks of rice. People shovelled down rice as they returned to their dormitories (ranged in rows between dusty trees) while peasant women salvaged waste from the bins. Xiao Wu insisted that they fed it to their hens.

After this meal, the last food all day, the students were free. The dormitories hummed like an airport lounge, resonant with voices, with the scraping of spoons in chipped enamel bowls, with the fierce gush of water on the washing slabs, with the flapping of sandals echoing down corridors, with the tuning of guitars and the practising of scales on the violin. A few students played basketball but in time they all went back to their books. Lights went off in the dormitories at eleven, and Jan and I would watch from her window as torches beamed in room after room.

Classes ceased at lunchtime on Saturday, but the afternoon passed in political study (which most students loathed), spring cleaning of classrooms, dormitories and grounds (not much less loathed), and long hours of homework. In the evenings the locals went home.

It was in these large, purpose-built, all-in walled units that society functioned as the Party meant it to. The unit was the building block of Chinese society, the embodiment of the Party, the middleman between government and people. Everyone had a unit: the peasant had his township and village brigade, the worker his factory, the doctor his hospital, the inhabitants of traditional lanes and houses the invisible organization of the neighbourhood committee. It was one of several aspects of modern society that appeared part and parcel of the communist machinery but was in part a continuation of the status quo. Alien though the concept may seem to a Westerner, the Chinese had always formed part of a group, the Big Family or clan. An individual was responsible to the family; together they rose and fell. If one of their number was officially recognized then everyone gained fortune and fame: if one fell from grace the whole group might face death. Under the Confucian code of morals people had an obligation to both family and society; their duties depended on their position in the hierarchy under the absolute rule of a patriarch at the head of a cohesive, nationwide clan.

Little had changed. The walls themselves symbolized the Chinese inclination for privacy and secrecy. Sedan chairs were curtained. Big houses were walled; the Forbidden City was closeted behind a fifteen-foot wall. Walls and secrecy surrounded everything in China: units, activities, people's innermost thoughts and fears. Even phone books were secret until 1980. Barriers kept the outsider outside.

The old Big Family was being riven by politics (for it had too much power and was too great a focus in people's lives) to be replaced by the new Big Family, the unit. The divide-and-rule policy shifted function and control on the government in the shape of the Party Secretary, the head of each unit, providing welfare, security, education, child care, guidance, discipline and the illusion that life held a purpose for everyone. Emotional clan ties still survived, but to what degree? And for how long?

If the idea of an all-embracing unit in which people are subjected to laid-down principles seems alarming to Westerners, the response of most Chinese to our society might be more dramatic still. They have never known freedom in the Western sense; in the Chinese language the word does not exist and its mere concept is tinged by a libertine indecency. Since the Chinese were almost never alone they could rarely feel lonely or alienated; when I asked people if they liked to be alone my question seemed incomprehensible. The unit provided an identity for its members. The regularity of their lives produced a stability and calm. Habits were simple. Work was not penance for the freedom it bought, but an end in itself. People were known; the boundaries of right tightly circumscribed.

At mid-autumn festival the following year Jan accompanied a group of students on a two-day visit to some hot springs nearby. 'We congregated by the unit entrance an hour before the bus was due, for "group photos",' Jan wrote. 'Anyone who strayed was quickly brought to heel in bossy boy scout tones. Once up in the mountains, everything was regulated. Our group leader was ever present to tell us when to get up or go to sleep, rest or bathe, swim or not swim, eat, take photographs, chat to minority people or burst into happy song in celebration of our wonderful outing, as if he were our collective conscience absolving us from thought or responsibility of our own. He told us nothing we couldn't have conceived for ourselves, yet the others seemed bewitched, as if their personal desires had been placed in abeyance for the sake of the smooth functioning of the group. Private wishes were overridden and my bids for independence, even for a few minutes, caused grave consternation. The essence of our outing was to do everything "together" . . .'

Many Westerners in our so-called democratic society pity the scrutiny the Chinese must endure, the constant exhortations to be clean, public-spirited, of high morals, uncomplaining, unfailing in dedication to the cause. But there are those in China who prefer the security, who pity us in turn for being propelled through advertising, via the media and those around us to drink, to smoke, to compete against our neighbours but look after ourselves, to make lots of money and cultivate our sex lives – unhealthy and ultimately demoralizing pursuits of potentially self-annihilating capitalist rule.

8

The Untravelled Coast

There was nothing alluring about a Special Economic Zone, but since I was passing on my way into China I stopped off at Shenzhen. Shenzhen was the largest of four SEZs, three years old and about half-built, located on the border with Hong Kong. As part of Deng's Open Policy regime its aim was to generate economic ventures between the mainland and foreign companies, with China providing land, labour and raw materials (which it had in abundance) and acquiring capital, equipment and expertise (which it lacked). In addition to the four major SEZs, fourteen coastal cities and Hainan Island have since been opened for foreign investment. The investors, while profiting from short-term gain, might in the long run lose out; the Chinese learnt fast, and soon will be exporting the same quality goods at prices far cheaper than the original company could make them for. China was unique among developing countries in that it had no foreign debt.

In the distance Shenzhen appeared wholly Western, pale tower blocks against pale clouds, but on closer inspection the blocks were still mingled in that characteristic urban-fringe land-pattern of vegetable plots, close-planted and weedless, and the makeshift shanties of the 80,000-strong construction force. I'd been wrong in my summary assessment of Shenzhen, as I'd been wrong in my censure of modern planning elsewhere: Shenzhen, in the eyes of most Chinese, was the revolutionary poster come alive. It was a place of opportunity for those allowed to live there, proof that the Party was true to its word. Here was the reality of gleaming new tower blocks and dual carriageways fitted out with lollipop trees. Here were bulldozers to lessen the workload and salaries twice what they were elsewhere. Here was housing with air-conditioning and lifts going up to the twenty-fourth floor. Near here there would soon be a nuclear power plant, a base for nuclear industry. That there were also fleets of taxicabs, and a golf course and funfairs and a video arcade, and imported merchandise and exclusive facilities for overseas businessmen, and yet other items of a somewhat less revolutionary tone, one could conveniently ignore.

Shenzhen was an experiment in capitalism, the antithesis of a city under communist rule; what was forbidden elsewhere was allowed in Shenzhen. Since China wanted to learn from the West, overseas businessmen had an almost free hand. But being so small and surrounded by a fence to contain its contaminating influence it could always revert if the experiment failed. Visiting leftists, muttering darkly about feudalism and exploitation, sincerely hoped it would.

Shenzhen was packed with tourists! Not foreign tourists – there was nothing there for them – but mainland Chinese, more visitors by far than I'd seen at the best-known historical monuments, gazing with awe at this monument to their future. What to many Western visitors was just another ugly place that alienated people from their natural environment like any in America, here represented, by the looks on peoples' faces, the most wondrous creation on earth. Their pride was touching; their pleasure infectious. They stared open-mouthed at the tallest, palest and shiniest buildings they had ever set eyes on; they gorged themselves on double-decker burgers and ice-cream sundaes in fast food bars; they cast sidelong glances at the made-up waitresses in scarlet skirts; they lurched drunkenly up escalators as if in a fairground and pondered the prices of imported produce in lonely supermarket aisles. At £1.50 an 8oz can of Heinz baked beans and just under £20 for 10oz of cold cream the tills were understandably quiet.

Put the same people down on the streets of Hong Kong and their wonder might well turn sour. 'Why has all this been kept from us for so long?' they could not be blamed for asking. 'Why in thirty-five years of so-called Liberation are we so little better off than we were before? If all this can be achieved on a few small islands with minimal resources why cannot we, with the third biggest country and the largest population on earth, do the same?'

But Shenzhen could never be like Hong Kong. It lacked the geography, the spectacular slopes, the forested hills and blue sea. It lacked the history, the mixing of cultures and the exhilarating tension between the two. It lacked the energy of being only temporary. It lacked the expertise, the injection of Western design and techniques. It lacked the diversity and soul.

The road up the coast was breaking fresh ground. The trail was too long, too uncharted for travellers who moved in the fast lane. The air was warm, the markets leafy with vegetables. It was April now and men were in shirt-sleeves and girls in summer frocks.

We left Shenzhen along puddled roads. Trees dripped slowly on dark moist earth. Cucumbers clambered on latticed canes; water chestnuts tufted flooded fields. The vegetable landscape was peopled by cultivators, wigwammed by field beans, fertilized by waste, by goodness trading back and forth. Here again was the China of my childhood imagining, of straw-hatted peasants bent over in paddy fields, of bamboo groves and upswept roofs, of ducks being marshalled like children in playgrounds, of buffaloes and bicycles and shoulder poles.

Building styles changed as we drove north towards Shantou, from plain to patterned, from grey to ochre to white and back to grey. The older houses mellowed gracefully, New Year couplets fading round the doorways, woodwork silvering, roof tiles mossing, brick walls softening with the patina of age. Between them the newer ones rose like scars, flat-roofed, rendered, their walls discoloured by dust and rain.

The hills in the background were scattered with graves, mounded, horseshoe-shaped or upstanding stele. Grave urns gathered on the lower slopes, rows of jars holding exhumed bones awaiting transference to their final home. In the absence of hill-slopes grave mounds up to six feet high were built before 1949 on the edge of each family's land, or outside the walls in the case of a town. They had gradually submerged large quantities of farmland, and were levelled when land was collectivized. But to disturb a grave mound was to insult the spirits who influenced the fortunes of the living clan, and in protest old people had taken their lives.

Shantou was a large and rambling city, its central streets narrow, colonial and congested, its suburbs sombre, wide and grey. Faded black lettering of British trade companies anointed stucco building fronts. Pavements were planted with Bombax trees, their branches arranged in symmetrical whorls, their young leaves citron, folded in umbrellas, their flowers scarlet on half-bare boughs. Foodstalls

146

were embellished by garlands of produce strung from awnings, red speckled sausages, squid and octopus, onions and celery and silver fish. Taxis were bicycles with a plank on their saddle-rack on which the passenger had to ride.

I walked through a park where young palms were growing and old men were grading piles of torn polythene to the harbour wall. Terns were wheeling in a mackerel sky. Ferries were cruising to rocky islands rising grey-green from a silty sea. Fleets of junks in butterfly sail, pride-filled, spine-finned, floated in their wake. Small poled sampans plied the shoreline of the salt-smelling, spume-winded South China Sea.

Shantou was built of bamboo. Everywhere I looked I saw manifestations of its bamboo economy, in fences, balustrades, barricades and pergolas, chopsticks, chicken coops, baskets, hats and rain capes, mats, mugs, pipes, pegs, blinds, roofs, crates, sieves, fans, flutes, beds and fishing nets, parasols and fishing rods, sandals and steamers, pens and paper, ladles and measures, tree-guards and furniture, gutters and sail battens, porches, pushchairs and fan-shaped brooms. Whole buildings were made of bamboo poles supporting overlapping leaf-scales sandwiched between frames. Housing blocks were textured by a shadow-doubled lattice of balcony and window screens, thief-proof, child-proof, supporting climbers and shading the sun.

Throughout South China bamboo grows naturally, rising in fountains to a hundred feet. Bamboo is the national symbol of endurance, a favourite subject of painters and poets; it bends with the wind yet does not break. In Guangzhou Botanical Gardens alone there were more than fifty kinds. Some were tree-like, with stems thick as forearms and coarse rattling leaves. Others were delicate, like paintings on porcelain. One had black stems, another was green with a soft white bloom. Some were fragrant, some grew in zigzags, some were striped and some had spines. Some grew in thickets but a few grew singly, throwing up canes a yard apart with fragile, brush-stroke leaves. Yao, the botanist, stroked them fondly and explained how each was used. 'This one produces the edible bamboo shoots. This one has a thin stem wall and is used for weaving mats and baskets, while that is a thick one, used by boatmen as oars or by peasants as shoulder poles. Those three are used for scaffolding and several more can be pulped. See this one here?' It had bulging internodes, golden and smooth; I had seen it planted in temple courtyards. 'We call it Buddha's Belly! But this is my favourite of all.' He pushed between the fronded stems and squatted beside a clump in the shade. 'Feel its canes!' I touched them and found they were square.

In the back lanes of Shantou I watched mats being woven from lengths of split cane. I watched hats being made from overlapping leaves, and stools being gouged and slotted and wedged with neither nails nor glue (the same stools sold in English shops for thirty times their Shantou price). The city abounded in craftsmen. I watched coopers making buckets and washing bowls and women shaping coloured paper flowers for wreaths. I watched woodblock printers gouging out characters and men making paper from wood and straw. There were lathe workers, scale makers, stencil sprayers, name-seal carvers and makers of oilcloth parasols the colour of cheese. Many household goods were still being made in indigenous materials to designs evolved over four millennia – the chicken-feather duster, the rice-patterned bowl, the wok, the pickle jar, the palm-fibre broom, the glazed ceramic plant pot – but there were others made only for the export trade and unavailable to ordinary Chinese. London craft shops sold numerous items which to me seemed quintessentially Chinese but which I never found in any-one's home. Where were the Chinese to value and promote their rich inheritance as many Indians did theirs? Craft was the living art of China, the art form least molested in the Cultural Revolution since it was produced by the people for everyday use. It had already been partly institutionalized in big state factories producing straw work, cloisonné, lacquerware, embroidery, carved ivory and jade, and partly destroyed in the Great Leap Forward when the need of the nation was thought to be iron. It would disappear in time, as it almost did in England, not because of Party ruling but through vulgar and uninitiated public taste.

In one particular back lane in Shantou I met a bridal party setting out for the groom's house with the dowry heaped high on two cycle rickshaws, a sad reflection of changing standards and cheap con-temporary design. The baskets were not the traditional kind, but the up-market varnished ones sold to visitors from abroad. The bucket, the washing bowl, the flowers, the sandals, even the suitcases were moulded in bright-coloured plastic in preference to bamboo, silk and wood. There were towels, a table lamp, a television, two thermos flasks and a mirror embossed with the double happiness sign. There was a sewing machine, some soap and shampoo, and synthetic blankets and satin-covered quilts. China was going through that adolescent phase when production not product was the general goal, when people wanted smooth synthetic goods that peasant hands were unable to make, when design meant status, not function or style.

Alongside the age-old peasant culture strode a strident, superficial and prosperous one, nowhere more visible than in Guangzhou and Shantou with their illicit trade with Hong Kong and Taiwan. Nowhere was there a higher black-market rate. Nowhere else had I seen so many street stalls, so many cheap watches or imported cigarettes, so much Coke or Pepsi, so much rural construction, so much advertising, so much curled hair, so many tight trousers, bright colours, heeled shoes or – a sure sign of growing prosperity – so many beggars. They followed me, pleading and plucking at my clothes, propositioned me on buses, serenaded me with song. I saw a man with long matted hair pick a scrap from the gutter and put it in his mouth. I saw people scavenging in rubbish bins and rolling cigarettes from salvaged butts and living in shanties of cardboard and polythene pressed up against the harbour wall.

Through an open doorway a painted mannequin in tinted glasses, fake fur jacket, leather skirt and stiletto boots was styling a customer's hair. Every other youngster was learning the guitar. Girls in tight pants swung their hips and knew precisely what they were at. A lorry driver made kissing sounds, and a man in a bus pressed his body against mine in an undeniably sexual way. Shops displayed photos of Chinese in white wedding dress, taken in the studio after the event. Young men swapped stamps and listened to rock and stayed out late playing video games.

So fast were the changes brought on by Open Policy all over the land that even during eight months I felt their force. The Chineseness of cities was being swamped in a way that no outside culture could ever endanger the Englishness of ours but would simply enrich it, containerized in zones for us to sample or ignore. For the first time in China I saw signs in English at stations and English announcements on trains. 'Time is money', read a notice in a window, and Chinese were being chivvied to get moving and achieve. Shops displayed foreign electrical goods for the get-it-while-you-can consumer urge, disguised by the Party as economic growth. Advertising was beginning to employ romantic imagery, following the West in its search for the ultimate dream. A fast food store appeared in Beijing with synthetic ivy and moulded chairs, selling hot dogs and chicken legs to a modish leather and jeans clientele. Western movies played at cinemas and Beatles music bellowed from rock bars. Foreigners flooded in with hotels and cafés and craft shops in their wake. A German traveller was asked for a tip. Luxury hotels boasted swimming pools, and cocktails were sipped among potted palms; private taxis brought clients to the door and porters carried their bags. The day would come when the untouched, undescribed, untravelled coast would be despoiled by resorts and hotels.

And there was more to come. There was talk of widescale privatization, not just of agriculture and industry but of airline companies, transport and bus lines, hotels and housing, doctors, traders, colleges and schools. Shanghai businessmen were considering the formation of a stock exchange. There'd be cars on the roads and planes in the sky (in eight months I scarcely saw one). City centres would be mazes of subways and tower blocks and coffee shops and discos and late-night bars. Streets would be neonized. Lettering would be romanized. Fashion would be stylized. Marketing would be sensualized. Agriculture would be mechanized, the countryside netted by roads and wires. If Japan could rise from medieval feudalism to modern Pacific power so also could China, despite what Confucius had to say: 'A gentleman takes as much trouble to discover what is right as lesser men take to discover what will pay.'

It was in Shantou I met Liqing. On the face of it he seemed like any other young Chinese, polite and washed-looking, a geography teacher in the Gear Factory Middle School. We met in a shop where I was buying gauze masks to keep out the dust.

Liqing took me dancing. Dances had recently been reintroduced so that singles could meet a potential spouse. Of the half-dozen dances held every night we chose one put on in a cinema foyer, with discoloured walls and rough cement floor. Fluorescent lighting beamed without mercy; amplified music blared through the door. Couples were wheeling each other around, pairs of men mostly, but sometimes two girls or a girl and a boy. We sat on chairs lined up along the wall and sipped fizzy orange and watched the show.

Liqing would not listen to any excuse. He pulled me up, put an arm round my waist and proceeded to teach me the waltz. Aware of Confucian rules of decorum his proximity put me on edge. Nor was I a dancer; even without my boots and rucksack I would not have known what steps to take. Luckily most others were no better than I. It was just like the dodgems, a hundred would-be dancers with two left feet, whisking round the foyer in their anoraks and hats, treading on each other's toes and swigging fizzy drinks.

We met again. It was for people like Liqing that the revolution had been won. His background was impeccable, a poor peasant family in a mud-walled hut on the outskirts of town. As the city moved outwards building houses and factories his parents became workers and Liqing went to school. Both his parents were cadres in the factory and Liqing had the status of a teaching job. His shoes were polished, his trousers well creased; he had an upright carriage and was unusually tall. Were it not for the communists Liqing would be living the life of his father and grandfather before him, a life with no hope of having, or saving, or moving home.

Liqing also had a girlfriend. 'I quite like her,' he said offhandedly, 'but she doesn't love me.' This did not seem to bother him unduly since according to him she was neither beautiful nor intelligent.

'So what kind of girlfriend would you like?' I asked.

He looked at me pointedly. 'A foreign girl.' My mouth fell open as Liqing explained that Chinese girls didn't know how to love, that only foreigners were capable of that. Foreign girls were, moreover, beautiful, which Chinese girls were not. Many of his friends would marry a foreigner if they had the choice, not only boys but girls too.

I was stunned. Everything I had read and heard was to the contrary. 'But why?' I asked.

'Money,' he replied. 'Money and opportunity. The chance to go abroad and get out of this place.'

After a further day's journey north along the coast I came to Zhangzhou in Fujian. Compared to Shantou Zhangzhou felt parochial, remote and unwesternized, set astride a river among emerald fields. Its streets were narrow, its arcaded buildings painted brick red, mustard and dull fern green. Basketry and bambooware spilt out from shops, across arcades and into the road.

It was late afternoon when I crossed the river and ascended the slope to Nanshansi Temple. Barefooted peasants in bamboo-leaf hats trotted out of town with their shoulder poles. The low hill was dark in the shadow of a cloud. Buddhist monks had chosen temple sites in places of great tranquillity; the road would formerly have passed through forest but the trees had gone and fields and power lines lapped its walls.

Through a gatehouse defended by the giants Heng and Ha the complex unfolded in a sequence of courtyards, a symmetry of fluid, connecting space. In spite of restoration the leafy courts and half-empty shrine halls had a powerful sense of peace and place. A big silver dragon hung in a gallery, a flock of lanterns in a court at one side, elaborate confections made for a festival, tasselled with silk, embroidered or painted, pasted with cut-outs and hung with fairy lights and miniature dolls.

Nanshansi was reopened for the tourist trade. Walls were rebuilt, fresh timber carved, bright paint slapped on, new images made and an entrance fee charged to get in. But they were not the usual groups of sightseers scurrying about the courtyards and chattering among the pot plants, the camera-toting, dressed-in-their-best Chinese on a jaunt, but little old ladies in side-fastened shirts, carrying torches, umbrellas and black plastic bags. I watched and waited as more old ladies appeared on the scene, lit bunches of incense, bowed before the images, placed flowers and oranges in their gilded laps and burnt spirit money in a furnace for the dead.

Gradually everyone moved towards the Great Hall. Rows of low stools had been set before the image of Buddha rising huge in his lotus seat and flanked by two disciples. The old ladies laid claim to the stools they preferred with their torches, umbrellas and bags. Dusk was falling and the courtyards were growing shadowy and indistinct; inside the images glimmered in the gloom. In the gathering dark the little old ladies flitted like bats. They sat down, got up, adjusted their stools, hung their umbrellas on hooks on the columns, chatted to their friends, melted into darkness and reappeared, and came to see who I was. Was I a Buddhist? they asked. A hundred million Chinese still called themselves Buddhists. By mistake I said yes and was drawn into their fold. They raised their palms in salutation and offered me texts in Chinese. How many Buddhists were there in England? They gazed up at me, smiling, their heads below my shoulder. One of them took me by the hand and led me out through the charcoal-shadowed courtyards, up a flight of steps, down a passage, through the kitchen and up through a hall where grey-robed monks were preparing a painting of Guanyin, the goddess of mercy, to a small room beyond where the abbot had his home.

We sat at a table, the abbot and I, and drank green tea out of tiny cups and ate small white cakes embossed with the double happiness sign. Green meant eternity; white meant peace. The abbot smiled as he watched me eat. More dishes were heaped on the table before me, fragile fried noodles with green beans and fungus and a bowl of seaweed soup.

By the time I returned to my place in the hall the ceremony was in progress and the night velvet-dark. In the dimly lit interior the painted ceiling was almost invisible. But the images smouldered like dying firelight, and the altar table embossed with dragons and the shaven monk who stood before it in robes of gold and scarlet splendour shone by the light of the lamp.

Men and women worshippers faced each other across the aisle in which the monk stood. They chanted in unison, page after page of vertical text, in the long black gowns they'd donned in my absence, gowns with mandarin collars and sleeves falling almost to the floor. Their faces glowed like moons in the dark. Then the rhythm changed to a single line repeated ceaselessly as the scarlet-robed monk led off in procession around the hall, followed by the men and finally the women, palms closed in front of them in a snake-like chain. I processed in my turn, conscious of our deliberate pace, of the Buddha looming flame-like in indistinct space, of walls where once there'd been paintings and statues, of the tolling bell, the gong and drum. How different it was experiencing a temple not as a tourist, walking in and quickly out in the white light of day, moving indiscriminately, glancing at anything that caught the eye, hunting for the original photographic angle among dozens of others doing just the same; how different it was to be present as a worshipper, moving and intoning in a circumscribed way, absorbing the reson-ance of the echoing walls and the serenity of the images as I passed them by, observing the prayer hall from different viewpoints and again and again on consecutive rounds. By the fifth or sixth our passage had become a kind of meditation and as my body grew tired my spiritual energy seemed to increase. The procession flowed on, a continuous line of black-robed forms gliding smoothly along the half-seen walls. The big drum boomed, the great bell tolled, the images glowed and a pall of incense made a haze about the lamp. For the first time in China I stopped being in charge and delivered my will. I felt calm and cleansed yet somehow strong.

After more than an hour we returned to our stools. While one side chanted the other side knelt, foreheads on stools, palms upturned on either side. It was as restful as sleeping. My body was loose, my mind without thought. A feeling of happiness welled up inside me. Then suddenly it was over and the little old ladies were unhooking bags and collecting umbrellas and switching on torches and asking if I had somewhere to sleep. If I hadn't they'd have offered their homes.

Before Liberation Buddhism and Daoism were the faiths most widely practised by the Han Chinese so it was these the Party stamped on with the greatest force. Of the two, Daoism was the more antithetical to communism and it was not until the eighties that it began to re-emerge. In the end I located a Daoist temple complex in a pink-painted neighbourhood, but functioning Daoist temples were rare. Half of it was demolished in the Cultural Revolution to make way for a factory but the monks were returning to take up their old quarters in the half that remained. A knot of women earmarked the entrance selling mulberry-coloured joss-sticks and tomato-red candles. The roofs of the shrine halls peeped over pink walls.

Only one of the shrine halls had been restored. A life-sized image of a Daoist immortal in butter-yellow robes was canopied by patchwork and tasselled silken lanterns and surrounded by renderings of temples in landscapes, Dufy-conceived, with paint-patterned frames. I peeped through a hole in the paper-backed lattice, until, seeing my interest, a young man led me to an inner courtyard where the monks had their cells. It was a garden such as an artist might have had, frilly with chrysanthemums, strewn with stones and shells and gourds and planted with life-prolonging herbs. The object of Dao was to be in harmony with the universe and this could be attained by contemplating nature with intuitive knowledge, by sitting with a blank mind. True Daoists sought to extend their lifespan through exercise and abstinence and magic herbal brews.

We entered the cell of the oldest monk, a wizened fossil of eighty-eight years who looked older still. He was lying in bed wearing a side-fastened jacket and black padded trousers and black cotton cap and white cotton gaiters the young man called socks. His long hair was knotted on top of his head. I asked why.

'Previously in China everyone had long hair,' the monk explained. The Manchu rulers had forced their subjects to wear pigtails, or queues. 'When other people cut their queues in response to a ruling by Chiang Kai-shek, we kept ours long.'

The old man lay on a bed of planks. It was the first room I'd seen where everything was old. There was a dark rosewood table with brackets shaped like clouds. There were blackwood chairs, large and uncomfortable with marble seats. There were porcelain cups, a pewter tea caddy and a black lacquer box containing dried fruit. I was offered a mandarin and the monk sat up to watch me eat.

He seemed not to do much, but that was the point, learning through unlearning, realizing through inaction. Some of the other monks practised *qigong*, the rhythmical deep breathing to imbibe the universal force. Some practised sword play to improve their balance and keep malignant spirits at bay. There was one who could cut through a brick with one finger, to what purpose I failed to ascertain.

I travelled on to Sima, a smaller, more intimate version of Zhangzhou spread out at the edge of the sea. According to my guide book it was open to foreigners but the way people stared I began to have doubts. Everywhere in China, but especially in Sichuan and Fujian, I was stared at continuously – but it was never like this. The media sometimes warned about staring at foreigners since a few foreign students had got so paranoid they would scarcely leave their campuses, but it had no effect. The Chinese custom was to stare at spectacles. 'We take photographs of them,' one traveller argued. 'Why shouldn't they stare at us?'

Schools of children followed me round Sima, pushing each other in their fight to get close. Women shelling oysters looked up, startled, mouths falling open, eyes widening in fear. One girl shrieked, and vanished through a doorway. Pensioners peeped through chinks in their spirit walls (woven screens hung on chains or propped on stilts before their open front doors). Some gazed in distaste; others hurried away.

I fled for safety to a first-floor noodle house looking down on the park, a small paved square with open pavilions and benches and trees. It was Sunday afternoon. The citizens of Sima were sucking pale yellow lollies in the deep green shade of mango trees. Story-tellers were performing to rings of spectators on low bamboo stools. Children were playing jumprope, higher and higher till they missed their step. Old women were relaxing, leaning on tree trunks. Old men were squatting, playing Chinese chess. Girls were parading, arms about each other's waists in the orbit of loaf-ing youths. Parents were walking toddlers, clairvoyants telling fortunes, vendors selling oranges . . .

Feeling out of things in the noodle house I ventured down to listen to a story but glancing up a moment later I counted more than two hundred pairs of eyes standing round me in a ring, all fixed on mine. When I moved the crowd moved with me, growing visibly as the news went round. I climbed to the top of a stepped pavilion where a man lay drunk in a pool of puke and the crowd climbed too. Then a policeman detached himself and took me by the arm.

Sima was a closed town. I was escorted to the Public Security Bureau where a room was unlocked for my questioning. Sit down, please sit down, their spokesman said in a definitive sort of way. I sat. What was I doing in a closed town? But I didn't know – the guide book, as ever, was wrong. Had I taken any photographs? I hedged, afraid they would confiscate my film. So they sighed and gave up, and escorted me through lanes to the harbour to catch the Xiamen boat, the boat I was leaving on anyway.

It was a romantic trip with its emphatic river sounds: the swishing of water, the chugging of engines and the hooting of horns. As usual I was the only foreigner in a boatload of peasants all barging on with their ducks in baskets and bundles of lotus roots and lumpy sacks, cursing and clashing shoulder poles and getting them caught in other people's ropes and shouting until their luggage was stacked and their poles propped in corners and their fish parked in basins overflowing the floor and they were safely installed in their seats. We chugged down the estuary past boulder-strewn hillsides, the sea slowly silvering as the sun broke through, and in two hours reached Xiamen, or Amoy as it used to be. Amoy was one of five treaty ports opened as a result of the Opium Wars. By the end of the nineteenth century China was virtually a semi-colony, with control over shipping and railways and telegraphs in the hands of Western powers.

Xiamen had a flavour of provincial France: France at night in the canyon streets where grey-bunned matrons leant from windows framed against the light of high-ceilinged rooms and shouted to men in the street below; France in the stucco, the ironwork, the shutters; France in the food, the shellfish and oysters; France in the evening, chattering streets, the gaiety and paintwork of light bright blue.

I caught the ferry to Gulangyu Island and followed the lanes along the beach, over a headland bristly with trees and down to a small secluded cove. Through acacia woods the path wound on, sunk deep in the soil, the banks damp with moss. Birds sang in bushes: barbets and virios. Pink and yellow wood sorrel starred the woodland floor. This was not the China I knew.

Breaking out from the woods I came upon a mansion, mellowing, Mediterranean, shrouded in palm trees and gazing out at the still blue sea. Its sun-warmed stucco and shadowed arcades reminded me of dreams, of childhood holidays and novels half-forgotten. For a moment I felt proprietorial, with a greater right to be there than the group of workmen chiselling stone, rebuilding steps and paths and walls for what would become a public park – but the feeling soon passed.

The grandest houses in colonial China were built in Xiamen on Gulangyu Island. Turning inland, winding in alleys up and over hillsides between walls and iron gateways there were dozens, perhaps hundreds of stuccoed halls, pierced by arched and balustraded verandahs, their colour fading cream, pink and blue. I could feel the colonial presence there still, haunting the galleries, whispering in the palm trees, promenading at dusk at the edge of the sea. Strains of Chopin floated through a window. Ferns grew in drainpipes, chickens pecked in yards. There were pantiles and pine trees and pot plants on parapets. Cats slunk in alleyways, vines covered pergolas; virginia creeper swung from railings in the tangled romance of a bygone age.

It was foreigners who created the enchanted, flower-blown,

birdsong place: without them the island would be sparse and dry, peopled by fisherfolk and factory compounds, the scrub hacked for firewood, the birds killed for food. The trees they planted had reached full size. Yellow Thunbergias threaded through the branches of leafless flame trees patterning the paths. I walked in a paradise of white Bauhinia and flapping banana leaves and dense green mango and frangipani and loquats studded with golden fruit: the colonial emblems of a tropical Eden entwined with honeysuckle memories of home.

A few hours further north was the old port of Quanzhou. Once one of the busiest harbours in Asia it had silted up and there was no sign of sea. A man approached me in a narrow lane, tall and stooping, an eager look in his hamster eyes, his ears small and high on his head. His Western jacket was three sizes too large and his chisel-toed shoes were coated with dust.

We strolled along alleyways paved with stone, down lanes of scented Bauhinia trees. Their branches met above our heads and some of the women wore blossoms in their hair. At first I barely heeded Jiao's words for my eyes were everywhere, looking at the flowers and beyond at the houses, an extraordinary medley of materials and styles. There were walls faced with quarry tiles and long granite slabs, with stucco and glazed blocks, with ornate panelled woodwork, with kiln-patterned bricks, with mud reinforced by broken tile that resembled peanut brittle. It was a town of few roads or vehicles, a town as towns should be, overflowing with flowers and people-sized lanes. I drank it all in as Jiao babbled on.

Jiao was persistent: he enjoyed speaking English, especially with one whose accent was British. We met several times and each time we talked I appreciated him more. He was gutsy, earthy and bounding with life. As we wandered down lanes he pointed out wells where girls were pulling buckets from unprotected holes among cyclists and rickshaws and pedestrians and carts. He pointed out temples, this one a park, that one a school, a third a workshop, a fourth a library, a fifth a teahouse, a sixth a cycle park and a seventh, prominent beside the hotel, a reconversion to its original use.

'People wonder what we're looking at,' Jiao remarked with a smile. 'Some are too young to know these buildings had a former use.' Disfigured as they were by wires and scraped-off fragments of political slogans and infill development and blocked-off courts it was sometimes difficult even for Jiao to tell. And harder still for a young Chinese to understand the logic of rebuilding what had so recently been smashed when religion was thought of as a 'cultural relic' and when money was needed for people to be housed. 'A decade ago the Party told us to destroy the old. Now the same Party is putting it back.'

Jiao and his wife were low-ranking cadres and lived in a single room. It was dominated by the bed with its bright pink canopy, Jiao's favourite colour, and each piece of furniture was labelled in English: Wardrobe, Cupboard, Table, Chair, Window and Wall. They married for love and as yet had no child.

A girl required permission from her unit to get pregnant. Each unit had its quota of births for the year. 'The wife of a friend of mine became pregnant without asking and her unit demanded she have an abortion,' Jiao recalled. 'This was their first child too. They refused to comply and the girl gave birth, so the cadre concerned spread a rumour that the child was conceived out of wedlock. She was old and bitter, and she did it out of spite. My friend confronted her and when she tried to slap him he got in first and kicked her on the shin. She took to her bed and refused to get up till my friend had been sentenced, so they put him in jail. It was six months before he was put on trial – the permitted maximum is supposed to be one – and the court sent him to labour camp for a further year.'

I had once tried locating a labour camp, but found nothing more compromising than walls and barbed wire. So I asked Jiao instead: of the Chinese I made friends with Jiao was the most forthright of all.

'I spent six years in the PLA and we sometimes visited labour camps. They are freer than jails, though prisoners are still locked up at night and watched over by day as they work in the factories or fields. Should they stray outside the demarcated zone a warder will shoot, first over their heads but the third time straight at them to wound.'

'Why did you join the PLA?' The PLA was generally out of favour. Though some were friendly, others were rude, more like archetypal servicemen than archetypal Chinese. I had watched a group in a noodle house in Xiamen, sitting round a table – though they didn't stay that way for more than seconds at a time. Some, or all, got up, sat down, or marched across the room striking metal-tipped heels on the tiles. They shouted, threatened, gesticulated and leered, snapped lighters, rocked chairs and flung tealeaves behind them over the floor.

'It was the Cultural Revolution then,' Jiao replied. 'It was safer to be in the PLA than anywhere else because soldiers were often the least involved. A soldier earned a reasonable salary, and had special facilities, and easier access to Party membership too.' Jiao glanced at me sideways. 'When I left the PLA I joined the Party.' I stared at him and he laughed. 'You didn't think I was a Party member did you?' I shook my head. 'Only four in a hundred are Party members. There aren't many as young as me, but it was easier then with my PLA background.' Jiao was in his early thirties, his wife five years younger. 'It's worth being in the Party for the better-paid jobs and faster promotion that membership brings. But it's mostly just a way of keeping out of trouble. For a monthly subscription of only three jiao the Party trusts us. They even made us cadres. All we had to do was swear allegiance to Marxism–Leninism–Mao Zedong Thought. We don't believe in it of course,' Jiao grinned, 'but we sympathize with some of it.'

We were sitting in a noodle house overlooking the park. Rick-shaws were passing, tinkling bells. A loudspeaker was playing a popular song. Groups of masons were fashioning granite into fair-faced slabs and the tapping of their chisels was echoing all round. As we watched and listened, an old man went by, beating a gong.

'Do you know who that old man is?' Jiao asked. I hadn't seen such a man before. 'We all know him by his gong and we run out to stop him,' he explained in his eager tones.

'What for?' I asked.

'He castrates cocks.' Jiao paused and I prodded. 'To make a rooster fat and delicious you have to castrate him. That man is so quick the whole thing is over in minutes,' Jiao said. He'd had his own cocks done the week before, so he should have known. 'The old man holds the rooster down and makes a cut beneath the wing. Then he severs the testicles with a single hair from a horse's tail and scoops them out with a spoon. He plugs the wound with a feather and it heals in two or three days. It's a pity I didn't think of it at the time,' Jiao mused. 'We could have chased that man and watched him work.'

Instead he grew sad. Perhaps the castrator had put him in mind of his own lack of progeny. 'My only worry is that my wife may die. She has an unknown disease and has been in and out of hospitals ever since I've known her. I knew when I married her we might not be able to have any children but I married her anyway because she'd been kind. We'll wait another five years or so, and if nothing turns up we'll adopt a child. It won't be the same of course, we'd rather have our own. But if she died my life would lose all meaning. I don't know what I'd do.'

9

Willow-patterned Plates

From Fujian I went on to Hangzhou, where I boarded a boat to travel overnight on the Grand Canal to Suzhou. The broad eight-hundred-mile canal from Hangzhou to Tianjin (south-east of Beijing) was part of an extensive network of waterways dug by hand with shovel and shoulder pole, begun four thousand years ago. Thus marshland was drained and floods controlled, silt was intercepted on its way to the sea and spread to fertilize fields. The Grand Canal itself is fifteen hundred years old, built to ship food from the richer fields of China's south to the depleted lands in the north. Canals were still being excavated in the 1980s, sometimes by hand, because transport by boat was still cheap.

The Grand Canal was black and foul, reeking of sulphur and apparently fermenting. Dismal factories blanketed its banks, broken here by a power station, there by a slag heap. Strings of reinforced concrete barges plied the black water, hauling baulks of timber and rocks and bottles and gravel and cabbages and bricks.

Thus I arrived in the morning at Suzhou, city of silk and old Chinese gardens and women of legendary but unapparent beauty, one of the least despoiled cities in the land. Suzhou's main shopping street was shaded by plane trees, the pavements stippled by soft yellow sunlight, the shops selling cake and ice-cream. Behind the tree-lined vehicular streets were narrow cobbled alleys of whitewashed houses with scrubbed wooden buckets leaning up against doorways and padded winter clothing dripping from poles, and bunches of bamboo leaves drying on strings for packaging rice to be steamed in cones.

It was here I met a surprising man, a middle-grade cadre who lived in a whitewashed courtyard house on a cobbled lane – and was proud of it. A slight, suited figure with languid eyes he played the hammer dulcimer, read Tang poetry, practised calligraphy and trained bonsai trees. He respected his heritage, the only Party official I met who admitted to having such cultivated tastes. As his father had passed on his skills to his sons so the young man would encourage his only child. He denied that traditional culture was dying (as millions like Weimin, themselves estranged, imagined it was); families such as his would keep it alive.

At five every morning students of *wushu* (the correct term for kung fu) practised beneath the plane trees in the square. Lulled by a rhythmical swishing of brooms as women swept the dawn-grey streets I watched their movements, ebullient yet controlled, elegant yet warlike, impressive not only for their physical skill but in the harmony between master and student. Sometimes it was difficult to tell them apart for the teachers were as likely to be learning from their students as the other way round, and the students were helping and encouraging their colleagues. So intense was their level of concentration that the sweepers, the joggers and the fringe of spectators might not have been there.

As dawn turned to sunrise the *wushu* students retired to have breakfast and start the day's work, and the elderly gathered to practise *taiji*. They in their turn were succeeded by cycles that filled the square in an interlocking sculpture of saddles and spokes, watched over by old ladies on stools. Shutters folded back and shop doors opened and the pavements chattered with footsteps and wheels.

Towards evening the bicycles started to thin and a different rhythm pervaded the square. Youths hung around benches, strumming guitars. Vendors set up stands of traditional street craft; one cut a likeness of a customer's profile, exaggerating differences, cutting without drawing, completing each outline in a minute or so. A dough man moulded figures in rainbow-coloured dough, miniature fantasies of operatic headwear and elaborate robes.

Evening performances in the theatres round the square ranged from light entertainment to full-blown operas in authentic local style. The Eight Revolutionary Exemplary works staged exclusively in the Cultural Revolution had given way once more to traditional tales. The performers were gorgeous in embroidered satin gowns with elongated sleeves and platform shoes. The audience was less so, patched and faded in their everyday clothes, foiling concentration with their animated chatter, not just on and off but most of the time. They ate, they drank, they coughed, they spat, they moved about, came late and left early – yet none of this indicated lack of interest or poor performance, rather audience participation in traditional village style. When the interval came they stampeded out in their plastic summer sandals and battered straw hats to the foyer for a smoke. Others, wanting ice-cream, had to fight their way blind through the fog.

After the interval the performance resumed, the babble of chatter, the creaking of chairs, the shuffling of feet and the cracking of melon seeds drowning the voices of the singers on the stage. Having seen the same opera numerous times they had no need to concentrate, but I had to do so doubly hard. For there was meaning in everything: the style of the headgear, the colours of the gowns, the beards, the expressions, the make-up, the hair; half the story was presented in code. Yet though unable to interpret it I could at least follow the general theme and appreciate the opera on a visual plane. Movement followed curves, like the lines of a painting or the edges of a leaf. The mask-like make-up, the exuberant clothes, the exaggerated gestures, the falsetto tones, everything was remote from real life. Descended as Chinese opera was from travelling troupes who performed in the countryside, walking between villages carrying their props, the stage was almost bare. At the end there was almost no clapping at all, and the peasant audience was up on its feet and making for the bus stops before the curtains had even closed.

On another occasion I happened by chance on a puppet rehearsal of *Journey to the West*. I sat on the stage and watched the puppeteers moving high on the gangplanks manipulating paddles of thirty strings, speaking and acting the parts as they did so, even making the relevant facial expressions and projecting their voices to the back of the hall. Western puppets had eight or ten strings and were far less versatile than the Chinese kind which could move their eyebrows, their eyes, their mouths, which could write and ride bicycles, ride horses and dance. Both performers of opera and puppeteers were artists of multiple skills. They were singers and dancers, actors and acrobats; but their arts were spurned by many younger Chinese and it was hard to foretell what their future would be.

I had come to the Orient searching for the China of the willow-patterned plate. Since early childhood my images of China were of angled bridges and latticed pavilions with upswept roofs and contorted trees like bonsai miniatures grown full-size. My initial disillusion took weeks to overcome. Even visitors to China at the turn of the century bemoaned the fact that the Orient was not one endless latticed fantasy with coolies and mandarins and fishermen in sampans, and that trees grew leaves just like trees in England and those porcelain trees producing feathers and footballs were nowhere to be found.

If the willow-patterned plates once existed anywhere they existed in Suzhou, in the gardens of the wealthy literati. But their images were more than just picturesque playgrounds for noblemen, for behind the willows and painted pavilions lay a thousand years of custom and ritual based on the philosophies of Confucius and Dao. Screened from the noise and bustle of the city by twenty-foot walls the gardens were totally self-contained. Women of such households rarely went out but passed their lives within the courts, dressing, cooking, managing, embroidering, while the men entertained and practised calligraphy and painted and wrote poetry and sang. Every activity had its place. The women remained in the women's halls and the servants had their quarters nearby. Children studied in the schoolroom; ancestors were worshipped in the ancestral hall. Tutors, friends or concubines were housed in separate courts.

Each garden consisted of a series of courtyards of varying size and use, some interlocking, others secluded, enclosed in each case by the rooms or pavilions or halls that made up the house. Some were linked by galleries, some were open-sided and set among foliage or over a pool. Men gathered to contemplate and philosophize.

The gardens of Suzhou were an emblem of an age, a surviving testament to vanished dynasties of Chinese history developed in the Song but coming to fruition in the Ming. In their lack of symmetry, their play on emotions, they diverged from orthodox Confucian theory and seemed closer to the tenets of Dao. Contemplation of a water-worn rock could bring one closer to the mythical mountains that housed the Immortals; to understanding the nature of being. Comprising rock and water, plants and walls, the garden represented an ideal world.

In China a garden wasn't planted but built, its spaces defined by buildings and walls. Its structure was architectural, the planting like the furnishing of its rooms. Courtyards were paved in intricate pebble patterns with the richness of carpets and set with arrangements of water-worn rocks. The abundance of stone made the gardens too yang, too hard and masculine for most Western tastes accustomed to landscapes predominantly yin – too yin for the Chinese mind. The Chinese believed in expressing the duality of yin and yang by setting them off in pairs – space and solid, light and dark, still and moving, open and closed, full and empty, mysterious and predictable – to complement and dramatize in a manner never matched, only seldom perceived and still less clearly understood in the West.

In the orientation of pavilions and entrances and the positioning of furniture *feng-shui* played a vital role. No building should be windowless and bridges were angled or arched. The positions of rocks and trees and pools were adjusted with the help of a *feng-shui* man. But though the planning seemed complex and the limitations considerable, the effects of the gardens were ultimately simple: a glimpse of a courtyard through a circular moon gate or the pattern of a shadow on a whitewashed wall. Such delicate vistas could be far more subtle than the massing of shrubbery and lurid green grass in the garden of the Englishman's dream.

My favourite was the Garden of the Master of the Fishing Nets, at an acre the smallest of the Suzhou gardens yet giving the impression of endless surprise and unlimited space, of pavilion after courtyard after gallery after pool. The acre of land had been layered and divided using light and shadow and mysterious glimpses over and under and through. The garden-makers had achieved their aim of making a small city plot seem large by allowing only part to be visible at a time, by taking the visitor on a circuitous route, by scaling things down in texture and size, by creating vistas through doors and lattice and foliage and grilles that enticed the eye and slowed the step, by spatial variety – a constant progression from light to shade, from small to large, from inside to out, from formal to asymmetry – and by the use of concealment and neutral tones: the soft grey walls that receded like mist and the browns that symbolized shade.

Like all good gardens it was more than its photographs. No picture could convey the fluidity of space, the unfolding of views and the progression towards the central pool, the spiritual, religious and cultural context and perhaps most of all the degree of restraint.

Grey pebbles, grey paving and pitted grey stones. Whitewashed walls and stained brown wood and water a soft grey-green. Plants deployed as sculptural form, flowerless foliage tracing lines, suggesting and echoing details of buildings, framing, shading and filtering light. Plants fulfilled functions and symbolized qualities the Chinese admired: the pine for longevity, the lotus for peace, the plum for renewal, the peony for rank. Grass was excluded as being too bright; grass was fit only for cows.

Even interiors were simple and dignified, with cold stone floors and long dark tables with upturned ends, and high flat chairs with marble backs and stained brown beams and plants on stands and scrolls upon the walls. Since the time of Confucius in the fifth century BC reticence and harmony had been cultivated by 'gentlemen', and subconsciously externalized in daily life. Colour had a place in corporate activity, in the fantasy of festival, the fervour of worship and the fanfare of parade; it had a place in architecture used symbolically to balance the yin and yang of its parts; but it was disparaged when used to promote the self. Bright colours were boastful; they blazed, they sang. They deflected attention from symbol and meaning and the quiet contemplation of form. Painters of past dynasties portrayed the landscape as the early literati constructed their gardens, in a limited palette of greens and browns, even monotone shades of grey.

Sunlight in the Garden of the Master of the Fishing Nets had a quality almost magical. It streamed over walltops and intensified the glow of whitewashed walls. It flowed through the filigree of window grilles. It sieved through the latticework and patterned the floors in slanting jigsaws of diamonds and crosses and triangles and squares. It bounced back from mirrors and reflected from pools. It was filtered and fragmented by foliage and it dimmed in the shade of magnolia trees.

Less subtle than the Garden of the Master of the Fishing Nets but much more fun was the Garden of Joy, the garden the tour groups eschewed. One knew why at once. An odious smell pervaded the courtyards, issuing, it seemed, from a public loo. Tickets were half price and the place was full of peasants, bringing with them from the countryside their tattered garments and rustic speech and garlic breath and generally lowering the tone.

The garden was charmingly overgrown. Trees had surpassed

their intended size. Jasmine flowed like waterfalls. Loquats draped their boughs across roofs and virginia creeper spilled down walls. Somehow the planting set the stage: the plants being seen to be doing as they pleased – unusual in a Chinese garden or park – the peasants assumed they could too. They rested their plimsolls on top of the walls and scrubbed their sandals in the lotus pools. They littered the path with sunflower-seed husks and rolled up their trousers as if still at home in the paddy fields. They flannelled their faces and spat in the lake, the nucleus of the garden where the 'moon washed its soul'. No soft-class overseas visitors here; this was the garden of the proletariat and the Party seemed bent on keeping it so.

Visitors to gardens in dynastic times were sometimes requested to name a pavilion or compose a couplet which distilled its essence in a handful of words, which embellished its mood and itself became part of its ongoing history. Visiting a functioning Buddhist temple far from a town it once fell on me to participate in this ritual whose origins went back a thousand years. I drank tea with the monks in one of the shrine halls and after a while a book was fetched and placed upon my knee. Within its cover of coarse yellow cloth was a continuous concertina of heavy hand-made paper, on each page of which an epithet or a couplet or a poem was inscribed. The contributors had taken their task to heart and constructed each character to the best of their ability, and composed their poems on the blank white sheets with a natural eye for balance and form. Roman script was no match for Chinese characters and I politely desisted, but the monks held firm. So I wrote two lines of anticipated eulogy – only lofty ideals were permissible at such times, in spite of requests for 'spontaneous thoughts' – and dated and signed them as others had done. The sun shone down making patterns of the latticework and the monks smiled their pleasure in their quiet grey robes.

Calligraphy is to a Chinese garden what classical statuary is to a Western one: it defines its context with historical analogy and metaphor. The names of courts and bridges and pavilions were inscribed in stone; poems were written on vertical scrolls. Pre-Liberation Chinese characters had a rhythmical harmony and inner vitality unequalled by the modern simplified ones, and their perfection took years to achieve. Personality was judged by how one wielded a brush.

Through an introduction by a friend I watched a serious amateur calligrapher practising at his home, working without a break for four hours. For the first half-hour he screwed up each sheet and threw it aside, for it took that long to get in his hand. But he continued to scrumple two sheets out of three when he'd misjudged a character or forgotten the shape of one of its twenty or thirty strokes. That, he said dismally, was the mark of an amateur, of one yet to achieve the measure of his art.

He painted while we talked, while our friend spat out husks of sunflower seeds on the newly swept floor, while neighbours came in to peer. He painted on his desk, on his bed, on the floor, depending on the size of the brush he chose. He painted fast, poising the brush above the paper, then blackening its whiteness in a lattice of strokes, then leaning back to assess its work, almost as if he had not been part of it, as if the brush had done it all on its own.

The River Li coiled a path through the mythical mountains south of Guilin. For a thousand years they'd been a source of inspiration to landscape painters who travelled for days to see them for themselves.

I saw him first on the hotel roof where he went each day in the dawn and dusk – as I did too – a man of quiet dignity in late middle age with thick wavy hair going grey. He was not like the others, who though artists themselves just came and stood and looked at the mountains shining in the river and the last light orange in the western sky and said wasn't it beautiful and went away. This man stayed, and drank in the landscape with his heart and soul, and didn't say a word.

Wei Meng had brought a group of his students to paint the Guilin mountainscape. I would see them at their easels working in oils, not in the Chinese style but in the manner, I suggested, of Cézanne. They laughed. 'Cézanne is our teacher's favourite painter!' So they tried to paint like him too.

That they loved and respected their teacher was plain. They sat close by him and sometimes touched him, taking his hand or stroking his knee in an act, I felt, that was close to reverence. They addressed him familiarly as a father or friend but never, in my presence, showed off.

There was a kind of wholeness about Wei Meng that intrigued me too – not separateness exactly, for he had no arrogance, but acceptance of himself and the way things were. So much in China was unspontaneous that it was a relief to find someone who said what he thought. Whereas most people said I spoke good Chinese Wei Meng pronounced it enough to get by, so that three months later when we met again and he said I'd made progress I was pleased as for once I knew it was meant.

Though the clothes he wore were orthodox proletarian, shabby and frayed, on him they seemed almost bohemian. They were faded and comfortable, they expressed him and were part of him. His coat was so old its blue had gone grey and its cotton was smooth like old jeans. His trousers were darned and his olive-green plimsolls were held by short laces between two holes. Millions of people wore clothes like these, but not with such style, and they would rather have worn something else.

One morning I found him painting the river, filling his canvas with that sure Chinese speed, painting and looking simultaneously. Sitting behind him I tried to respond to the scene through his eyes, to learn from his skill. Never pausing in his painting he pointed things out, the curve of a rock, the light on a stone, relating to me not as a foreigner, but as a student or an artist; certainly in a way no other Chinese had treated me before. I watched the landscape growing on his canvas, wondering why he paid no heed to the details that interested me – the elegant bamboos on the opposite bank, a row of trees on the side of a rock silhouetted against the sky, a band of yellow sunlight shining on the water – but concentrated wholly on colour, luminosity, mass and form. His mountains were solid; his sky breathed with life.

I told him of a path I had found in the mountains that patterned his canvas, a woodcutter's path that wound up and up between the peaks, where there was nothing and no one but tinkling cowbells and scented scrub. But his expression changed and he told me not to go again for there were snakes among the rocks and in the scrub. I said I could stamp my feet. But cobras didn't run away, they reared their heads and struck. I said I couldn't be living my life according to the perils that might befall me, and that cobras didn't matter, I wasn't afraid. They *did* matter, he insisted, treating me still as a child in his charge, and he cautioned his students too. He forbade them to swim in the river when I did or to take long walks in the fields. But when he thought I wasn't listening I heard him say that I had 'big courage', *dazi da*.

Talking frankly, as the students did in the presence of each other ('Your painting is awful') and Wei Meng did with me, signified friendship and respect. It was impossible in China to be less than polite with any but one's friends. In return for this trust I told him, when he asked, that I was writing a book. Most Chinese were less concerned about what I did than how much it earned me, and with the bewildering fact that I was travelling alone, but Wei Meng didn't question either of these things. Instead he asked me what I wrote and why I wrote, what motivated me and whether I was disciplined and wrote every day, and who would read the book I wrote and how it might benefit anyone else. And I asked the same of him. He painted because it was what he most loved. The State paid his salary to teach and write on the theory of art, so in normal life there was little time spare in which to paint. At home in the city he couldn't paint landscapes; it was only on field trips that the opportunity arose.

Of all the people I met in China it was Wei Meng with whom I felt most at home. We shared a passion for land and its expression through art. I spent hours in his company, determined for once to overcome the maddening barrier of language; my Chinese was poor but Wei Meng spoke no English at all. Born of poor peasants in Anhui province he spent his childhood in the fields. There was often no food and in famine years the family almost starved, eating bark and grass to stay alive. When Liberation came he was twenty-two, and showing an aptitude and a correct class background he was given the chance to study painting in Beijing.

The Marxist view of art had been puzzling me so I put him the question: 'Mao asked, "What is art? And for whom?" How would you reply to him?' I enlisted a student to help translate but his English was as limited as my Chinese and our discussion lasted hours.

'The purpose of art is to serve the people,' Wei Meng replied. 'It should express the aims of the new society and be related to daily life. It should stimulate political consciousness, typify struggle and point a way forward. It should alter perception. Most of all it should appeal to everyone, not an enlightened few.'

Not yet knowing his background at that time and deciding Wei

Meng had a mind of his own I prodded him. 'You're just saying that,' I accused him. 'It's the current Party line.'

He laughed. 'No, I'm not! It's what I really believe. There's a difference you see. In the Cultural Revolution art had to serve the masses, which was not the same thing as serving the people. The masses are the *gong nong bing*, the workers, peasants and soldiers.'

'And the people includes everyone? You and me? Intellectuals?'

'That's right. Art is for us too.'

'Art means different things to different people,' I objected, 'but its only legitimate message in recent years has been propaganda. Expression has been stifled and the artist loses his dignity.' A country that repressed creativity was fearful of confronting the truth: an artist could illustrate the collective consciousness before its mood was generally perceived. Who but an artist could describe the way things were?

'Our ideals were confused in the Cultural Revolution,' Wei Meng replied. 'All we could paint were socialist monuments and landscapes prominent in Red Army history – like the caves in Yanan – and portraits of Mao Zedong. But it's different now,' he said.

Ten years previously art had been something to be ashamed of. Artists were thought feckless and unreliable. Old themes had been given a political context: a landscape might be embellished by a smoky factory or a hydro-electric dam. By persecuting art the Party had in fact made it more desirable than before.

I wanted to know how landscapes and still-lives in the manner of Cézanne raised the people's political consciousness. Should art be enjoyed as well as being instructive? 'Your paintings reflect the world as it is,' I said. 'Yet according to the Party this is not the purpose of art. In their view people should be presented with something to aspire to.'

'If people enjoy my paintings they will look at them more carefully. If they look at them carefully maybe they will learn; Western techniques are still new in China and being so different people may be shocked into seeing the land in a way they never have before.' Wei Meng's paintings did not question or criticize the communist regime and as such were no longer banned.

I explained the approach of the Western artist. 'Western artists paint any subject or abstraction that comes to mind and in any manner they please. Modern Western art is anarchic. For the first time in history artists have no constraints; they are not even bound to please their buyers or sell their work for the State will support them when their funds run out. Western painters have only themselves to satisfy. They paint with their minds, or their feelings, or their passion, or both, or all. Sometimes they don't know why or what they are doing, though they may be able to provide a rationale in hindsight, and even if they don't the critics will find one for them. Art is sometimes used as a means of attracting attention, as a short-cut to fame.'

It was never so in China. Chinese artists always worked within the confines of culture and society. In traditional painting there were correct techniques for rendering a rock or a boat or a tree. 'The approach is so different. You aren't allowed to paint your feelings,' I told Wei Meng.

But he disagreed. 'Perhaps it seems so on the surface. But underneath our aims are the same. Chinese artists paint because they want to, for personal satisfaction. When I see a scene that moves me, something stirs me to paint it. I *have* to paint it. But this does not mean that my painting has no use for others.'

Again I quoted the words of Mao, 'Art for art's sake, art which transcends class or Party, does not in fact exist,' but Wei Meng just grunted and didn't respond.

I told him of artists at home in the West who painted by computer, or with spray guns or their feet, for whom a work of art might be a slash in a canvas, or the canvas itself.

'What use is that?' Wei Meng challenged me. 'Do people understand what they're trying to say?'

I sympathized. What was art, and what were its standards? Surely Mao was not wrong to ask? Art at the whim of individual artists expressing something indefinable and interpreted variously by different critics – did this art serve a purpose? Was it not more positive to encourage and motivate than dampen and depress, even if a painting was future objective not present reality? Even Westerners laughed at 'original' art for the artist and critic and investor-collector. Marxists interpreted esoteric art as a protest against capitalism, an expression of its decline, believing socialist values suppressed by the system lay buried beneath. 'Most people don't understand it,' I said. 'Most people don't even like it.'

I was later to visit an exhibition at the China Art Gallery in

Beijing, crowded with people of all ages and kinds, appealing to a wider cross-section of the public than abstract Western art could ever hope to do. A nationwide event staged every five years it was the equivalent, in principle, of the Royal Academy's Summer Exhibition. Artists submitted work, which was selected by a panel.

The display was as diverse as its English counterpart, and for an outsider, more enjoyable. Among the exhibits were watercolours on silk, oils on canvas, woodcuts, photography, etchings, lithographs, paper-cuts and sculpture. Subjects were contemporary, and though sometimes stereotypic they told of China in the 1980s, its realities, its hardships, its aspirations – and its lies. But above all each work was understandable; it conveyed a message available to all.

Though censorship had softened, most paintings still carried an underlying political theme, not of Mao's ideological struggle, of heroes of socialist self-denial, but of prosperity and production, the revolutionary goal of Deng's China. The construction site was still there, but seen as a backdrop to workers on tea break swigging Coca-Cola, or in the distance through a window of a cramped Tibetan home. The hydro-electric power station was still there, but as a detail in a landscape of towering crags. The peasants were still there, but no more did they toil in communal industry; instead they sat and counted out banknotes and smiled at their shiny new television sets. They were examples of Deng's slogan: 'To get rich is glorious.'

One small woodblock seemed to have escaped the Party's censure. Throughout the exhibition peasant life (as depicted chiefly by urban artists) was as cheerful and faultless as an English picture postcard. The woodblock possibly came nearer the truth: it portrayed a man bent double in a rice field, his clothes in tatters, his face in anguish – a suggestion that peasant life wasn't all the Party made it out to be.

Coming from isolated rustic backgrounds, China's new leaders had still to arrive at any definite conclusion in their policy on the arts. With little interest or knowledge in the subject themselves they nevertheless presumed to dictate what was good and bad. The inclusion of the woodblock showed a certain relaxation but the ultimate dictate still held sway, that it was wrong to propagate any idea inconsistent with the principles of socialism, and that art should serve the people's needs.

Looking round the display and returning twice more I found it easy to accept the overall view that art should be for everyone. But not all Westerners saw it that way. The large exhibition hall on several floors was so crowded with workers in everyday clothes that a girl from my hotel dormitory exclaimed: 'What are all these ordinary workers doing in an art gallery?' Galleries, as this Westerner understood them, were for cultured people only: foreigners, intellectuals and the artists themselves.

Chinese art was putting out feelers, learning from the methods of the Western world in an attempt to evolve a style of its own. After three thousand years of growth in isolation there were paintings reminiscent of Rembrandt and Vermeer, Monet and Van Gogh, and others that moved the Chinese style towards bolder, semi-abstract, apolitical themes, the beginnings, at last, of a Cultural Restoration. Judging by the talent of Chinese artists resident overseas, the latent resource of artistic brilliance within China itself, untapped and unrecognized, was a wholly reprehensible waste. The Beijing exhibition was no more than a note of optimism in an otherwise barren contemporary scene.

Wei Meng himself was unrecognized. I searched for his work in the gallery in Beijing but he'd been in Guilin at submission time. Though employed as a teacher he had never been offered a public show, and since his work was so powerful I wondered why. 'Maybe I'm too young,' he said softly, rather than let his country down. 'At fifty-seven? Then what about Hu Yiwen?' I asked.

Hu Yiwen was an artist of international fame. She had recently been on a visit to Paris, displaying her paintings, meeting French dignitaries, promoting goodwill abroad. Her work, though eclectic, was vigorous and diverse, comprising Parisian monuments, animals, portraits and operatic themes. Hu Yiwen was eight years old.

Wei Meng laughed. He had no position, no back-door connection with the cadres concerned with promotion of the arts. Artists were selected with a certain degree of arbitrariness, not on the grounds of exceptional talent but as representatives to further a political cause. They were pawns in the game of international friendship, bait to succour international support.

Months later I visited Wei Meng at his home. His wife and daughter were at work in their factories so Wei Meng cycled to the market to buy food, leaving me alone in their ground-floor flat. An ordinary dismal grey block on the outside, inside, without trying, was an artist's home. By Chinese standards the flat was a large one, with one room as a studio crowded with paintings, landscapes, townscapes, portraits and still-lives. The familiar blue coat hung limp from a nail. A pot of paintbrushes bristled on the table among books and papers and *objets trouvés*, rocks and shells and lumps of twisted root.

I walked through the sitting room into the garden, an extraordinary courtyard, almost square, bounded by high grey-rendered walls and roofed by a pergola of vines. Beans grew up strings that striped the walls and the soil sprouted vegetables, mint and potatoes and Chinese onions reached along narrow brick paths. Raw compost was strewn to rot where it lay. It was a peasant's garden, a vegetable plot, and a strange and mysterious green room. Even the light, filtering through the vine leaves, was still and green. On the wall of the shed hung a blackened pig's leg. 'Why?' I asked when he came back from market. 'I will paint it,' he replied.

We had lunch at a desk in the sitting room. Wei Meng had brought bread in sliced white loaves to save time cooking rice. He made soup of dofu and spinach leaves and a dish of fried chard. The room was big and full of books. Though individually every item of furniture fell prey to that desperate Chinese ugliness, the overall atmosphere was neither clinical nor gauche, but generated rather the spirit of its occupants, comfortable and cared-for and worn. We dunked our bread in the dofu soup and looked out upon the green of the garden room.

By comparison with the immediacy of Wei Meng's landscapes, the black ink paintings of Chinese-style artists seemed hackneyed and remote. They moved trees and buildings and mountains as it suited them, added sampans, invented villages, formalized, formularized and dramatized the scene before their eyes. Slopes were exaggerated, bamboos isolated; non-existent pine trees hung wizened from crags. The resulting mountainscapes seemed two-dimensional, expressions of an old ideal whose point they seldom understood rather than sketches of a living, evolving land. Though I loved their Chineseness, their stylistic allusions to the unattainable Orient of the willow-patterned plate, they failed to distil the spiritual essence, the currents of energy flowing through the land. Wei Meng's paintings were solid and inviting; he painted light, he painted what he saw.

The expertise of the traditional painter was not expressed in innovation, but as virtuoso interpretation of a rigid set of rules. By re-evaluating an ancient theme the artist attempted to elevate consciousness through harmony and balance and line, creating gardens on paper, as the garden-maker's aim was to translate the perfection of a two-dimensional painting into space. Void meant as much in their drawings as line. What wasn't said, but suggested or implied, was as meaningful as that which was.

Though it had always been representational, China had 'modern' paintings and poetry long before the West. Brush strokes were deft and impressionistic, capturing the essence of a bird or a branch. In Guangzhou I had watched a group of artists perform before an audience in the Cultural Palace, the former Sino-Soviet Friendship Hall. Their subjects were traditional: mountains, flowers and bamboo leaves. Colours were predominantly black and grey. The artists worked as calligraphers did, gazing at the paper, contemplating its blankness, dipping the brush in the watery ink and draining it just the right amount, holding it poised above the sheet and then attacking it suddenly, as a blackbird catches a worm. Blob: a petal. Drag: a branch. Flick: a leaf. Then after some minutes when the painting was done and seen to be satisfactory, a dedicatory poem was added down the side, ending in the artist's name seal in red. The pictures were poems; the poetry visual. Despite working to formulae the finished paintings, pegged to a washing line, held freshness and appeal.

How these artists performed to an audience was bewildering to me. But a painter was a craftsman, and craftsmen were used to being watched while they worked. Accustomed to performing in the presence of others it must be possible, I supposed, to learn to be alone when in company, to turn off the outer world and concentrate within. Millions of Chinese must do that to stay sane.

A few Chinese artists were fortunate enough to be employed just to paint. The State paid their salaries and sold their work, paying the artist a small portion of the proceeds over and above their habitual wage.

Huang Jing was retained by the military unit in which his father worked. He was obliged to execute five paintings a month which were given as gifts to visiting delegations. Like a peasant under contract, everything he produced beyond the first five he was free to sell. He completed a painting in an hour or so and sold it surreptitiously to unsuspecting foreigners like me. So long as he continued soliciting custom he was sitting, for a Chinese, on a goldmine. Already he had purchased a Japanese motorbike, acquired through illegitimate channels by his father, a high-ranking officer with considerable pull.

Jing laughed at my cynicism. 'It's not as simple as you think,' he insisted. 'Many of my paintings I have to discard. There's a high element of chance in the Chinese approach.'

His paintings were elegant and well composed. But later in the Shanghai Museum of Art and History (in which, as in all museums, the only exhibits were Chinese), I discovered a replica of one of Jing's works. Probably the others were somewhere to be found. Yet Jing was no charlatan in the Western sense, for copying was a talent not to be despised. The government craft stores sold copies by the thousand: students learnt by mimicking others' works.

In Wei Meng's studio a passable Pissarro hung upon the wall.

10

The Man from Xian

Nobody knew which queue I should be in. Two dozen long lines snaked across the ticket hall, orderly at the back, Asiatic at the front, a babble of irritable would-be passengers confronted by the clerks who wanted their lunch. Several times over, having stood and shuffled for half an hour and fought for counter space, I was directed to the back of a different queue. Until finally I was pointed to the foreigners' ticket hall where I had no intention of going. Chinese railways charged a special rate for foreigners' tickets, which had to be paid for in FEC and were almost twice the ordinary fare. This double price standard, devised as a means of generating foreign currency to buy foreign grain, infuriated many visitors for it smacked of the very inequality and exploitation the revolution had fought to destroy. Especially since China was now exporting grain.

'Why should we have to pay more for our tickets?' I asked the clerk.

'You're a foreigner. You're rich.'

'Not all foreigners are rich.'

'Your salaries are far higher than ours. You must be rich to be in Shanghai – I couldn't afford to visit your country.'

The argument went on for another five minutes while the queue behind me grumbled and shuffled and tried to push in front. I was on my way home and hadn't enough money for a foreign-price fare.

'I cannot give you an ordinary ticket, you don't have a Chinese student card. You must talk to the clerk in the foreigners' ticket hall.'

Instead I waited near the back of the queue for I had one last chance. People with tickets they could no longer use would return to the station and sell them to someone in the queue. Sure enough, along came a man with a Guangzhou ticket which I promptly bought off him. In the background I heard mutterings of 'Na bu xing!', that won't do. Many Chinese supported the Party's belief that foreigners should bolster their economy. Yet others condoned the travellers' attempts to obtain cheap tickets by asking a friend or paying a Chinese to buy it for them or using a fake student card, for they'd have done exactly the same themselves.

Getting on a train anywhere but a terminus involved confinement in a waiting hall until the train was actually approaching the platform, and then squeezing through the barrier to stampede down the platform, and over the bridge or under the underpass and sprinting towards the doors of the hard-seat carriages to push and elbow those trying to get out with shouts of 'Go on!', 'Don't push!', and 'Get a move on!', and procuring the last seats before anyone else did, ignoring the protestations of supine passengers and their cries of '*You ren!*' (the seat is occupied) because by *you ren* they only meant that the seat was occupied by their ankles. In consequence the process of getting on a train took three times as long as it ought to have done, with people wedged in doorways, their luggage entangled in other people's shoulder straps, their shouts vilifying other people's origins while those still stranded out on the platform hurried helpless from door to door.

Normally foreigners were spared all this. With their foreign-price tickets they waited for the train in comfortable armchairs with tea in china cups, far from the hubbub of the hard-seat passengers, the former third class. When the train came in they were led to the doors of their sleeper coaches. Nobody pushed or shoved.

Shanghai being a terminus my ticket had a numbered seat. When I entered the carriage two minutes before departure everyone else was comfortably settled (and would have been that way for the past half-hour). Their belongings were stowed in tiers on the luggage racks; zip-up hold-alls, boxes, baskets, net bags bulging with packages and fruit. Their face towels hung from the innermost rail. Their tea mugs nestled in clusters on the tables, patterned enamelware, tea-stained and chipped. For the moment there was peace: everyone had a seat.

Chinese trains are green. The seats are green and the carriages are green, the deep dull green of cedar trees. The hard-seat coaches in which I was travelling followed the pattern of English trains, of seats around tables on either side of a central aisle, only the seats were firmer, flatter and more upright. Each numbered coach had a 'blue girl' in attendance, who looked every bit a pawn of the Party in baggy blue uniform and cap. She was charlady, tea girl and disciplinarian, bringing round water in steaming kettles (sometimes brass ones with wickerwork handles and delphinium cosies), berating and bossing, sweeping and mopping and emptying containers of ash.

No sooner had I extracted my mug and settled in my seat than a man demanded to know my age. I had stopped telling people my real age for it aroused too many looks of consternation, and replied instead that I was thirty, at which age I could still be both a student, and therefore poor, and unmarried, and therefore alone. To travel alone with no purpose in view was to many Chinese a pointless exercise, a waste of time and energy, an abuse of hard-earned cash.

Questions continued with where was I going and what was I doing and what was my salary and my job? Yet most queries related not to me but to China: 'Are you accustomed to life here in China?' and 'Are you able to eat our food?', people never quite believing that either might be possible. They asked each other similar questions: 'Where are you going?' and 'Where are you from?' and 'What is your unit?', the last of which was the most revealing, the equivalent of caste, an identity tag.

The man who first addressed me had a pock-marked face and solid frame. At nine in the morning he was already on the booze, with a bottle of *mao tai* clamped between his knees, alternating liquor with mouthfuls of steamed bun and hot pickled greens. A younger man opposite was chewing gum and revealing scarlet ballooning long johns and effeminate shoes, all straps and heels. A thin girl sat next to me, twiggy and knitting, and the others were youngish, unremarkable men.

Having extracted what information they could, given my reticence and limited Chinese, the five in my section settled down to discuss me and compare Chinese with foreigners. I caught odd remarks like 'Very big boots,' and 'Those are Chinese trousers she has on you know,' and 'How many metres do you think she is?' Curiosity was a social virtue. The anonymity of Western city life where people kept themselves to themselves was incomprehensible to most Chinese.

Listening to Chinese conversations generally the word 'China' came up with unfailing regularity. The Chinese were more conscious of their history and nationhood than any race I knew: they clung to it and it hung from them, absolving their present inadequacies, stretching far back in unlimited horizons of culture and power. Yet they shattered its memory on the orders of Mao only twenty years before.

Like the British a century or so ago, the Chinese had little conception of themselves as part of a worldwide society. Believing themselves larger, older and more civilized than any other nation, it was China they cared about, and if others were trampled in their race for advancement it meant nothing to them. Their history lived on as part of the flow of today and tomorrow: the religion of the Chinese was China.

'Welcome to our train.' The voice rang loudly from loudspeakers at intervals set along the coach. It was almost always a woman's voice. Nobody took any notice. 'Our journey from Shanghai to Guangzhou is 1134 kilometres.' There followed a list of the stations we'd be stopping at, with arrival times and lengths of stay and times of connecting trains at each, with finally Guangzhou: 18.05 the following day. The litany continued with information about mealtimes and sights to be seen on the way. Party propaganda, blasted throughout China in the Cultural Revolution, had died with Mao and was replaced in the eighties by the 'Red River Valley' and 'Auld Lang Syne'.

As with industry, education and health care, so with the railways: the system was startlingly new. While Britain had been closing non-profit-making lines for the past thirty years, China was still building, forging out across deserts and mountains to Kashgar and Tibet at the peak of its railway age. Many lines weren't built until the 1950s and the network was still sparse, even in the populous eastern seaboard: in Shandong, a province the size of France, there were only two lines, a main one running north–south and a branch line crossing it. What seemed, therefore, like crowded trains gave a false impression of a nation on the move. So few were the trains that each had a number by which it was called; ours was number 49. There was only one a day.

Normally the system functioned smoothly. Trains left, and even arrived at destinations several days away, on time. A 'Summary of Railway Travel Knowledge' gave explanations of train types and carriages, baggage allowance and timetables. Children less than a metre high travelled free, and each passenger was allowed twenty kilos of luggage. If no coach was available the railways provided what the booklet described as a 'covered wagon substituted for carriage', by which it meant a cattle truck, in which people sat on the floor in darkness.

I gazed through the window at the passing of Shanghai. Due back in England within four days I was sad already, leaving before my time. At first it seemed I was already in London, so much did Shanghai's urban railway backlands resemble the seedier purlieus of King's Cross in their smoke-blackened brickwork and dust-fogged windows, their weedy wildernesses burgeoning between sidings, their railway workers shovelling cinders, their willow trees and tramline wires. The sky was grey; overcast London. I was half-way home.

Steam locomotives were shunting in sidings, black-bodied, red-wheeled, billowing smoke clouds and funnelling steam. More than half the Chinese engines were still powered by steam, an embarrassment to the Party who lumped them together with pedicabs and sampans and donkeys and hand-carts as backward and feudal, and would prefer foreign friends not to notice them. Wonderful as they were, having spent the previous journey from Xiamen to Hangzhou brushing smuts from my clothes, rubbing them from my eyes, scraping them from my ears and shaking them from my hair I was thankful to be travelling in a diesel-powered train.

Gathering speed we left the city for the sub-rural green of vegetable fields. And then it was country, and whitewashed villages straddling canals, and ripe stands of wheat and flocks of fat ducks, and rape gone to seed and flattened in whirlpools by wind. The land rolled past, criss-crossed by a grid of ancient canalicules dug by hand with shovels and shoulder poles, fragmented like frames of slow-motion film by metasequoia trees lining the track. Wheat stood in stooks, or lay drying on field bunds or under the trees on the bank.

It was the end of spring, a time of transition to summer crops. Squares of young rice in their nursery beds nestled among the wheat. The wind rushed in through the open windows. I dozed on my forearms, half-aware of the wind, the whirring fan, the smell of liquor and the rhythm of the train. But a hand on my shoulder prodded me upright, a uniformed man checking tickets. Having scrutinized mine he went off into flights of gestures and words.

Assuming he was doubting my Chinese-price ticket and demanding more money I deliberately didn't listen, feigned incomprehension, but a girl was fetched, a speaker of English, impossible to ignore.

'The comrade calls you to the bedroom,' she said.

How many times on long train journeys had I queued and struggled for the privilege of a berth, sometimes waiting twenty-four hours, sometimes never getting one, for the coaches would be full and government officials waving papers from their units would take priority. When for the first time I was actually being offered one I hadn't any money.

'*Mei you qian*,' the girl explained to the knot of passengers who had gathered round, and they seemed surprised. I thought that was the end of it, but my neighbour with the bottle was busily writing on the back of an envelope, chewing his pencil and furrowing his brow. He thought, he wrote, he gave me the envelope. 'Ther is bet,' it said. At stations people called through the window that berths were available, but I was happy where I was, tired enough to sleep in a third-class carriage, savouring my last few hours in the market place, so to speak, rather than among the privileged in a berth.

Inland the fields had already been flooded to receive the summer rice. The ingredients were all there, the archetypal features of the age-old Chinese landscape – paddy and bamboo, peasants in blue, villages and pools – yet compared to Sichuan or Fujian the country lacked soul. The fields had been rationalized, netted by a grid of drainage canals. Marching pylons diminished villages. Flat-roofed houses sprung up among old tiles. Then again there were vegetables, the approach of a town.

'We are approaching Songjiang station,' announced the disembodied voice. 'Do not go to the toilet while the train is in the station. People getting off should do so as soon as the train stops. Take all your baggage with you and pay attention when you disembark. We will be staying at Songjiang for seven minutes.' People scrambled off with sacks, followed by half the remaining passengers, bored and already on the prowl for food. Girls in white cotton jackets and caps were spaced along the platform selling bread buns and fruit.

At each new station more people forged on and clambered down the aisle over boxes and baskets asking anxiously at each section, 'Is this seat free?' After each new station the railway rules were announced again. 'Sit down. Don't block the aisles, don't block the doors, and don't take up unnecessary space. Don't put your luggage on the seats or the floor, nor hang it on the coat hooks; put it on the rack. If you go to the toilet don't leave your belongings with people you don't know. If your little friends [children] want to go, don't let them soil the floor but take them to the toilet. Don't let your little friends get on or off the train by themselves . . .'

There were five minutes of regulations such as these, during which a new man sat down opposite and regarded me with interest. He was large for a Chinese, with side-parted hair and heavy-framed glasses, dressed in standard summer uniform of light grey trousers and short-sleeved shirt. I must have replied to his opening questions with the reserve he expected, for he asked why the English didn't socialize on trains, but hid from the world behind magazines. He, I noticed, a man from Xian eight hundred miles distant, was engaged in a card game – a kind of gin rummy – with three complete strangers within half an hour of boarding the train.

Along the carriage further groups of men were playing the same game; everyone knew it and the rules never changed. Others were rearranging luggage on the racks, or shuffling down the aisles to replenish their tea mugs from the hot-water urn, or standing by their seats to ease their backsides. At the end of the carriage a mother was spanking a screaming child to a background of music from the *Nutcracker Suite*, crackly and flat. The thin girl next to me with the pinched sour face was knitting something fiddly in acid yellow. Her needles jabbed my elbow; she nibbled pickled cabbage between rows. Three peasant girls sat in a line nearby, soft and round, their mud-stained socks balanced between thighs on the opposite seat, gnawing at sugar-cane and spitting out the refuse to tumble to the floor. The speakers had switched to a Taiwanese pop song and the girls sang too, between mouthfuls of cane, not the tune from Taiwan but a melody of their own, written in numbers on a printed songsheet which they took it in turns to cover their faces with when, later on, they slept. Otherwise the carriage was filled with men, alone or in groups, young or middle-aged, mainly belonging to what would become an emerging urban middle class. Women, children, peasants and the elderly stood out as individuals but the men appeared one collective soul, eating, drinking, spitting, coughing, talking, reading, passing round comics and magazines, poring over papers, raking through and through for anything they had missed, folding and refolding the cream-coloured sheets.

And smoking. Smoking was already a growing habit at the turn of the century, popularized by the British-American Tobacco Company. By 1984 it was the compulsion of the majority of Chinese men, nowhere more offensive than when travelling by train. Fortunately I was not a man. If, as a man, I refused a cigarette I would humiliate the offerer and shatter his hopes of a Kent or Marlboro in return for his Peacock or Double Happiness brand. However much the government campaigned – and campaign they did, on the radio, in the papers, even in song – and however much the wives complained it made no difference, except among the minority of intellectuals. On long train journeys most men chain-smoked. They smoked away their stress and boredom. They smoked away my peace of mind.

'Personally I don't smoke,' said the man from Xian, a confirmed intellectual, having finished his card game and noted my distaste. 'The government says it's bad for the health. My wife says we can't afford it.'

I never asked his name. He was returning to Xian from a conference on pollution, appropriately enough, and at thirty-five was an expert in the field. I stared through the fug at the crowded compartment. 'Where do you suppose all these people are going?' I hoped it wasn't far. In a land where people needed papers from their units to do almost anything I was always surprised by the crowded trains. Few would have had the money to travel even were it allowed, and it was dangerous to forge a letter from a unit, though that was exactly what some people did.

'Most of them must be travelling on business,' replied the man from Xian, 'attending meetings like myself or buying equipment or selling their produce. The three I was playing cards with belong to an urban collective in Guangzhou, and not being state workers can travel where they wish. Maybe some of the people in this carriage are on holiday, going to visit relatives or friends. Those who have worked in a unit for a decade are now entitled to a month's vacation every two years.'

It was still the men who had the freedom, the men who drank, the men who smoked, the men who played cards, the men who gathered in restaurants and played the Chinese finger game, the men who travelled by train. 'Why are there so few women?' I asked.

'We don't believe women make good salespeople. Most women are employed in the service industries, in transport and catering, or light manufacturing. It is not a woman's nature to be pushy and aggressive.' Such revelations, in a land of legendary female crane operators, were capable still of surprising me.

Since previously most Chinese had had little chance of going anywhere at all, I wondered if travel was still a novelty for them. After four months in China I personally watched the passing land far less than I had at first, but the Chinese barely glanced outside. If they did their eyes had a faraway look.

'For those who don't travel much, it must break the monotony of their daily lives. These hard-seat carriages are comfortable for a while, though on longer journeys the novelty soon fades.' He grinned conspiratorially, shifted his buttocks and put one socked foot up on the edge of his seat. I remembered the doctor who healed me in Chengdu. 'I don't want to go *anywhere*,' he had told me firmly, looking drained of vitality just with the thought of it. 'It's too tiring.'

The man from Xian wriggled his toes. His eyes roved along the carriage. 'Even the peasants are travelling nowadays,' he mused, 'visiting relatives and tourist spots.' As he spoke a peasant family passed along the aisle, silently searching for space to squat, a man, two women and a child. 'Look at the change!' he observed with some pride. 'They wear nylon shirts and terylene trousers. There are no more patches on their clothes.' I imagined that these were the luckier ones, but even I could tell they were country folk by their ruddy complexions, their raggedy haircuts and a subtle humility in their mien. 'Just now,' he went on, 'I noticed some peasants at work in the fields wearing nylon hats! I never saw such a thing before!'

'Can you always tell who people are by the way they look?' I asked him. 'Can you, for instance, tell the cadres apart?' A mystique surrounded even low-ranking cadres, an élitism not shared by low-grade officialdom in the West.

'I can usually distinguish the high-ranking ones by their clothes and their manner but they wouldn't be travelling in a hard-seat coach.'

I could tell them too for they were stouter than others and wore high-buttoned suits made of classy material and had pens in their pockets and carried black plastic hold-alls and their hands were stained brown by nicotine. And they sometimes looked through you as if you weren't there.

'The lower ranks would be harder to tell for they look much like anyone else. There might be five or so lower-grade cadres travelling in this carriage – five out of more than a hundred I suppose – but I doubt if I could pick them out. Recent Party policy has been to encourage younger people. Previously cadres were exclusively elderly, and usually poorly qualified. In a way this recent reformation of outlook bears similarities with the Cultural Revolution. Then, as now, young people were encouraged to question and criticize, to share the power in a move towards greater democracy.'

This was the opening I needed. Away from their units people were relaxed, less careful over what they said. In a train there was endless time. No one was in a hurry to be doing something else. No one but ourselves spoke English. 'Then the Cultural Revolution was not wholly destructive?'

'The Cultural Revolution was a reviewing of ideas, a chance for people to speak their minds; it illustrated the widespread dissatisfaction at that time. Its aim was to root out counter-revolutionary people and ideas, to instil a sense of self-reliance among the peasants and workers and prevent a cementing of the growing élite. Young people were encouraged to become Red Guards and destroy the last shreds of bourgeois individualism and reinstate the declining spirit of revolutionary zeal.'

He reeled off the usual communist clichés. 'But it wasted ten years of your lives!' I said.

'We don't all see it like that. Revolution was necessary because many were forgetting the purpose of socialism and were even beginning to criticize the State. Change is a part of moving forward. Our history goes back four thousand years; our whole future lies ahead. As I said the ideals were good. People were shaken out of passivity, forced to think, to question what they formerly believed. Children left school and travelled around in bands of Red Guards, creating revolution. Factories stopped producing and workers argued moral issues with the management, learning to participate in a greater democracy. Medical practitioners were sent to the countryside to train the peasants as barefoot doctors. Office workers went to labour in the fields and learn humility from the rural people. Not only that; there has been a lasting benefit of the Cultural Revolution, in the thousands of new schools and clinics in the countryside.

'I look back at that time as exhilarating and positive. We travelled the country fired by idealism, and people denied us nothing. School-children now look on my generation with envy, jealous of our freedom, our exciting lives.'

Non-Chinese visitors found it hard to understand the potency of mass commitment which caused such upheavals in the Cultural Revolution. They also believed that when people criticized Mao they were being frank and daring, when in fact all they were doing was following the current Party line. It was current Party policy to denounce the Cultural Revolution as wholly bad, and the so-called Gang of Four as the sole cause of its evil, yet in reality not everyone shared this view. Though the 'Gang' had fallen they still had many followers who knew better than to speak their minds. Those still nostalgic for the Maoist era were gradually being purged, and locked up in jails.

So much had things relaxed since the fall of the Four in 1976 that rules were being broken all the time and people were getting away with it. It was forbidden to take livestock on Chinese trains, yet a kitten was tethered beneath my seat (fortunately our blue girl affected not to notice as she went down the carriage refolding face towels in the orthodox way). At stations there were posters banning the carrying of explosives and picturing maimed passengers, their faces distorted by blood and burns, but people paid them little heed. When the inspector arrived a number of passengers vanished discreetly from the end of the carriage. I asked the man from Xian.

'They'll probably be caught,' he said. Sure enough we later heard that the inspectors had rounded up quite a collection, found lurking in coal holes, squatting beneath basins and hiding in loos. 'Ticket dodging is a major problem,' said the man from Xian. What I had paid for my Guangzhou ticket was the equivalent to a Chinese of a good new coat or two weeks' wages, so it was hardly surprising they weren't keen to pay.

We fell silent and I looked around the coach. Our blue girl was approaching, once more with a broom, heaving a mountain of mandarin peel, chicken bones and eggshells, sunflower-seed husks and cigarette ends, paper and polythene, mud and dust down the aisle towards us, adding to the pile with supplementary collections from each section of seats. She repeated her journey with a mop and cold water, and as a grand finale before vanishing to her room, she spat on the floor and slowly rubbed it in with her shoe.

Newcomers had arrived on the bench across the aisle, a man with a voice and a golden-skinned girl who hung on his words. I watched him push other people's mugs aside and lay out some paper and a chicken complete with its head and feet. He tore at the wings and gnawed on the bones. Grease fell down his shirt and spattered the floor. The girl nibbled delicately, her expressions, her gestures, pregnant with sexual innuendoes. I remembered the riverside park in Shanghai replete with thousands of courting couples leaning on the river wall, sardined along benches and hiding in hedges, faces turned inwards in anonymity, but they weren't behaving like this. Other passengers on the train had turned away and buried their attention in pamphlets on palmistry or the straps on their luggage or something that might be about to fall . . .

Their hunger satisfied the couple settled back for a snooze. They sat entwined, ostensibly in order to sleep more comfortably but in reality, instinct told me, because they couldn't keep their hands off each other. She laid her head in his pin-striped lap and his arm enfolded her round backside. They behaved if they were the only ones there, as if the rest of us were blind.

'Why are they doing that?' I asked the man from Xian. Given such an excuse he gave them a long, pondering look, devoid of any emotion. Then he shrugged and looked away. 'They must be a honeymoon couple.'

'They are behaving rather oddly,' I remarked. 'What would people make of them?'

'Everyone is embarrassed. Physical love should be expressed in private. In public men and women should maintain a certain distance.'

Confucian decorum demanded that members of the opposite sex should not even touch in front of others but remain impersonal, maintain composure. Confucian ideals still permeated society, and many still felt awkward shaking hands.

'What if they'd been Westerners?' I had seen Western travellers behaving even more shamelessly, swimming topless, kissing in public.

'They would feel just the same.'

Such small aggravations did nothing to disturb the impression I had of the overwhelming gentleness and accommodating good manners of most Chinese, their lack of imposition on others. Their sense of mutual consideration gave the illusion that the Chinese were all of one family with me its adopted member. They were not of course, and I was not part of it; my foreignness prevented it and would have however long I stayed.

A crackling on the speakers signalled the preambles to lunch. People perked up; there was a general hum of anticipation. Fourteen times the menu was repeated: stewed pork 1 yuan, mutton and cabbage 1 yuan 2 jiao, dofu and sausage 8 jiao, rice 1 jiao. Those in the know got out at a station and bought steamed dumplings, and eggs from a vendor who plied the aisles. The rest wolfed down box meals in about ninety seconds, scooping up the rice and casting the cartons out through the window and on to the platform where a thin old woman in ragged peasant black was darting about, gathering them up again and flattening them down in her bag. No state employee applied that degree of assiduity to the task in hand. I gave her some eggs which she stuffed down her apron and asked the man from Xian who she was.

'I don't know,' he replied. 'I never saw anyone collect cartons before.' The Chinese had no wish to advertise poverty or need in their society, whether they knew of them or not.

'Perhaps she'll use them for fuel?' I suggested. 'Or sell them to a recycling co-operative.' Receiving no satisfactory reply I asked what China was doing for such people.

'As yet we cannot afford social aid. The Party recognizes that much remains unsolved, that perfection is almost impossible to achieve. But it's not specifically a Chinese problem; beggars exist in almost every land. For the moment the responsibility lies with each family to support its relatives.'

'What if the whole family is out of work?' In villages people had access to land, but in the cities there were millions of unemployed, especially school leavers and people returned from the countryside.

'There is always temporary work,' he said vaguely, with the negligent air of one who doesn't have to find it. 'In winter there are jobs in boiler houses. In summer they can sell ice-lollies. An ice-lolly seller makes more than a teacher when the weather is good. He applies for a licence, buys the lollies wholesale and makes half a fen profit (one sixth of one penny) on each one he sells. In one day he could earn three yuan. His tax is very low.'

Many Chinese turned their backs on the beggars, on the lepers like the man I saw in Guangzhou, his face hanging down like a sack to his waist, on the colonies of squatters scavenging in tips, on the Shanghai slums half-hidden in back lanes where alleyways threaded between houses of mud and battened-down polythene so small it was inconceivable how people could live in them; they tossed them off, saying people could work if they wanted to.

The man from Xian had finished his lunch and was peeling an apple. The Chinese peeled everything, quartering oranges and sucking their juice so their lips shouldn't touch their chemical skins. Beyond the window the weedless fields rushed by in a slur of half-grown green. Ankle-deep in water, trouser legs rolled thigh-high, arms and legs encased in mud, straw-hatted peasants were applying themselves to their plots of land, scattering night soil or granular feed, feeling for weeds between their toes and hoiking them out with long poles.

China's three revolutions were happening simultaneously: heavy industry was paramount while Mao was in power but computers could take over in a decade or so. Agriculture, meanwhile, though updated near cities and in some state farms, continued in neolithic simplicity elsewhere.

There was method in this, though not by intent. Since one man with machinery could produce more grain than several hundred cultivating by hand, mechanization would cause mass unemployment. But the man from Xian shook his head. 'Most of the grain the peasants produce is consumed by themselves, so in spite of higher yields nothing moves forward. China's policy is to build a network of communications serving the villages and the new rural factories where the displaced manpower will be absorbed, supporting Deng's move to quadruple production of industry and agriculture between 1980 and the year 2000. This is what the peasants want. They are setting up collectives free from central planning control.'

'My own country's in a position where machinery and computers are fast displacing workers in the industrial sector too. The solution for some is to go back to the land, to intensive cultivation and small craft industries.' China had better look out, I warned him, but the man from Xian found all this too remote to be worth even considering. He scratched his head and looked perplexed. In practice it was simpler to mechanize, to indulge the trend so strong in mankind it had become near-instinctive all over the world.

The Chinese idolized industry. They were proud of their factories, unconcerned about their smog. Industry was progress. 'We have achieved industrialization without the disastrous side-effects of exploitation, social upheaval, undernourishment and eventual unemployment that the industrial revolution brought about elsewhere.'

'So far,' I agreed. 'But what about pollution? Terrible!' I chided him. 'The pollution level in your cities is beyond a Westerner's comprehension.' In Wuhan it was sixteen times the US permitted maximum. In Kunming my hotel overlooked a smoking vehicle depot. Pollution was responsible for lung disorders, my own included. Urban waterways were foul. Even the countryside was assailed by vapours of undigested night soil; clean air was like a precious pearl. 'What can be done?' I challenged him.

'By the year two thousand,' the man replied, 'China will be a modern and developed country.' This was the goal of Deng's new policy, the Four Modernizations of agriculture, industry, military defence and science and technology. But few believed he could carry it off. 'To achieve something worthwhile,' he continued slowly, gazing into space, 'there is always the need to suffer for it.' Was this a contemporary yin–yang syndrome or was he merely offering platitudes, finding convenient justifications? 'China has to grow through this phase of her development just as Western countries have done. We cannot afford to devote our funds to controlling pollution at this stage.' Though there had not yet been a national campaign, I had seen the signs, or more accurately one sign, of an embryonic awareness of conservation, in a poster depicting flying white geese passing through a smoke stack and coming out black. 'What we *can* do,' he continued, 'is move industrial plants and their workers out to rural areas, at least in the short term.'

'Does it help to spread the same pollution over a larger area?'

'In the short term, it must do. In the long term there will be less pollution.'

'What about the workers who are moved out?' I asked. 'Do they like being shifted?'

'As an example,' he replied, 'a new industrial city with a population of a hundred thousand has been built in north-east China. Some people like it there, but others would rather go back home to their small cramped flats, to their relatives left behind and the cultural life missing from the satellite towns. We Chinese love new things. We search the department stores for any new lines. We browse in bookshops for new translations or new Chinese works. We want to buy the newest records, wear the newest fashions, see a new film when it first comes out, which is only possible in the major towns. But at the same time these places are overcrowded and in my opinion more new cities should be developed in the countryside.'

'What about economics?' I asked. 'Is it not more efficient to concentrate production in a few large centres than disperse it around the countryside, duplicating machinery and wasting resources?'

'Perhaps, in a country like yours,' he replied. 'Chinese thinking must begin from what is good for the people and the present conditions of our country. Since communications are still difficult and energy insufficient we must produce things where we can. We must ease the pressure on our eastern cities and create work in the smallest villages. It's called walking on two legs, simultaneous development of both large and small projects.'

There was a further reason for dispersing industry. Every year tens of thousands of rural Chinese migrated to the cities, some of them legally, having bribed a cadre for a resident's card, but most without permits, either 'sent-down youth' returning home or peasants seeking new work and new life. Within fifty years some rural regions would change dramatically, with mechanized farming, satellite towns and peasants getting jobs in industrial co-operatives. As factories gradually denationalized, the onus was on the peasants to set up craft industries and workshops themselves.

The man from Xian leant back in his seat and closed his eyes. But not for long. Someone tapped his elbow, wanting to know what he'd been telling the foreigner, wondering why she was interested. He explained our discussion – in a watered-down fashion – while I turned my attention to the westering sun. Each time I looked out the wind seemed warmer, the rice higher, the scene greener. In the soft evening light we passed mile upon mile of continuous beehives lined up along the track and clouded with bees. Then standing in a station a further encampment was parked in a siding, hives stacked high on open wagons and atop them the beekeepers, unprotected and unconcerned with their cooking pots and bicycles, among the buzzing browsing bees. 'It's a specialist activity and a risky one,' observed the man from Xian, following my gaze. 'A family could get rich, or lose all its capital. Many rural people have taken up beekeeping, moving all summer from place to place, following the flowers. Some move as far as two thousand miles from their winter home.'

Day turned to dusk and dusk to night. By nightfall the carriage was so overcrowded it was impossible to move. People were standing all down the aisle, leaning on those who occupied aisle seats and stepping on toes. Some had small stools or were squatting in corners or perching on shoulder poles balanced between the seats, or lying underneath them on newspapers. No meals could get through, no water for tea. No one went to the loo, but crawled through the windows at stations instead. Refuse piled up, stewed tealeaves lay stranded like seaweed on mug sides, the windows were closed and the air filled with smoke. Unable to sleep the men resumed cards and the lights stayed on all night.

Outside the sky was clear. Stars pierced its coal-black dome. A crescent moon flickered through the trees along the track. I leant on the table and slept until dawn.

'Today is Tuesday the twenty-third of May. It is six a.m. and our music programme will soon commence. Noodles will be on sale from the trolley. In fifteen minutes we will be arriving in Zhuzhou. Passengers for Changsha, Wuhan and the north should get out here and await their connection . . .'

People straightened up, yawning, and stretched their arms, grateful to be absolved from their pretence of sleep. Songs struck up, full-morning volume, popular melodies from Hong Kong and Taiwan, Western tunes sung to Chinese words and classical music that captured the delicacy of bamboo upon a scroll. The songs never varied, but neither did they lose their tuneful appeal. People hummed along as they gathered their toothbrushes and pulled down their face towels and clambered over obstacles and queued for the loo. They splashed about the basins, scrubbed their faces with their cold wet towels, wrung them out and dabbed them dry. They gurgled and spat. They opened the windows to tip out their tealeaves and poured in some fresh ones and held out their mugs for the boiling water and clamped on the lids to infuse the flavour and savoured it slowly in scalding sips. Conflicting streams were still fighting up the aisle to fetch noodles from the trolley and down it with their toothbrushes, tea and damp towels.

The man from Xian alighted at Zhuzhou, going on to Wuhan to visit his sister and thence to Xian. Our train swung south, through Hengyang, Zhenxian and Shaoguan to Guangzhou.

Shortly before we reached Guangzhou the blue girls began spring cleaning the train. We lifted our legs, moved our bags, stood up, sat down, squeezed ourselves flat on the back of the seats as floors were mopped and mopped again, walls and tables wiped with a cloth and ashtrays emptied around seven score people and their bundles and boxes and baskets and bags. Outside the land was hot and green. A woman sat in the shade of a tree. In the sultry evening crops were wilting, mud was drying on buffaloes' backs. Tomatoes were ripening, cane was heightening, squash rampaging, bananas furling, pine trees bushing in their new season's growth.

Everyone was up and ready to get off. Their torpor had vanished; they grew chirpy and active as they piled their bags in a barrage by the door.

And then I was back where I'd begun.

The Government Service Workers' Hostel where I stayed in my first two weeks in China had changed its tune. The hotel manager had discarded his suit and donned a pair of natty white shorts. I took the last bunk in an infinite dormitory, lit by red and green ceiling lights and cooled by fans. Laid-back travellers on Asian tours lay dozing in the indolent heat. Rock music mingled with dope and sweat. Mugs of half-cold half-drunk tea sat festering on rim-stained table tops. Waste bins and ashtrays overflowed. Off-white clothes hung limp from strings; sarongs shrouded sun-bronzed skin.

I left China next morning with my back to the engine. I didn't want to go. But there was nothing, I decided, to prevent my return.

11

In the Country

In October I was back in China. I had left it on an upsurging wave when the weather was warm and the food was good and the days too short to contain all I wanted to fill them with. From Guangzhou I took the overnight river ferry westwards to Wuzhou and a bus and another bus over hills and plains to a small riverside village I shall call Shuliang in the mountains near Guilin.

It was winter when I first came to Shuliang, when the fields were brown and the saw-toothed pinnacles lifting from their midst were dim and drizzle-misted, fading to infinity in interlocking ranges of diminishing grey. Citrus trees smudged the watercolour landscape and bird flocks spattered the sky like ink. Villages comfortable in their biscuit-coloured mud-brick crouched under grey-tiled roofs. Bamboo stems creaked, and their foliage rustled in the cold winter winds.

The autumn rice lay in ripe swathes between church-spire rocks and leaves were jungle-dark in their late season's flush. My bus came to rest beneath a big spreading tree from which lanes and paths led into Shuliang. The air was clean, the sky was blue: there were birds and butterflies and my spirits soared with them. I crossed the fields to a friendly guest-house where instead of forms to fill in there was tea and talk and the staff turned out to carry my bags and rid my room of dust. There was a well in the courtyard and a sediment of silt in my thermos flask; strands of boiled riverweed floated in my tea.

Walking beside the river I entered another world, a gentler world it seemed to me then, dictated by seasons and the labour of hands. I moved through a land of limitless green: the golden green of rice fields, the emerald of vegetables, the laurel green of citrus leaves, the acid green of scum on pools, the neutral green of bamboo fronds, the eau-de-nil of distant peaks and the charcoal-green of shadows. The river swam slowly on its pebbled bed, clear as washed wine bottles, streaming with weed like Ophelia's hair and fringed by fountains of giant bamboo. Men poled into shore, their rafts heaped with riverweed, and piled it on the beach to drain. Girls washed radish leaves at the water's edge. Boys rode bareback on buffaloes.

As day cooled to evening I wandered round the village streets of wood-panelled houses where old men sat and smoked their pipes, and children tumbled in passed-on clothes, old and faded, the red dimmed pink, the white gone grey, their bottoms protruding through back-slit pants. With the shutters drawn back the streets were a warren of rural industry, of ropemakers, carpenters, blacksmiths and tailors stitching cotton-padded jackets for the approaching cold. Beyond, the houses disappeared far back in mysterious interiors of lofts and courtyards and hidden inner rooms.

Past boatbuilders and noodle-makers and herbal doctors and sweetmeat stalls the lane sloped down to the river beach, shadowed by a headland shrouded with trees. I swam far out through armfuls of weed to the clear green deeps in the middle of the river. I could see round the bend to where the cormorant fishermen poled their rafts in the shadow of the cliff. They lived on the beach on the opposite bank, boats moored in the shallows, rafts shelved upon the stones, fishing nets drying in the sun spilling down in yellow-green shafts over high scrub-sprayed cliffs. Beyond on a meander there were people drying persimmons, peeling them, spreading them, moving them, turning them, pressing them flat into sun-bright discs.

I watched as the sun set fire to the river, as the mountains darkened to silhouette and the sky glowed apricot in the valleys between their peaks, watched as it turned to aubergine and the boat people lit their paraffin lamps, watched until the stars came out and the night was sensual velvet-dark, for I could not bear to tear myself away from the beauty and stillness of that perfect place.

I left the village one morning in the dew-silvered dawn and skirted the tapestried vegetable plots. Ripe pomelos hung yellow and pregnant and persimmons shone copper against the deep green darkness of the shadowed fields. The path plunged beneath the foliage of a high plot of sugar-cane that brushed my face and wet my clothes as I parted its leaves, and hissed and flopped in my wake. It curved on past old gravestones and through clumps of bamboo and broke on to a flatland patterned by small irregular plots and bisected by channels and bunds. A wadding of mist still felted the fields that lapped at the foot of the peaks. I passed children carrying bags to school and women thumping laundry on a step beside a stream and men hauling stooks to the sides of their fields to commence the day's ploughing while the earth was still damp. Autumn wildflowers clouded the bunds, a lace of ephemera in a landscape uncluttered by roads or wires. To get somewhere you walked. To move something you carried it. China's shoulder poles and field paths were our articulated trucks and motorways.

A man with a plough was walking a buffalo out to his fields. I fell in beside him, observing, as I greeted him, his furrowed face, his faded clothes and his hair a fuzz of new-grown stubble; peasants shaved their heads to evict the lice and save on barbers' fees. Although his feet were cracked he walked on the verge for the path was stony and the soles of his shoes worn thin. But at least there was the buffalo. Visitors to China as late as the sixties saw six-man teams yoked to ploughs.

'Isn't it beautiful?' I said. The morning was pearly still. Dew sparkled on the fields. People usually liked their homeland to be appreciated by outsiders.

Not this man. 'No. It is not beautiful.' But at least he understood Mandarin; most peasants spoke only the local Guangxi dialect.

'What do you find beautiful?' Never travelling, I supposed, he might have no notion that his mountains were unique.

'Guilin.'

Guilin was awful, ugly and grey. Rebuilt after Japanese bombing in the thirties, its pulse had been quickened by the influx of tourists. It was grim and grasping, on the lookout for deals, and its shop signs were written in English. The handicraft stores sold nothing more ethnic than polyester clothing and plastic beach-balls. There were prostitutes in late-night eating stalls. There was a new supermarket where the goods on sale were almost double their cost elsewhere, but some would pay it for the status of being seen there. Prices were rising, the cost of fruit had soared above what the locals could afford and Coca-Cola had arrived. Guilin was growing fast, growing big; it was spawning hotels and Kathmandu-style cafés, and its visitors fuelled the expanding black market. The boat trip on the River Li, which is why the tourists came to Guilin, cost eighty times more than my journey in a peasant boat, and earned China tens of thousands of yuan a day.

I told the farmer I disliked Guilin, but that Shuliang was one of the most beautiful places I had ever seen.

'Do you have mountains in your country?' he asked, assuming I was just being polite.

'Not like these. Our mountains are a different shape.' The humps and spires and columns and cones that rose around us were karst mountains shaped by underground water.

'What about rice? Do you have rice?' I told him it was imported. He asked what we ate, and whether I liked Chinese food. Then I asked if he was happy, how he felt about the political regime. I was forever reading in the *China Daily* and being told by officials how good life was for the peasants now, how much more money they had, how much better was their food, how much greater their freedom, but I wanted to hear it from the peasants themselves.

'Our lives are bitter,' came the reply. 'We still eat bitterness.' He kept repeating the word bitter, *ku*, and I often heard it in conversation. Our word coolie, *ku li*, means bitter strength.

'Surely things are better now?'

'Scarcely at all,' he replied, at which he turned off on to a narrow bund with the abruptness of a character in *Through the Looking Glass*. I continued, saddened by the plight of the 800 million farm people for whom life, according to this man, was scarcely better than it ever was before. From across the fields I heard ploughmen calling from plot to plot: 'She comes from England! She speaks Chinese!'

No longer in China did I feel uneasy, wandering paths so narrow I seemed to be trespassing on private land. No longer did I feel an intruder, trampling heavily across something fragile. For a couple more miles I followed small paths, selecting, where they branched, the track that appeared to travel further. I circumnavigated a plot of jute and emerged by a gathering of mud-walled farmsteads, sheltering under eaves and shadowed by lemon trees. Their walls were a collage of maize cobs and rape seed, of strings of drying cabbage leaves, of straw hats and sieves. Women squatted in yards chopping foliage for their pigs. Then a voice called, 'Hello!' and there was a man as different from the peasants almost as I. The cut and cloth of his light grey suit buttoned up to the neck, his tall weedy frame, his shoes, his glasses and his hair combed flat identified him instantly as a city man. So far from a road, so far from a town, I was as surprised to see him as he was me.

'What are you doing here?' he asked in English. Foreigners were rare around Shuliang.

I explained myself. 'What are *you* doing here?'

'I've come to visit my wife's family. My mother-in-law is old, and has been seriously ill. My wife was worried and begged me to come.'

Prompted by my interest he told me his story. He and his wife were an example of the several million couples still separated by their jobs. Zhang worked in a factory in Guilin and studied English in his spare time. His wife and daughter lived in Nanning, two hundred miles distant, and had no wish to return to Guilin, a smaller town with fewer prospects for promotion. Zhang, although he'd tried and tried, could not get transferred to Nanning. So they met twice a year, for three days at Spring festival and longer in the summer, but had neither time nor wherewithal to be together more often.

I imagined Zhang's wife as having entered university in the Cultural Revolution on the sole qualification of her peasant origins, and having outgrown her background to become snooty, even ashamed of it. It would explain Zhang's awkwardness in the earthy environment and his assurance that this was his second visit ever.

An old lady with white hair drawn back in a chignon and a long hollow face had followed Zhang out. Zhang introduced her as his mother-in-law, and she smiled and nodded and invited me in to share the morning meal. I hesitated, as was proper, but Zhang insisted, leading me through the doors in the mud-plastered wall to a passageway twelve feet square. One side opened on to the courtyard. A ladder led to a platform where timber was stored. A calendar was pinned to the pine-panelled wall, and above it hung an unframed portrait of Mao, smooth and smiling like Humpty Dumpty, with the wart on the left side of his chin.

'You scarcely ever see Mao's picture any more,' I observed. Though familiar to me from books, only twice in four months had I seen the Great Helmsman's image in a public place. The portraits had come down, the slogans were painted over, the plaster busts had been put away, the armoury of Mao badges with which people had studded their jacket fronts were on sale by the thousand in flea markets in Hong Kong. For a man whose name ten years before had been constantly on the lips of a billion Chinese, praising and thanking him for every small mercy, it was astonishing how rarely people mentioned him. His municipal statues had almost all been destroyed and his books were out of print. Blamed for the miseries of recent years, his name was almost a dirty word.

'I love Mr Mao!' Zhang replied with venom, his eyes shining black and small like currants behind his spectacles. He had declared himself: Zhang was a leftist, a diminishing breed in the onward rush for material gain.

'What about Deng?' I asked. Deng's portraits were as scarce as Mao's, for Deng would not be idolized.

'The same . . . Mr Mao and Mr Deng are the same thing. It is just their policies which are a little different.'

I might have argued on the grounds that Deng hailed what Mao had condemned and put economics before ideals had not Zhang's brothers-in-law, the Wus, appeared. They brought low stools and set them down around a portable stove on legs. While Zhang was pale and intellectual, the brothers Wu were sunburnt and muscular. While Zhang's hair was barbered, the other men's looked dusty, and stuck up in tufts. Zhang's suit was polyester; the brothers wore vests and open-necked shirts and green cotton trousers that were faded and patched and not particularly clean. On their feet they wore plimsolls and their toes showed through. They grinned at me nervously, each welcoming me in the Guangxi dialect for they spoke no Mandarin. Having never conversed with a foreigner before they would undoubtedly never have invited me in had it not been for Zhang. I felt their embarrassment, their loss of face about the unkempt house and their old cotton clothes, and maybe the fear still lingered on of retribution for consorting with barbarians. Zhang's motive for inviting me was a selfish one. He welcomed my intrusion to relieve his boredom, to gain sympathy for his having to spend three precious days in uncomfortable surroundings among uneducated peasants he barely knew.

From our low wooden stools in the passageway we looked out across the door slab (with holes for the posts that once kept out thieves) to a sunlit landscape bright with flowers. A blaze of scarlet canna lilies smouldered in imperial purple leaves. Their roots provided fodder, or were dried and powdered and fermented as alcohol. A stand of jute was ready for harvesting, cream hollyhock flowers on brown stranded stems. It was as if the house were no more than a shelter, its doors for security against rain and theft rather than protectors of privacy and peace. What was house and what was pathway, what was private and what was communal, what was in and what was out was hard to ascertain. Neighbours had no custom of erecting barriers between themselves and houses had no areas of personal domain. Peasants passed along the path, sometimes dropping their loads to lean, straw-hatted, against the door. And some came in and sat on a plank bench set against the wall.

One of the brothers fed the stove with straw and leaves and the embers flared up, melting the chill of the draughty passage. Chickens scratched in the courtyard beyond, where baskets and jars and cooking pots were stacked and a hand-cart leant up against the yellow brick wall. A wok of hot broth was balanced on the stove, a wooden plank upon the wok and dishes of sauce upon the plank, holding chilli and coriander in vinegar and soy sauce. Having said that I was vegetarian, Zhang and the brothers propelled dofu and scallions across the broth while fishing out chunks of pork for themselves: and for once I decided to ignore the meat because manners were more important than principles. We ate without bowls, dipping each morsel into the sauce and transferring it dripping to our mouths. Zhang fretted for his suit, but the others were silent while they ate. The brothers poked in twigs and roots and the broth bubbled like a witch's brew, and we ate of the food that represented such toil. The men drank *mao tai* out of handleless cups, and when the dofu was finished sticks of dried bean curd were drowned in the wok with squares of pale cabbage leaves. We ate and ate: I had breakfasted in Shuliang two hours before on hot soya milk and a warm steamed bun and should not have been hungry at all. But when the wok was empty rice was brought and we ate that too. Harvested only the day before, rice was never so fresh or good.

Zhang apologized for the food.

'What's wrong with it?' I hadn't expected such palatable food in a peasant household, guest or no guest, and I knew that Zhang was not being modest. Invited to share other family meals in Shuliang, I noticed they ate only chillies and rice. Yet I also saw that their enjoyment was as great as mine ever is of my rich and varied diet from all corners of the earth.

'It's rather crude,' Zhang replied. 'City people wouldn't eat this kind of thing.' Served at a London dinner party, our meal would have been the *ne plus ultra* of originality and sophistication. 'Food is by far the most important thing in these people's lives,' Zhang went on. 'They are better off now than they have ever been and eat meat or fish almost every day.' He was talking just like the *China Daily*, which, being a leftist, he would. His urban background held him apart, prevented him from seeing any more than he'd been told, any more than what he wanted or expected to see. 'Forty years ago a peasant family would have meat only twice a year. Today every household keeps chickens and ducks and pigs, and most have a dog. It is only when they have satisfied their hunger that they will turn to clothes. Only when they have enough new clothes will they turn their attention to their standard of living. You can see for yourself,' said Zhang disdainfully, waving his arm to include the earth floor, the unswept yard, the hand-made simplicity of everything in view, quite oblivious to the feelings of his brothers-in-law who most probably preferred their comfortable mud floors since you could write on them and spit on them and throw things on them and feel at home. Mr Mao smiled down from the dark panelled wall. 'In the city it's the other way round,' Zhang explained. 'Living standards come first, then clothes, and food last.' It was an interesting theory, explaining much about the gulf between city and countryside, about the contempt in which peasants were still held.

How many times had I heard how well clothed people were, how rationing provided sufficient cotton for two sets of clothing a year. But were people well clad whose feet were visible through the holes in their shoes? Were they well clad when their garments were torn and patched and stained, and insufficient to keep out the cold? In remote rural areas – and there were vast tracts of China more remote, less fertile and less prosperous even than Shuliang – whole communities were too poor to own a change of clothes, even, if witnesses were reliable, too poor to own clothes at all.

While the brothers were relaxing, eating good food and talking to their guests, their wives and daughters were at work in the fields. For the peasants, women's equality had no meaning at all except for the levelling of class. Women were often worse off than before, forced for the first time to share in field work while their men gave no help in the home. In more prosperous areas than Shuliang men secured factory jobs leaving women to toil on the land. Women still cooked and washed the clothes and gathered the firewood and cleaned the house and minded the children in addition to their work in the fields. They got up first and fetched water from the stream. Then they lit the fire and made the tea, often only boiled water which they called 'white tea'. While their husbands slept off the midday meal they gathered dry leaves or washed clothes in the stream. While they smoked or drank tea with their friends in the evenings the women mended clothing and swept out the rooms. While we sat eating one of the wives must have been in the kitchen preparing our food, too shy to come forward, to look a foreigner in the eye.

Rural Chinese women weren't supposed to have minds, far less brains. There were few female cadres in the countryside and those there were were often ignored. Women were resigned to their supposed inferiority, their ritual uncleanliness and the Confucian prejudice that for countless generations had held them down.

Throughout our meal a man from next door was sitting panning lice from his daughter's hair and snapping them between his nails. A girl was minding a neighbour's child, who for the hour I observed him sat motionless on the bench, his face puffy with bites, his hair dry and lifeless, his expression incuriously void.

'Peasant children are like that,' said Zhang. 'I can't understand it. My own daughter, a charming, charming girl of three, is constantly demanding something or other. If I give her milk she feels like chocolate, if I give her chocolate it is bound to be something else she wants. She is always active and talkative.'

It seemed clear enough to me. Zhang and his wife both pandered to their child. She ate the varied food their higher salaries allowed and got better medical care.

The brothers had finished, upturning their cups to indicate repletion, shredding tobacco from a cake-like block cemented with rape oil and filling their pipes. They brought me pomelos and showed me how to tackle them, quartering the rind and tearing it from the flesh, paring away the pith and twisting the fruit in two. I ripped the skin from each segment, spat out the pips and gnawed the flesh. The floor was littered with pips and pith and segments of peel, I saw as I bent to scratch my feet.

'Sandflies!' said Zhang gloomily seeing the bites. He was also being bitten, through translucent socks that looked like French letters, the latest in footwear. He despised the rusticity that attracted the sandflies and the old Chinese habit of strewing things anywhere: 'If my daughter throws something on the floor,' he said stuffily, 'I give her a slap.'

The Wus had coarse skin and the sandflies didn't touch them, but they scratched all the same just to be polite. From that moment on my enjoyment of Shuliang was blighted by the bites. They rose in rude lumps to cover my feet and itched in the sun and the hot afternoons and drove me insane beneath the quilt at night, and instead of disappearing only spread and got worse. I avoided the sun, sat in my room with my feet in a bucket, dipping them in the river when I went for walks and tearing at their burning skin in my sleep. Submerged in water for hours each day they began to rot; I paid dearly for my visit to the family Wu.

Straightening up I noticed a newcomer. One of Zhang's nephews had come in from the fields bearing two big baskets of rice on a pole, a strapping lad for a southern Chinese, exuding vitality from his well-formed frame. Half the peasants' lives seemed to be spent moving loads, of fuel, or grain, or water, or night soil, and I asked Zhang to ask him how much his load weighed.

'Eighty kilos,' he said promptly, proud of his muscles and sun-bronzed strength. Aware that my rucksack was a third of that I bent my knees and placed the pole on my shoulder and caught the ropes in its slots and strained to get the baskets off the ground. But they would not move. Neither could I lift either one with both hands. I had practised at the guest-house with a lighter load, steadying the ropes, keeping shoulders and back straight and moving from the hips with quick small steps to prevent too much bounce or sway. Even circling the yard with shallow baskets of sand my shoulder was sore for I had no furrows, no callus of hard skin.

Observing my interest in things that Zhang scorned or took for granted set his mind to work.

'When you go back to England you must write an article about peasant life in China. People should know what it's really like. The foreigners who come here just float down the river on tourist boats.

They watch the villages and rocks and river glide by and imagine the peasants lead perfect lives. They see them from a distance and understand nothing of their hardship and toil. They equate nice surroundings with hearts free from care. It is not so,' said Zhang. Visitors to China are encouraged to believe the peasants have got rich: papers and magazines do not help with their endless reports of peasants buying cars and setting up sidelines; revolutionary posters do not help, with their portrayal of perfection and undoubting fervour; and paintings of the countryside, of a busy and productive rural utopia, don't help either. Since we cannot stay in Chinese homes, since we do not speak the local tongues, since little of rural China is accessible to foreigners we will probably continue in our ignorance.

My memory shifted to early spring, when I first walked the paths around Shuliang. It was cold and damp and the lanes were clogged with mud. Villagers in sodden shoes hauled hand-carts heaped with stone. Doors were closed against the cold.

I perceived the same hardship even now. Behind the picturesque façade of gnarled old peasants and dilapidated houses were lives of poverty, disease and want. Passing along the village streets and greeting the old people who sat out on stools I discovered that many were partially deaf, that a few had goitre and some were blind. Their cloth-fastened clothes hung layer upon layer over bony frames; their hair was balding, their skin blotched and brown. Unable to afford the treatment they required they went on suffering, and at the commune clinic, in the rooms that weren't locked, I believe I saw why: unswept floors and discoloured walls and equipment rudimentary in the extreme. Things lay about, patients sat about, babies cried and nothing seemed to get done.

I realized now why it was that foreigners were not encouraged to visit Shuliang. Although open in theory the tourists didn't know about it and I passed a fortnight in splendid isolation. Not only was the infrastructure inadequate (the food and water caused intestinal problems even for visiting Chinese) but if people came they might see too much – the bitterness maybe, or the man whose bed was a heap of fern. If tour groups were taken to the countryside it was to newly built settlements, ideals of the Party, just as tourists in England visit the villages that represent the English people's dream.

To help with the article Zhang insisted I should write (I hadn't told him I wrote; I rarely told anyone since the Party's view was that writers sowed the seeds of dissent) he offered to conduct me round the house. Previous generations of the Wu family clan had built it themselves with the aid of neighbours, as most rural houses were still being built, in traditional styles with indigenous materials, limited by local skills.

But architects were at work in more prosperous parts designing Western-style homes that took up less space, that were easier to clean, that were fire and flood and earthquake resistant and more sympathetic to the upholstered furnishings it was expected the peasants would come to demand. Considering most peasants owned their own homes I'd be surprised if the proportion of state-owned property were not far lower in China than in England.

'If I worked all my life,' Zhang said with a frown, 'I could never afford to build such a house, nor, for that matter, a house of any sort. I'm thirty now, and if I work until I'm seventy my total salary for all those years would not be much more than 20,000 yuan (£7,000), only twice the cost of building a house. It is the peasants who have both money and opportunities, who can save up gradually and store materials, who live in large families and work jointly to pay for them, and help each other out in their construction.' Zhang would never have a house but in time he might own his own flat. City municipalities were beginning to build blocks for private sale. It would save them money since rents were so heavily subsidized.

More than four times the size of the average urban flat and larger than an equivalent dwelling in India, the Wus' house combined the traditional elements of symmetry, simplicity, formality and balance. By facing south with a stream nearby, and being sheltered from the north by a saw-blade of rock peaks, it collaborated with nature and conformed with the requirements of *feng-shui*. The ingress of evil was prevented by a spirit wall, while beneficial energy still flowed around the rooms that looked out on the courtyard in which we stood.

Someone was sent to find the person who kept the keys to unlock the doors of the rooms where anything of value was stored. We bypassed the kitchen, a bamboo shelter with a grass-thatched roof (but peeping in later I saw a water trough and rough-hewn quern, a bucket of pig-swill, a built-in wok and earthenware jars), and entered a room built opposite the entrance, protected by the spirit wall and empty but for piles of dust and chicken dung. New Year couplets were pasted on the spirit wall, the wrinkled paper faded pink. The remaining walls were boarded and bare.

'What do they use this room for?' I asked Zhang. I was startled by the quantity of unused space.

'It's a sitting room,' he said vaguely, passing on quickly to a small rear hallway off which two more rooms opened left and right. As the first door swung back there were thuds from inside, and rumbling sounds as of people playing bowls. A strange light filtered through the paper-packed windows. There was a bed in the corner, large and dark, canopied with netting like old lace curtains. And on the floor there were rolling pomelos and dozens more heaped high in mounds, glowing like moons in the prevailing brown.

There was no sign anywhere of religious impedimenta. The empty room with the spirit wall would once have housed the family altar, the ancestral tablets and shrines to the gods. Characters were once written on the spirit wall, *fu* meaning happiness and *cai* meaning luck. Shuliang itself gave the general impression of Red Guards having applied themselves thoroughly, and by comparison to, say, Dali or Fujian there was little visible evidence of religious belief apart from the odd mirror deflecting evil from a doorway, ancestral shrine or door guardian poster or brass Buddhist bangle or incense stall. Through force or volition, the power of religion had seemingly diminished.

'Do the family worship any gods?' I asked, Zhang interpreting.

'No!' replied the brothers. 'We don't allow that here!'

'What about your mother?' I asked. The old lady remained silent, looking at the floor.

'No. Nobody worships.'

'Did she not do so before?'

'No. Well, maybe a little, before Liberation.' The child obeys the father, the wife obeys the husband, the mother obeys the son. Evidence suggests that in spite of all those years of political indoctrination many Chinese adhere to their faith. During the Cultural Revolution they hid their altars and worshipped in secret. In spite of what her sons said perhaps the old lady still had faith too.

Three miles to the south-west on the fullness of a meander commanding swathes of green water and peaks upon peaks stood a temple in a cave, pelmeted with stalactites like rows of shark's teeth, pale against the awning space. The temple was a shell, destroyed by Red Guards in the spasm of zeal to obey Chairman Mao and destroy the 'Four Olds': old ideas, old culture, old customs, and old habits. They smashed the gilded images, burnt the carved woodwork, covered the wall paintings of gods and dragons with whitewash and slogans and Mao Zedong Thoughts for as far as their arms could reach. The site was sullied by their misplaced fervour, sad in its silence of abandoned walls.

The Shuliang authorities probably imagined that no foreigner would bother to walk that far, crossing the river by man-poled ferry boat and following its banks along small earth paths. Relics of Cultural Revolution destruction, though still abundant throughout the land, are out of bounds to foreigners; places only open once their 'sights' have been restored.

Zhang was hopping from foot to foot, dying to get out of the house. He suggested we take a stroll. As we continued down the path away from Shuliang he extolled the virtues of rural life in guide-book clichés I suspected he didn't really feel: the 'beautiful scenery', the 'clean fresh air', the 'singing birds' and the flowers by the stream. For a moment he'd forgotten the flies, the floors and the crude peasant ways and was seeing the country through a visitor's eyes. 'I would like to live in a village myself, so long as I was able to get to my factory and draw on the privileges of a town,' he said. I gazed out over the fields of rice, marvelling at Zhang's sophistication and wondering how long it would be . . . 'These peasants,' he continued, conscious of his position as one of China's urban élite, 'their values are so different from ours. They know of nothing except food and pigs and chickens and crops. And home and family,' he added as an afterthought. The extended family and the obligations it implied was the most enduring legacy of feudal China, persisting in the countryside for want of a means of breaking it up. 'My brothers-in-law do nothing useful with their free time. When television comes it will be a good thing. It will open their eyes to the outside world.'

For me it was pleasant to be in a place without amenities. Walking home from the river down the unlit village streets each evening I saw through every open doorway people talking in interiors the colour of old oil paintings. The Wu family had no electricity. They had no piped water, no bathroom, no drains. They had no bicycle, no bus, no road past their door. Years of toil had made them resilient and frugal, so that even were they to make more money they would be careful how they spent it. They worked hard when it paid them, but if they were not permitted to bear sons when they wanted they could not be expected to work indefinitely for abstract political goals.

I sympathized with their plight. After thirty-five years of promises and idealism, of fundamental swings in which the farmers themselves never had any say and which as often as not made them not better but worse off, the peasants had the right to feel bitter and confused. In 1949 the rural population fell into three basic categories: the landlords and rich peasants, the poorer of whom might own as little as three acres and have reached that position by dint of hard work; the middle and poor peasants, by far the largest group; and the rural dispossessed, the beggars and bandits. Shortly after Liberation teams of raw young cadres were sent to the countryside to seize the land and distribute it equally in a movement known as Land Reform. The landlords were victimized: four million were killed. But with no animals or tools the poor still could not work the land. So groups of households were gradually amalgamated, first into small-scale co-operatives and later into larger ones in which land was held communally, equipment was pooled and labour shared. The conclusion of this policy was the Commune Movement, part of the Great Leap Forward of 1958. Belonging now to a Beijing-run commune each comprising tens of thousands and broken down into Production Brigades and Production Teams it was the State you worked for, the State which made decisions, the State which owned the land and the State which reimbursed you according to a system of workpoints (even then the system was not truly egalitarian, with a strong person earning up to four times as much as another who was weak). Private property vanished, plots and livestock were confiscated and free markets were closed. Half the peasants' income came in the form of the so-called Seven Guarantees: food, clothing, health care, schools, housing, births, marriages and funerals.

Though logical in theory the communes failed to produce results. People worked a minimum of hours and as slowly as they could, reluctant to put in any more effort than the others in their team. The organization was too centralized and its methods unscientific; trees were felled and burnt for fertilizer, forests and pastures cleared for grain and the peasants enjoined to dig the fields for coal. Changes were fast and radical, new cadres unskilled and often corrupt. Crop failure followed, exacerbated by floods and drought. In three years grain production dropped to the level of ten years before. Twenty million died from shortage of food.

In 1966 Chinese villagers again lost their insurance (given back to them in the meantime) in the form of their fruit trees and vegetable plots, their capitalist chickens and pigs. They had to share their land with a further influx of urbanites, seventeen million of them, sent down to the countryside to humble themselves and 'learn from the peasants'. Until in 1979 the policy changed yet again. While land remained under ownership of the State, income was once more linked to production. Under the new Responsibility System a family contracted to grow so much grain on its allocated land, or in a Specialized Household to produce so much timber or fish or meat or eggs or craft goods or transportation, the surplus of which, the greater part, it kept for consumption or sale. Those who gave up their land were compensated in cash. Those who kept it were guaranteed use for fifteen years. Land could be leased and labourers hired. Sideline production was once more allowed. Private plots were returned and peasants regained the right to gather wild plants and trap animals in the hills. Though village-wide assets such as irrigation schemes were still managed collectively, Mao's state-run system of communal agriculture had finally come to an end.

Although the term 'commune' was officially out of use it was often retained in speech. Even the address of the family Wu, given me in order that I might send their photographs, remained unchanged: People's Republic of China, Guangxi, Yangshuo County, Shuliang Commune, Qimen Production Brigade, Wu Liguo.

The Wu family was not a Specialized Household. Nor did I notice any evidence in the area to suggest a specialist undertaking. The implementation of Deng's new policy had been painfully slow and thousands of villages remained as they were. There was no mechanization in Shuliang, no amalgamation, no sign of any new 'village and town enterprise', no solar heating or bio-gas plant. Shuliang was slow and old-fashioned, allowing prosperous areas to forge ahead. The Wus grew rice under contract with the State and their pomelos were a sideline which they sold in the market in Shuliang.

For twenty years the local market had been closed. It had reopened recently and every three days several thousand peasants poured into Shuliang by boat and on foot to sell the produce from their fields. Once more they were able to leave their 'communes' so some sold their produce further afield, and purchased goods from the cities and returned to sell them in Shuliang: watches, clothing, crockery and tools. Some set up libraries, some shaved hair, some sold medicines and some cooked meals.

'Why don't the Wus become a Specialized Household?' I asked.

'It could be that they aren't prepared to put in extra labour,' Zhang replied. 'It might be that they are wary, or lack the special skills or the motivation. Perhaps they have no example to follow — the peasants are conservative and specialized teams must make decisions for themselves. But everything is open to those prepared to work,' he said.

Specialized Households were seen by the Party as pioneering units to encourage the less skilful or enterprising. While recognizing that the policy would exaggerate inequality it would not, they argued, be the polarization of pre-Liberation society. Families in need would be aided by the State. For all Mao's rhetoric, Deng had done more in five short years to increase production than the Chairman had ever achieved.

But while in many ways an improvement — grain production had doubled since it came into force — the Responsibility System was not without its faults. Rural birth-rates had risen, families wanting more sons to increase their earning power. The less capable suffered and collective projects did not get completed; some former schemes were even dismantled and their materials shared out and reused. Tools were insufficient for everyone. Land was divided so that each got a share of the good and less good soil; thus fields became smaller and harder to mechanize and people's plots were widely spaced. Many leftists opposed the new liberalization and there was a labour surplus of a hundred million rural unemployed.

'What was the family's status before Liberation?'

'Poor peasant,' Zhang replied. 'They were always in debt, owning too little land to support themselves and paying half the harvest of their rented land to its owner in Shuliang. There was so little to eat in the winter months that they spent them in virtual hibernation.' He reminded me of the before-and-after propaganda, subdued now, but a decade before an obligatory litany at every port of tour group call: 'Before Liberation people lived in straw huts and dressed in rags. There were no rural schools or clinics and the peasants died from hunger. Now we have dykes to control the floods, everyone is fed and the children go to school . . .'

The Party's interpretation of pre-Liberation history was not the whole truth: people had been taught to 'speak bitterness' when remembering the past. Many older peasants felt freer before, for at least they could travel if they wanted to, and there was more in the shops when they had money to buy. They could worship their gods, have as many sons as they wished, grow what they chose and keep the produce from their land. Not all the old landlords were vile rapacious capitalists; some new cadres, in their own way, were worse.

I thought of something else. 'I know it would be hard for you to join your wife in Nanning,' I said, 'but what if you wanted to work as peasants?'

Zhang's currant-like eyes wrinkled up behind his glasses. 'The government still welcomes peasants and anyone wishing to become one.'

But while Zhang envied the Wus their new opportunities he would still not wish to be in their place. Land was still punishment in a country with a relatively recent feudal past. Just as Zhang aspired to a clerical posting and the white-collar worker to become a professional, so the peasant longed for a factory job. For all the verbal idolization, for all that they fed the population, the peasants were still the serfs of the system. In 1980 the national average peasant income was 83 yuan (£28) a year, though most grew their own vegetables and sold their surplus and had coupons for rice and oil; two-thirds of the peasants lived at or below subsistence level, 120 yuan a year. Poverty was worse in less-developed hill lands: in the mountain villages of western Fujian the peasants survived on sweet potatoes and bamboo shoots and looked two or three times their age.

It was hard to believe that a farmer should yearn for a job in a factory, especially now that means existed for making out and getting on. Yet to a Chinese peasant a factory job represented shorter hours, easier work, better conditions, increased status, higher wages, security of income and benefits such as pensions. Were more small-scale factories to be sited in the countryside people could have all this without severing family or cultural ties (that they might wish to do so was another matter), bypassing the social dissolution that accompanied industrialization in the West. At the bottom of the pile with nowhere to fall to, and the majority still so hopelessly unequal, their plight scarcely recognized in countries outside China, it was no wonder that the peasants still spoke and ate bitterness. Were they given the chance to express their views on the Party and its policies the peasants would be the most condemnatory of all.

The sun had lifted half-way to its zenith, melting the mist and the early morning dew, shortening the shadows and warming the air. Across the landscape groups of people were harvesting rice, dust displaced the dew and the sounds of labour drowned the streams. Sickles swished as they sliced through the stalks; one cut, one clump. Girls exchanged talk as they carried the sheaves to the threshing machines and pumped the treadle and tied each bundle with a couple of straws and stood up the stook on the stubbly field. The scene was once more deceptively reassuring, the movements steady, the noises rhythmical, and once again I almost envied them their unquestioned belonging and the healthy simplicity of their lives. Almost.

Zhang looked on with disparagement in his eyes. When I attempted to operate the nearest treadle I was tired within seconds, my leg muscles aching, my forearms prickling, my eyes and nose choked with dust and sweat running down my face. I could not have performed the work of these peasants, and neither could Zhang. I could not have borne the sultry heat of summer, or the long winter cold. I could not have carried their heavy loads. I could not have eaten their food. I could not have laboured those endless hours, from dawn until nightfall at harvest times. Even so, countered Zhang, the peasants had more freedom than city people did. They could work hard and make money, or sit about and be idle: there was no one to clock up their hours.

Away in the distance men were still ploughing, showering their beasts with the curses so pervasive in the earthy peasant speech. Only the sick and elderly remained in the shade of their rooms and yards, preparing food and minding the young, or turning the grain on the threshing floors with flat wooden paddles, or washing clothes in the stream. The spirit of China lived on in the countryside, in the fields and the crops and the farming techniques, in the buildings, the hats and the shoulder poles, in the rhythmical ballet of everyday toil. While cities like Guilin grew more and more Westernized it would be several generations before Shuliang lost its soul.

Our field was full of teenage girls, members of three families taking it in turns to help each other out. Zhang's indignation rose by the minute. Why weren't the men out helping in the fields? And why weren't the girls at school? He asked them their ages; thirteen, said one, fifteen, twelve . . . For how many years had they been to school? Three, said another; the first three years of primary school, that building by the stream their parents had helped build when farmwork was slack. Zhang sounded off on the value of education but the girls just giggled and looked away.

In most rural provinces more than half the young people could neither read nor write. Girls of ten and more were needed at home to look after toddlers or help cut grass as fodder for the buffaloes or assist their mothers when doing the cooking or washing the clothes. By their middle teens they could produce more grain than they could consume. Books were expensive and learning played no part in the village people's lives. It paid to keep the children at home.

As sometimes happens with places, I fell in love with Shuliang. If I close my eyes I can be there still, watching the sun set in the folds of the mountains and light the sky with fire, walking through the rice fields on a dewy morning or swimming in the glass-clear stream. When I finally left, driven out by sandflies and the fear of approaching winter in the north, I lamented the loss of Shuliang as soon as I boarded the bus. I lamented it all the way to Guilin as the landscape deteriorated into wires and concrete, and I knew I wouldn't find its like again, would never escape other foreigners for quite so long, never match the elation that in spite of the discomforts I had felt while I was there. Guilin seemed more ghastly than ever as I waited for my bus by a sanitary fittings shop. And I thought, at least I'm still in China. How shall I leave China now?

It was the only time I felt like that.

12

Out North-west

The train was in darkness. I followed the railway employee through carriage after carriage until we reached the last but one. Above the mechanical jolting of the wheels I could hear the muffled breathing of hundreds of sleeping Chinese. It was four in the morning and I had just changed trains; everyone else had got on in Shanghai.

A shadowy finger motioned upwards at the last free berth on the train. There were bunks in three tiers, the uppermost close to the roof. Two folded sheets were dropped in my arms and a towel to protect the pillow from my hair.

I had already been travelling for thirty hours. At one in the morning the previous night I had boarded the Beijing-bound train in Guilin. By Chinese standards it was a short run to Zhengzhou where I had to change trains, just 23 hours, and I made no attempt to fight for a berth. Kashgar was seven days' journey away, eighty miles from the Soviet border, two hundred from Afghanistan, and half-way back to England. Being permitted to enter China only via Hong Kong I had, in effect, taken a three and a half thousand mile detour to get there. (The borders have since been opened to tourists from Nepal and Pakistan.) India, my next destination after Kashgar, was a forbidden day's bus ride away.

No sensible Han went north-west out of choice. From being a promised land of opportunity in the years following the Revolution the vast north-west frontier province of Xinjiang was viewed in the eighties as a kind of Siberia; people were sent there to build brave new worlds, to tame the desert or build factories, to dig canals or lay roads and railways, to civilize and administrate and patrol its borders with the USSR, not for any crime they might have committed but to ease the pressures on poor rural areas on the eastern seaboard and to benefit the beloved motherland. Built in the fifties the railway was instrumental in the desert's development, allowing people to move in and produce to move out; cotton, garlic, sorghum and sunflower seeds. Xinjiang was still a virgin land with an unexploited wealth of mineral reserves, aluminium, manganese, uranium, nickel, copper, oil and coal. It lacked capital, industry and expertise but by the year 2000 would be the focus of China's new economic growth. Over the past thirty-five years between four and five million Han Chinese had been resettled in cultureless communities, doubling the former population, imposing an oppressive colonial force, sometimes pushing the established Muslim tribes on to poorer and poorer lands. Most Han Chinese disliked Xinjiang; they disliked the food, there was little to do, and home was thousands of miles away. In winter temperatures fell far below zero. In summer the scorching continental sands made Xinjiang one of the hottest regions on earth.

North of Changsha it was autumn. The parchment-dry foliage of yellowing bamboos rattled in a wisp of wind. The rice was almost gathered in, overflowing threshing yards in bulging straw stacks. Plane trees glowed, autumn-golden-brown. Beyond Wuhan, astride the Yangtze, willows and poplars edged the fallow fields; lotus leaves withered like crumpled paper bags. I leant on my forearms and slept on the table and towards midnight woke up to change trains.

China's busiest railway junction was crowded and lively even in the middle of the night. People snoozed in the forecourt under heavy cotton quilts, or dozed on benches in cavernous halls, or squatted on hold-alls, or stood dejectedly in queues. PLA men with yellow armbands on their uniforms strutted about the echoing halls, making people pick up every last fallen crumb in an over-reactive anti-litter campaign. With four hours to wait for my connecting train I retired to the ladies' waiting room where men and their luggage took up most of the bench space and babies were cradled in cast-iron cots. I unrolled my sleeping bag on the floor and slept, and woke in a pool of pee.

Five hours later I was making up a bed in two and a half vertical feet of darkness. Below me five heaped and blanketed forms snored softly in what sounded like trusting sleep. Yet in reality the Chinese with their jangles of keys secured to their belts and their luggage tied down with bicycle chains were as suspicious of each other as people in India where lights in sleepers stayed on all the time.

When I woke next day the sun was up and the five other

occupants of my section of the carriage were sipping hot tea on the bottom berths. There was instant silence as I dropped to the floor: necks craned upwards, mouths fell open. I was the only foreigner on the train – I generally was – and the end of the line was three days away. A middle-aged couple and their grown-up daughter were returning, disconsolate, from an annual visit to relatives in Shanghai to their involuntary home in Xinjiang (as an incentive to stay there Han wages were one-third higher than wages elsewhere; they were going home loaded with new radios and clothes). The remaining two passengers were in PLA uniform, he pleasant, she prissy and complaining of cold or over-bright light, flicking hairs from her jersey and swatting at dust on her high-heeled shoes. She avoided the journey by staying in bed, and the young man leant over her and spoke to her tenderly when he thought himself unobserved. Were they married, I asked them. No, just colleagues, said the man, and the girl turned away in embarrassment.

Outside it was winter. I gazed through the window, smudged and blurred by days of dust. The land was wider north of the Yangtze; paler and drier. People seemed larger, their faces less round. Gone were the rice fields and smooth-hilled softness of south and central China, gone to wheat and millet and sorghum, to a stark land of gulleys and stony fields. Hand-sculpted terraces carved the steep hillsides. Cave dwellings pierced the soft loess cliffs like the naves of Norman cathedrals. Dried-up watercourses patterned the valleys with the abstract precision of Japanese rock gardens. Last leaves hung yellow on rows of young poplars and fluttered, lonely, in the wind.

Only on extended overland journeys could one directly experience the size and diversity of a country like China, and this journey was the longest I had ever undertaken all in one go. I was racing against winter; seduced by Shuliang I stayed in the south far longer than I'd planned. On my return from Kashgar the following month this land I now travelled looked dead. No crops in the fields, no leaves on the trees, no people with ploughs; just frozen streams and dusty rocks and smoke blowing sparsely from distant stacks.

But on that journey outward to Kashgar it was not just the land that was new and surprising, but the presence among the passengers of a people I didn't know. They moved in packs, untidy-looking men with passionate eyes and aquiline faces that should have belonged to musicians and herdsmen. They tore at rounds of hard flat bread and wore razor-sharp knives in their belts. They were Uighurs, I learnt, the most numerous Muslim minority in Xinjiang. I feared their immediacy; envied their food. Islamic soul songs blared from recorders, better by far than the rules and tunes that came from the intercom (which I'd blocked with a blanket and someone's umbrella to the satisfaction of the others who loathed its persistence but were too mindful of authority to take action themselves), and bursts of a guttural Turkic language detonated down the corridors. While the Hans were quilted in layers of long johns and wads of stuffing the fiercest Uighur slopped brazenly about in a see-through shirt unbuttoned down the front. 'Churchman?' he growled as he slouched past my seat. 'No,' I said meekly, intimidated by his knife-sharp eyes and the undergrowth of hair upon his chest. It was a day before I realized it was dollars he was after, that he was asking me if I'd 'change money'.

Compared to the Hans, to whose Confucian reticence I'd become accustomed, the Uighurs were all-intimidating. Their smiles were broader, their voices larger, their gestures more real and their eyes contained lust. From time to time a pair would descend on a group of Chinese, offering *mao tai*, regaling the Hans with snatches of song and frightening them out of their wits. Thereupon they would rise, tiring of neutrality, and return to their own kind, leaving the Chinese glancing sideways at each other and muttering about their barbarous ways.

It amazed me, at first, that the Hans should have brought such a virulent people to heel. They imposed their policies. They exploited the land and its natural resources. They banned the use of the Arabic script, then relented and condoned it; thus a youthful Uighur could write to his grandfather but not his father, who communicated only in romanized script. Government aid was aimed at absorption, teaching Mandarin in schools, imposing rationing and health care and laying down the law. Although a higher degree of autonomy was propounded than in any other province save Mongolia and Tibet the reality was powerful military control, partly because of the Soviet border, partly because the Uighurs resisted through armed opposition and underground resistance and imposed a threat to Han rule. A Uighur uprising had been quenched in the early eighties and there'd been several small riots since then.

While the Uighur men were handsome and extrovert, expressing joy and resentment with unbounded pride, their women seemed silent and morose. I watched them tottering on high-heeled shoes, skirts swinging from the hips, stockings stretched like sausage skins over pink or green long johns bunched up in folds. They sat knees akimbo, layers of long johns and bloomers on show, and listened to their men. The men swigged *mao tai* and the women sat still. So long accustomed to the unisex clothing and behaviour of the Hans I found it astonishing to see such marked differentiation, the women's flowered headscarves a form of token purdah, the dresses an expression of their men's desire.

In the afternoon we reached Xian, set in a plain of rectangular fields. Filmed with a haze of young winter wheat the land looked more prosperous and peasants were abroad, riding bicycles, hauling hand-carts, enlivening the lanes with the blues and olives of their padded winter clothing tied up with string to conserve the warm air they confined.

At Xian and other major stations half the passengers would descend from the train but once out on the platform they looked about helplessly, not knowing what to do with themselves. There was little to buy and less to look at, so they stood in cautious knots by the doors until the whistle went and the blue girls ushered them back inside. Gymnastics had once been compulsory at stations as in factory tea breaks and restaurant queues, but with Mao's death the impetus died too.

The train had a life and community all its own. Far from the engine, far from the crowded hard-seat coaches where for four days several hundred sat or stood, people with sleepers lounged on their bunks, eating, reading and sleeping away the time. A continuous stream moved up and down the aisle, of passengers hoping for new horizons, of those who could afford it filing to the dining car, of blue girls in their pumpkin padding, sweeping, mopping and filling our thermos flasks, of one of the Uighurs topping up our tea mugs with a watering can.

During the night we passed the city of Lanzhou, astride the Yellow River and the ancient Silk Road, approximate geographical centre of China. Beyond and for five days to the Soviet border there was desert, the Gobi, ravaged and eroded, creeping outwards through lack of foresight or care. Much had once been forest and pastureland, but the forest was felled, the pastureland ploughed; wars devastated what remained. A new Great Wall of poplar and willow trees as long as the original was already part-established in the hills to the north to check any further advance.

It was colder in the morning, and dark until eight. Snow glazed the distant mountain slopes, blush pink in the rising sun. The sky was high and bright and blue, but everything else was brown: earth, grass, hills, sheep, rock, roads, roofs, walls, an all-pervading dun brown. Dust eddied from ox-drawn ploughs; vegetation withered in the wind. Under that huge sparkling sky all else seemed diminished; villages were as toys, even the shadow-moulded hills were as fistfuls of clay. We would be gone, even the desert had its lifespan; but the unconquerable blue sky would remain.

We drew into a halt: a few huts, a siding, some heaps of abandoned coal. Ragged children were picking them over but they turned and ran for the sleeper coach windows, holding up chipped and coal-blackened bowls for fragments of yesterday's bread and *baozis*, pork-filled dumplings. In poorer regions such sights were common and were multiplied a hundredfold in the early years of the Cultural Revolution when millions of starving countryfolk flocked to cities and stations to beg food. Guiltily superior people drew up the windows and put their stale food in the children's hands, believing it demeaning to drop it in their bowls. But the band of children, rosy-cheeked and beautiful beneath their soot and rags, were too busy stuffing to care.

By the fourth morning it was colder still. Snow had blown into the couplings between the carriages, and an icy blast blew through the hole that was the loo. The Mongols called this land Gobi, meaning desert, and the Uighurs knew it as Taklamakan, 'you go in and never return'. Nobody seemed inclined to get up.

Each day brought dramatic change. On the fourth day we crossed a desolate wasteland of stone-strewn desert and our train lost impetus, puffing very slowly uphill through the wilderness as if weary of the ride. The Hans had grown daily more morose but the Uighurs, though dirty, were joyful and vociferous as they neared their home. Unable to take food from the hands of pork-eaters they gnawed at stale nan bread and hunks of pickled cabbage procured three days previously in Shanghai.

I was warming to the Uighurs. For a while I'd been torn between the gentle Chinese courtesy that I had grown used to and the passionate Uighurs with their enlarged sense of life, but by the fourth day I knew where my sympathies lay. Having known other Muslims I understood the Uighurs and what they believed in; with the Hans it was often still hard to tell. For most Hans life ended at the borders of China, while the Uighurs held a more generous world view. I spent the last afternoon with two Uighurs in their thirties, strongly built people with proper men's shoulders and coarse healthy skins. It seemed crazy to have to be speaking Chinese with people who originated in the Middle East but because of their limited Mandarin vocabulary and their omission of tones we were fairly well matched; conversation was easy. I loosened; responded as I would to friends. When they laughed they roared a full-throated belly laugh while the eavesdropping Hans sat silently on. They were able to let go, to enjoy, look foolish and even be hurt. We regarded each other with mutual respect.

And at last I could feel the romance of the railways, of endless distances unfolding in dreamscape, of the big black engine with its scarlet wheels rolling away the desert plain, of the meetings and partings and spilling out at stations in Siberian cold, of the steaming mugs of tea and music of a stinging Middle Eastern mournfulness, of the multitudes packed in the hard-seat coaches and the soft-berth carriage all shrouded in lace, lit softly by table lamps and occupied by cadres in solid middle age.

At dusk we drew into Daheyon and I left the train and walked out into a town of wide and dusty dusk-darkening streets, and window-less houses and driverless lorries and men in flapping, fleece-lined coats. Daheyon was like a frontier town with its faceless walls and people passing through, its loneliness of steam trains shunting in sidings, its sun-lined faces and smell of dust. There was nothing to see, nothing to do, but it conveyed a poetry all its own.

My hotel was in keeping with the streets outside, rough in its tin-shack homeliness, set down in a square about a mud-rutted truckers' yard and occupied solely by Han Chinese. Rough yet welcoming was the comfort of the coal stove in the centre of each hut, the cheerful camaraderie between strangers abroad and the sharing of intimate needs. While women soaped their feet in alu-minium bowls, their men spat a volley of melon-seed husks in a spray on the floor. Steam rose in clouds from a line of wet socks. The tin roof bellowed in the desert wind. The walls peeled back in discoloured chunks and my bill was forty pence.

Dawn crept over the flat mud roofs as we waited for the driver of our bus. Melon-seed sellers squatted in the dust. A shunting steam train threw a perfect smoke ring among the aerials etched against a paling pink sky. 'Voi che sapete' from Mozart's *Figaro* rang out in the cold morning air.

Kashgar was still three days away, west along the Silk Road, the ancient trade route that bore grapes and roses, jade and spices, silk and porcelain through desert and mountain to Antioch on the Mediterranean coast. Kashgar was a trading post, the first on entering China from the West, in existence for two thousand years. Along that path of history came Christianity carried by missionaries, Islam by Turks, Buddhism by Indians, and the arts and produce of all their lands. Along that path came the Muslim tribes to settle the desert in the fourth century AD, long after the Silk Road was established by the Hans. Along that path came Marco Polo travelling east in search of wealth. In those days it was a five-week journey from Beijing to Kashgar by camel caravan and in 1984 the railhead was still five hundred miles away.

It was no warmer in the bus than out in the wind. Our driver was closeted in a separate compartment warmed by the engine while the passengers huddled on the seats behind, Uighurs and Hans in uncomfortable unheated proximity. The men rolled tobacco in strips of newspaper and pulled up their collars to keep out the cold. They turned towards me and checked on my long johns, one inadequate pair to their three.

We rode out of town to a desert of grey shale. The sun was rising behind a barricade of barbed wire on which snags of torn polythene were blowing in the wind and catching the light, an image sharpened by a brittle eggshell sky. We crossed a flat of no-man's-land and pierced a range of eroded hills crouched dragon-like in hummocked folds, and wound and laboured up a convoluted valley, light-flooded, dust-clouded like a fallen Valhalla. At its head we broke on to an easy plateau and from then on, for three days, our progress was smooth, and drama lay in light and emptiness that released the mind to float and dream.

I had hoped the trade route might still be plodded by caravans of camels, untainted by anything more modern than our bus. But the

Silk Road was now a coal road bearing load upon load of coal heaped high in Soviet-style wagons a dour deep green. Telegraph poles fenced us in from the landscape in a rapid flight of flickering frames. The desert verges were rumpled by the tracks of caterpillar tyres and the road itself, its surface melted, its edges dusted, was an oily smear across the clean desert plain. It humped and hollowed, erupted and fissured and slumped into valleys to carry away the snow-melt from the Mountains of Heaven to our north. The smoke-belching vehicles, the long strip of tarmac, the coal heaps and cabbages stole the romance from travelling the Silk Road, from crossing one of the world's great deserts to a far-flung outpost of the People's Republic, closed to foreigners until a few months before.

Yet a romance still lingered, not the age-old simplicity of days measured by camel strides, but a striving restlessness, a Victorian surge of moving, thrusting, striving, changing, exploring uncharted territory, of hardship and discovery and pioneering spirit. It was a land on the move: people, vehicles and the fuel to sustain them. We passed a platoon of PLA men mending the road with shovels and washing bowls, a passage from the past, a travesty of socialist construction. Our bus carried tradesmen, soldiers, cadres, involuntary migrants from the eastern provinces crossing the desert to an alien home.

After half an hour's lunch stop in a treeless town we came to the first of a string of oases watered by snow-melt borne in underground channels, lining the Tarim Basin's southern rim. Donkey carts impeded our passage, and I peered down lanes close-planted with poplars, the sun slanting low across the sorghum fields and striping the lanes like a tiger's skin. Hoofs dug deep in the donkey-coloured dust. Women in white headscarves washed vegetables in streams. Old men in a yard were threshing and winnowing, loosening the grain with heavy stone rollers, separating the chaff with shovels and wind. Glimpses through arched and latticed doorways revealed vine-shaded courtyards and wells and clay ovens and sheep and straw and strings of peppers drying on walls.

Between the oases stretched hours of arid shale, broken once, mid-afternoon, by a pattern of salt flats and brine-sodden marshland. The Hans looked astonished at the sight of clusters of reed-hooped huts, of the type constructed by the Marsh Arabs of Iraq. Here lived people whose lives were reeds, cutting and carting, building and burning, selling reeds for roofs and fences and fuel, supplementing their earnings with goats and sheep. Though it was 1979 when the Responsibility System was introduced it was the mid-1980s before it was implemented here.

Towards evening we crossed another oasis. The sun streamed low across the sorghum fields, glinting in their grain-filled spears. It shone through poplar and willow trees in yellow lozenges of leaf-sieved light. It caught the sides of straw stacks in threshing yards, and heaps of cotton and cones of grain, and butter-yellow corn cobs garlanding walls. Rumbling through a land of low mud houses and dusty lanes and smoke curling upwards from evening chimneys I was back in the Asia I knew and loved.

At dusk we came to Korla, an ugly modern industrial town, and braked beside a large hotel. 'What are we stopping here for?' the passengers stood up and yelled at the driver through his partition wall. He gazed at us sullenly, then without a word reversed the bus and drove through town to a long low mud block on an unlit street. This time everyone filed out quietly, and we crowded round the counter and paid our forty pence. No one asked for my passport or wanted me to fill in the usual forms. Was there heating, I enquired. 'Mei you.' No heating. 'But it's cold!' I complained. 'It's not cold,' they replied. 'But there's ice on the road!' 'It's only November the tenth,' they said. Winter in China began on the fifteenth.

Since there was no hot water a boy lit some straw under an oil drum to warm some. Since there was no loo we went down the road to the public one, as squalid an inconvenience as I ever hope to see. Since there was nothing to eat we crossed the street to the only noodle house within our reach, which was about to run out of food.

At this point my notion that Chinese politeness went only as far as it suited people was once again confirmed. In their anxiety to eat, to get on a bus, to purchase a ticket or procure a bed when they and I were both in the running for what might conceivably be the last of something, manners did not come into play. I was pushed and shoved and barged in front of and left until last in every fight. Giving up a seat on a short city bus ride when a member of the neighbourhood committee might be watching was one thing; giving up a meal on alien territory another one altogether.

We left in the morning two hours before dawn. We huddled in our seats, each nursing our cold. An icy wind streamed through the gaps round the windows, and I stuffed mine up with paper screws. Others pawed helplessly at the flapping panes and again the analogy came to mind of China as a boarding school with the people its pupils, learning by rote, doing as they were told, not bothering to work things out for themselves and never stepping out of line.

Long after the sun rose, weak and colourless in an ice-white sky, we sat cold and silent. Then suddenly we were hot, sweltering in the layers we couldn't peel off since most of our warmth lay in underwear. As the sun sank down the temperature plummeted and the cold rose about us and we huddled back within ourselves, hunching our shoulders, drumming our feet, pulling our scarves up over our ears and our hats down over our eyes.

But at first, that day, the desert was bountiful. Beautiful even, rucked into small and regular hummocks, each one crowned by a clinging crimson herb. The dimples gave way to tangled thickets of cinnamon willow and low thorn scrub of harmonizing hues like the shade card of an illustrious paint-making firm: sage, lavender, straw and mushroom, marbled and mingled beneath a pearly sky. Having moved for days through a camel-coloured land it was pleasant to come upon a palette of pastels, an interlude in the unrelenting grey. But the colours soon paled in the strengthening light. A gentle flap of glistening crows lifted from the road and the emptiness entered my soul.

And again there was desert, stark and pure, and again we were alone with the endless shale and relentless sky. Again there were oases, but it was winter here and the leaves were gone and the fields were grey and brown as the shale. Traffic was sparse and bicycles few. There were fewer Han Chinese and no Chinese eating-stalls. When we stopped for lunch at a smoke-blackened mud hut where bearded Uighurs in ragged fleece coats were slurping down noodles with conspicuous zest the Hans in our party sulked and whined; just as the Uighurs would eat no pork the Hans would not touch food not their own.

In Uighur society eating in company bore a moral obligation, cementing friendship ties. Uighurs ate with Uighurs, Hans with Hans: I, by this time, was eating with the Muslims when someone questioned me on the black-market rate. Since a cadre was present I didn't reply. But the cadre assured me: 'It's all right, you can talk. We have eaten together. We know each other. We are friends.' On the bus the division was equally clear. Hans talked to Hans, Uighurs to Uighurs, and a steadfast reserve was maintained between.

They were different in everything – as different, almost, as two peoples could be. Different in beliefs, in appearance, in attitudes, different in culture and creed. They used different shops and their children attended different schools. While a Uighur would urinate up against a wall a Han could only function behind the privacy of a screen. While Hans might be dirty in their personal habits – not washing their underclothes all winter for example – they would be loath to show it to the outside world. A Uighur, on the other hand, must be ritually clean before visiting the mosque, but scarcity of water absolved his shame if his clothes were dusty, or greasy, or stained. In our bus was a boy in his early teens cracking sunflower seeds between his teeth and letting the husks scatter on his clothes without pausing to brush them down. Dirt encrusted his hands and face and grew like a mould in his ears, the edges of which had fissured like dried mud. He wore four cotton jackets, all equally filthy, and stuffed paper in his cap and sockless boots to insulate his body from the cold.

As evening approached the Silk Road began to live up to its name. We were driving due west straight into the sun, through oases netted by the shadows of trees, past carts stacked high with gnarled desert willow to be used as fuel. The sun slanted silver in tangled seedheads of old man's beard and gold in swathes of reed. Towards us came hundreds, if not thousands of donkey carts, returning from Sunday market in Aksu, each donkey driven by a wild-looking Uighur with uncut beard and matted sheepskin turned up against the cold. The rest of each family sat behind on the quilt-covered cart, bundled in shawls, backlit silhouettes against the sun.

By the third day my senses were numbed by noise and cold. The engine rumbled; the windows rattled; music crackled on the inter-com. On return from Kashgar there would be three more days of desert and discomfort, three more days of ethereal mountains floating soft-shadowed, of carts and trucks and telegraph poles, of winter oases and expanding towns, three days of flat plateau land and then down and down the long winding valley, bouncing like a rowing boat bobbing on the water, flowing down the cleft between the dun-coloured dragon-rocks, and down, and out on to the plain of Turpan and the railway station at Daheyon.

On the third day the desert was pure expanse. There was so much light, not the hostile light of the Indian plains where everything is drowned in a blinding glare but a gentle light that danced and shimmered with the tender touch of fingertips, and paled and silvered and glowed ghost-like in the dust. When the mountains drew close there were colours in their flanks: jade, coral and amethyst. In the distance they were folded like English downland, creations of shadow and light. My memories of Xinjiang are memories of light, of sunshine illuminating translucent leaves and glancing across dust lanes in tree-trunk stripes; of light rays casting silver filaments of smoke and swirling in steam, and sparkling in roadside poplar-sided streams where flower-frocked women washed vegetable greens, and haloed in the dust around donkeys' hoofs; of sunbeams slanting in bars across roofs, throwing buildings and rocks and figures and trees into silhouette. Inanimate things like smoke and dust and air and fire all breathed with life in Xinjiang.

We stopped to buy melons by a handful of houses burrowed below ground, with ramps going down and branches for roofs. Herds of camels grazed the dry scrub. Then, five miles from Kashgar, the bus broke down. 'That's it then,' said the driver with a faceful of gloom. We sat and waited for the engine to cool. Move, stop, sit; move, stop, sit: and thus we crawled into town.

Kashgar, at first sight, was not the fabled crossroads of Asia, of walled caravanserai and ornate woodwork I had imagined the culmination of a week-long pilgrimage out north-west to be, but the usual unprepossessing industrial outskirts of any Chinese town, of wide empty roads and factory walls, of Chinese on bicycles and telegraph poles. Out across the desert there were new oases of tamed and irrigated plots of land, with communities of Hans growing cotton and wheat on large state farms, sheltering their crops with trees.

But once out and on foot I felt that shock of excitement which only a city like Kashgar can bring. Having opened recently there was no city map. There was nothing in guide books. No tour groups came, and the arduous journey deterred all but the stalwart and determined. In the centre of Kashgar the Hans were outnumbered six to one, by old men in black, Uighurs,Uzbeks, Tajiks, Kazaks, clunking down pavements in knee-high boots, and women in purdah hidden behind shawls. There was still a sense of surrounding space, of desert light, of a paleness and fragility absent further east. Faces were Asian, sounds were earthly: the smells were of Egypt or Arabia.

Beyond the mosque I entered the old world of mud-sculpted alleyways where walls were never vertical, where roof lines were never level and where fortress-like façades betrayed no hint of the layout and activity or the richness of interiors within. From the outside even the number of storeys was indeterminate. Beam ends jutted like abstract sculpture; chimneys protruded like pilasters. There were glimpses of carved woodwork and sometimes small yards, but most of the doors were barred.

For the second time in China – the first was in Dali – I slept in a room with a history, in a former consulate, far from the other guests billeted in barracks in the grounds. Its silence was so poignant it was almost audible. I was alone with the ghosts of merchants and diplomats, swaying in the old silk hanging on the windows, hiding in the dust beneath the Oriental carpets, waiting in the cold still room.

It was November the twelfth and there were three days to go before the official start of winter. North of the Yangtze the heating went on in state institutions on November the fifteenth, no matter the latitude, no matter the altitude, no matter the conditions that particular year. South of the Yangtze winter wasn't scheduled to happen at all and I later spent several days in Shanghai in an unheated room in a large hotel when the city was covered by snow.

For the first three days I stayed out of doors. Still on Beijing time (though three thousand miles west of it) it was dark until ten, cold until noon; at Delhi longitude there was a four-hour difference in time. When the sun set at seven the temperature plummeted and I paced the alleys and night bazaars for they were not as cold as my north-facing room.

On the fourth morning I was woken by clumps in the corridor and voicings of song and a trio of dirty, unshaven Uighurs burst in brandishing lengths of pipe. While I watched from my bed they moved my trousers with a pair of pliers, dumped a sheet of rusty iron in the centre of the priceless Oriental carpet, set down a coal stove and secured the flue to a hole in the wall with a length of wire. On return in the evening I discovered some slithers of desert tree and a small bowl of coal, apparently recycled, beside the mud-lined stove, itself a product of careful recycling and a hundredth the price of my coal stove at home.

The charm of Kashgar was nostalgia for a lifestyle threatened by the powers of Beijing. Behind its main streets two wide arteries renamed People's Road and Liberation Road which bisected at the bank and a ring road enfolding the former city walls, the unpaved lanes jammed with traders and craftsmen applying their skills, were a journey back in time. Each trade or craft had its street or zone in the manner of all Oriental bazaars, where the craftsmen benefited from companionship and solidarity and the customer from quality and control. Wandering through these streets each day was to be transported back to medieval trade guilds. Most everyday items were still made by hand, by craftsmen whose workshops were too small, too private, too cold for comfort and who thus performed in the street. There were blacksmiths and coppersmiths, cot makers and carpenters, cobblers and tailors, milliners sewing skull caps with gold and silver thread, turners working with the old bow lathe, bakers of nan bread in dome-shaped ovens, barbers shaving heads with fearsome knife-like razors, and potters and welders and scribes and goldsmiths and men who fashioned kettles out of old tin cans. There were vendors of gutsy haberdashery and underwear, and recyclers of rags, of tyres, of iron, and sellers of miscellaneous things in sacks like dried black flowers for polishing boots, and camel-thorn sugar, and camphor and jujube and saffron and bags of yellow fat.

The ancient response of the nomad to the desert held fast in old Kashgar interiors too: shut out the light (some rooms were lit only by a hole in the mud roof, like the smoke-hole of a yurt, capped during rain); insulate the dwelling from heat and cold; acquire only what is portable and enrich the rooms with pattern and colour as an antidote to the desert outside. Colour blazed in scarlet blankets, in patterned fabrics fixed to walls, in painted furniture decorated with landscapes, in floral linings to the men's black coats, in the women's dresses shot with gold and silver thread, shiny, tasselled, yellow and purple, green and orange, pink and turquoise, the ultimate in kitsch.

Sitting on a *kang* (a brick platform heated by a fire or flue) in a house in Kashgar, a bowl of green tea in the hollow of my hands, the overwhelming sense was of colour and warmth. Thick pile carpets covered the *kangs* and were pinned to the walls. Translucent ikats filtered the sun and scarlet geraniums flowered on the sill. Mirrors and calendars studded blue walls. Stencilled enamelware was stacked upon a shelf, patterned cotton cushions on the *kang*. Were it not for the angles, the window and the door it might have been a nomad's tent. There was nothing Chinese in sight.

Old Kashgar might not last. The immemorial mud lanes clogged with people and sheep and donkey carts, though aesthetically pleasing and fitting in a climate of extreme heat and cold, were narrow and dusty. The tight-clustered houses with their thick mud walls had no piped drainage or water supply. Nearby villages had no electricity. New brick blocks were gnawing at the seams of Kashgar's old-world heritage, taking bites from the labyrinth of zigzag alleyways and the Islamic privacy of the courtyards within. They towered in insolent visual barbarity, threatening a break in traditional community and a consequent change of lifestyle. However remote from the powers in Beijing, Kashgar was never immune. It had suffered its share in the Cultural Revolution when bands of Red Guards destroyed the old mosque and burnt the Koran and imprisoned the imams and beat believers to 'cure' them of Islam. They smashed Arabic inscriptions, closed down the markets and big Sunday bazaar and threw merchants and traders into jail. 'Why did you let them?' I asked a Uighur. 'There were too many,' he sighed. 'Ach, we would have been killed.' 'How many were killed in Kashgar?' 'It's hard to say. Ach, many – too many – thousands.'

Though Marxist ideology and the Islamic creed could never be anything but mutually exclusive the Party was now showing leniency; where violence had failed to elicit surrender an attitude of benevolence might yet succeed. Since Liberation dozens of mosques had been reopened and the principal one restored. Bazaars had returned to their former scale and almost none of Kashgar's trade was in the hands of the State. Only months before my visit in November China had signed new trade agreements with Pakistan, India and Nepal. The Pakistan border had been open for two years, the Soviet border for one. After a twenty-year interval, silk, cotton, tea and tobacco were once more leaving China by way of the Silk Road in exchange for vehicles and electrical goods. Those living near the border were once more permitted to cross it to visit their relatives, having been forced for two decades to travel by way of Beijing and Moscow, a detour of seven thousand miles. The bureaucracy meanwhile was addressing itself to what remained of Kashgar's colonial past, the well-proportioned and spacious buildings with pillared porticoes and scumbled paintwork that lined the two main streets. In place of those they'd already demolished there were housing blocks, turned away from the road and shielded from its gaze by unit walls, and modern department stores shuttered against the cold, their interiors dark, resounding with echoes and wasted space. The authorities wanted Kashgar to be modern and smart. Donkey carts were banned from People's Road and Liberation Road, the only streets wide enough to accommodate them comfortably; open-air food stalls were prohibited along their sides. In its urge to bring Kashgar's principal streets in line with socialist policy elsewhere the Party had made them the dullest in town.

I spent the evenings beside the mosque, dome-tiled-yellow, where on Fridays thousands of men in black prayed between lines of silver trees, kneeling, rising, silent, intoning, their prayer mats laid out in rows in the dust; and when prayer was done they shook their mats and lifted the dust and filed back out between the silver trees. By day the square was drab and grey but as dusk approached it came to life. Dangling light bulbs swathed unshaven faces with butter-yellow light, banishing distance to chocolate shade. Daytime space was disguised by darkness, colours muted by smoke and steam. The square smelt of charcoal and meat and marihuana (when one of the foreigners, caught with dope, was asked to point out the man who had sold it, the Uighur was sentenced to fifty years while the foreigner was let off free). Kebab sellers blew on their glowing coals and threaded chopped liver on skewers. Barrow boys set up displays of sultanas, jade, sepia, topaz and bronze, and sweet apricot kernels, and dried peaches and plums by the light of amber flares. Old men gathered. Girls gave alms. Beggar boys fought on the steps of the mosque. Melon and grape sellers clustered down the side of the small railed garden, dismal by day in winter hibernation but shadowed and mysterious in the dark. Groups of men squatted in the shadow of a wall, dealing out cards and passing round joints, thawing their fingers at a tiny fire.

Around the square were teashops and food stalls. Noodle makers practised their vanishing art, swinging the dough in elongating loops, twisting, stretching, doubling, flouring, making perfect spaghetti-thin strands. Topped with mutton and spiced vegetables and served with nan bread, hot and crisp from beehive mud ovens, they were standard Kashgar fare. Tea drinkers sat beneath tethered awnings, between walls of matting, on beds laid with blankets, stained by tea and muddy from the boots of the old men who sat in ancient padded black and mink fur-brimmed hats, cross-legged in companionable pairs.

Kashgar people stared at foreigners less than Chinese elsewhere. But if they stared I had no objection, for in Kashgar I stared too. If I spotted someone in an ikat fabric or in moulded felt boots I stared. In the Kashgar bank I saw a pale-skinned girl in embroidered cap and camel-coloured coat. Two heavy plaits reached half-way down her calves, indisputably her own. If she unwound them her hair would touch the ground. Never in my life had I seen such hair. And I stared.

13

Dissent

'You can't put your luggage on the rack!' the man shouted as I shouldered my rucksack and searched for a space. All the other passengers' bags were on the luggage rack and with minimal restacking there'd have been room for mine. But the man was adamant. When I tried to make room he got angrier still and pushed me away. I appealed to a blue girl passing down the aisle but sensing trouble and unwanted involvement she walked away. Too tired to argue I leant my rucksack against the edge of my berth and went to sleep.

When I woke an hour later we had left Beijing and were rumbling through frozen countryside. The night was dark, most passengers asleep, and my rucksack had fallen and was blocking the aisle. As I reached out to move it a warm, comforting, female voice reassured me in English: 'Never mind – I'll help you.' My rucksack was lifted and I subsided into memories, half-sleep images of the previous ten days in Beijing: of a flock of doves circling in the sky, bamboo whistles attached to their wings causing a fluting sound as the wind blew through; of the Forbidden City, dust-pink walls and yellow roofs, crumbling stone and wind-browned cypress trees, and the eternal passage from the outside in, up, down, along, through, under and over frozen moats, darkened halls, sun-haze-space, in and in, penetrating walls and courtyards like the layers of an onion, the consummation of what in China was least attainable, the desire to be alone; of Tian An Men Square in early pink sunlight when figures lacked detail and buildings swam in haze and the sun rose red in the eastern sky; Tian An Men Square, the hundred-acre centre of the nation that could hold two million, an appropriate symbol that defined China's vision, a reassurance of the Party's potency.

I woke in the morning to a motherly smile that matched the voice of the night before. She was a woman in her fifties with short waved hair and straight white teeth, wrapped in layers of soft grey wool. She smiled again and offered me tea.

Ho Yulan was travelling to Shanghai for the first time in her life to attend a conference on teaching in middle schools. I supposed it would be a change for her; she must be looking forward to doing some shopping and seeing Shanghai. Each city produced a different range of goods: people always seemed anxious to visit Shanghai where the choice was greater and the quality superior. But no, she said, there'd be little free time. 'The conference is bound to be dull,' she continued. 'People will get up and make long speeches on education but nothing new will come of it. We will have to sleep in one of the dormitories and there won't be any heating.' It was late December and snow was lying on the fallow fields. Unheated discussions in unheated rooms: Yulan would rather have stayed at home.

She pulled some schoolbooks from a plastic hold-all: English readers. Her pupils hated them, but she didn't know how to make the subject interesting. I suggested songs. 'But I don't know any songs!' she replied in desperation. 'Only "Jingle Bells"!' She made a sound to suggest that 'Jingle Bells' was not a great deal of use. 'I have no means of learning new songs. I can't get tapes and there isn't any money.' She taught at a middle school in the Beijing suburbs south of the Temple of Heaven. I suggested films. 'We can't get films either.' I suggested games. 'I would have to invent them. The first-year pupils like games,' she agreed.

Then without any prompting she began to talk of her family. It struck me fairly quickly that she needed to talk, to share her sorrows with a sympathetic listener. Though extraordinary to a Westerner who had known no real strife or humiliation, her story was not unusual for a mainland Chinese.

Yulan's father had been a professor, her mother a teacher in a junior school. She was the second of three daughters, with an elder brother now living in Beijing and a younger one a doctor in Taiwan. Until the thirties they'd lived in a large house surrounded by the culture and trappings of the West. But when the Japanese came they fled to Sichuan as refugees, returning only to lose their house and be hounded and criticized by the new regime.

'When we first saw the communists we thought they looked like tramps. The women cut their hair and dressed like men. They lost any sense of femininity or grace.' At this point the family could still

236

have fled: a million people followed Chiang Kai-shek and settled in Taiwan, and hundreds of thousands moved to Hong Kong, but they decided to stay and see.

They regretted their choice. Throughout the fifties the family was criticized for its rightist habits and bad class origins. Intellectuals were asked to speak out against corruption and maladministration in 1956, only to be castigated shortly afterwards in an anti-right campaign. In the Great Leap Forward the struggle sessions increased. 'The Great Leap Forward was such a calamity that for several years afterwards people lacked food. Everything we had that was made of metal was melted down to make iron. There was little in the shops and we couldn't afford coal. We sealed up our windows to try and keep warm.' But it was not until the mid-1960s that serious trouble began. Mao was convinced that the habits of the past weighed like a stone on the consciousness of the present, and his beliefs triggered off an extensive anti-Confucius campaign and the destruction of China's artistic heritage in the 'Four Olds' campaign, the extent of which was impossible to conceive. His vehicle for China's transformation from a society still riven by class hierarchy and capitalist tendencies to a new proletarian ideology was that section of the community most vulnerable to innovation and least tainted by the feudal past – the nation's youth. As militant Red Guards they took over first schools and colleges and then factories, then even local government and the PLA. They frequently acted without Central Party authority, killing and looting especially those to whom they bore a personal grudge, then splitting into factions and fighting each other until the army stepped in in 1968 to restore some sense of order and calm. They broke in to Yulan's family home during the initial frenzy and filled five sacks with books. They dragged them outside and set fire to them. They smashed the old porcelain and classical records. They ripped the calligraphy and landscape scrolls. They searched the cupboards for Western clothes and repeated the process in every suspect home. 'Keeping pot plants was bourgeois,' Yulan sighed, 'so we removed them from our sills. Nice clothes were bourgeois so we put on patched ones. Having dogs and cats as pets was bourgeois; they took them away and killed them. Taking photographs was bourgeois . . . anything, virtually, outside of politics was regarded as bourgeois and counter-revolutionary.'

Not to cling to the past was commendable in its way but the enforced destruction of a nation's heritage was arrogant and short-sighted. Treasures from the past could be learnt from and enjoyed, Yulan believed, without attachment to either objects or the society that made them. Even workers with nothing were opposed to the fruitless annihilation of the arts, mostly enacted by students and children too young to understand.

In other houses *objets d'art* were not destroyed but taken from their owners and locked in stores. Nearly twenty years later the more valuable items were being put on sale in antique shops to earn foreign currency from the tourist trade. Unsaleable items like photograph albums and Chinese books were put out in heaps for their owners to reclaim.

The ironically misnamed Cultural Revolution – Cultural Dissolution would have been more appropriate – effectively destroyed most of China's past but nothing has emerged to take its place. In the 1980s China is suffering an identity crisis, torn between a return to traditional values, the continuation of socialist ideals and the tempting comforts of the West. None of them yet has the upper hand and China is left alienated and insecure, not sure of the path to choose.

Of all Yulan's family it was her elder brother, a physicist, to whom she was closest now. He had emigrated to America in the 1940s but returned to China in 1949, not because he supported Mao's policies but because he was a patriot and wanted to lend his expertise in rebuilding the country and making it strong.

But his background was against him from the start. Science was suspect, having been introduced to China by the colonial powers. He came from a family of wealthy intellectuals and still had connections with the USA. He bore the shame of a series of struggle sessions until in 1966 he was arrested by Red Guards and sent to do labour in a camp in Qinghai. For twelve years he remained there, poorly fed and subjected to struggle until rehabilitated after Mao's death. Prisoners were made to denounce each other in political study groups in which even close friends could not be trusted and truth was no defence. They were set to sweep excrement and put to work down the mines. But letters told the family nothing except that he was still alive, for they were opened and censored by the camp authorities. No food or money or news ever reached him.

He was allowed no books, no paper to write on, and when finally released had grown so emaciated his family did not know him. Millions of victims were incarcerated in labour camps throughout the Cultural Revolution; just how many millions nobody knew.

It was common in China to meet people who'd been victims of Cultural Revolution atrocities. There was the hotel receptionist, the sole survivor of a once-large clan. There was the cutter of meat with a degree in French whose parents had been driven to suicide. There was Wei Meng, the artist, forbidden expression for more than a decade, paraded in the streets with banners and placards and a dunce's cap and set to clean out pigs. There was the teacher sent down to the countryside, half-starved on potatoes and kept up all night writing big-character posters so that ten years on she still could not sleep. There was the writer so badly bashed about that his head swelled up and his skin went blue. Anyone with academic or artistic pretensions (or wrongly suspected of having them) was slandered, tortured or banished to the countryside to 'learn from the peasants', a euphemism for labour reform. Wrong beliefs warranted imprisonment or death. Children and students tortured their teachers, people were thrown from fourth-floor windows or beaten by bars or crucified against walls. Hatred flowed in waves of vindictiveness, an infection whose target was basically abstract and could be switched from one hapless victim to the next. Western Marxists deduced at the time from the little that leaked out that the Cultural Revolution was a glorious festival of national awakening. For the school-age Red Guards who seized control perhaps it was. Violence was permissible in order to bring about change, to wipe the slate of China clean. Foreigners flocked to the new-born China of barefoot doctors and cadre re-education schools and intellectuals banished from the towns, oblivious to its aspect of terror and destruction, to the artillery battles between Red Guard factions both claiming allegiance to Mao Zedong but in reality fighting for power for themselves, to the extent of the murder, suffering and chaos. The Cultural Revolution claimed millions of lives in a cataclysm still not fully understood. Though its aim was to purify and rejuvenate, its reality was civil war.

The Red Guards were betrayed by Chairman Mao, the real defendant in the trial of the Gang of Four. He used them as scapegoats to purge the country of the pragmatist faction that threatened to usurp his power. When they took the initiative and thereby threatened to usurp it themselves he packed them off to the countryside where they could do no further harm. For the Red Guards concerned what had started out as a time of excitement and youthful rebellion ended in long and tragic years banished to rusticity and toil.

The Party now acknowledges that the Cultural Revolution was a grave mistake. Ten long years of a billion people's lives and the memories of their sufferings hanging over them like a nightmare are denounced by Deng as being a mistake. The destruction of China's heritage is absolved in the admission that it was all a mistake. Communization was a mistake. The smelting of pig iron in back-yard furnaces and the grain-first policy were, among other mis-guided campaigns, unfortunate mistakes. But confession in itself would not bring about forgiveness in the minds of people embit-tered for ever by needless loss. If the past was so full of avoidable mistakes what hope was there for the future?

Life in the early seventies was possibly worse than during the most rampant debauches of the Nationalists. In ten years Mao had undone the good he had built in the previous twenty. He was preoccupied, not with people but with perpetual revolution. He sacrificed friends for personal power. Most Chinese never under-stood his theories, though they learnt its language by heart. Their lives were governed by the slogans and jargon of the communist ideological arsenal, as if Mao had been picking up hints from George Orwell: '"How does one man assert his power over another, Winston?"' O'Brien asked in *1984*.

'Winston thought. "By making him suffer," he said.

'"Exactly. By making him suffer. Obedience is not enough. Unless he is suffering, how can you be sure that he is obeying your will and not his own? . . . Power is in inflicting pain and humiliation. Power is in tearing human minds to pieces and putting them together again in new shapes of your own choosing . . . In our world there will be no emotions except fear, rage, triumph and self-abasement . . . There will be no loyalty, except loyalty towards the Party. There will be no love, except the love of Big Brother. There will be no art, no literature, no science. There will be no distinc-tion between beauty and ugliness. There will be no curiosity, no enjoyment of the process of life ... always there will be the intoxication of power." '

For Yulan's brother release from labour camp was far from being the end of his suffering. Though Yulan slowly nursed him back to health, he had lost the best years of his life. Now at fifty-six he was still unmarried, for no woman would take the risk of a man with the stigma of a past such as his, in case of a future swing back to the left. Many political (and criminal) detainees had remained on release in the vicinity of their labour camps in preference to facing humiliation for themselves and their families at home. Too proud to impose on his sister's goodwill, Yulan's brother lived alone, ate out in noodle shops for he could not cook, and worked as a technician in a hospital. Return to America was out of the question. All he wanted was to forget, but with evidence of the regime that turned its back on him and the results of the Cultural Revolution all about him he was constantly reminded of what he had lost, of what he had missed and was never to be.

Worst of all, perhaps, was the effect his internment had on his father, Yulan's father. Being the eldest son and the cleverest of five children with a brilliant future ahead of him, he had been his father's greatest hope. When his mother died his father remarried, but nothing could stem the father's sadness and over the years he pined away, and eventually died of grief.

Yulan had suffered on her own behalf. For ten years before the Cultural Revolution she had been subjected to struggle, paraded, interrogated and denounced in mass meetings. She had to stand up in public and denounce her rightist attitudes and bourgeois way of life. She had to swear allegiance to Mao Zedong and promise to reform her ways. According to the Party there were three levels of consciousness, an outer or shared one, a middle level kept secret except from trusted friends, and an inner one known scarcely even to oneself. It was this hidden inner consciousness the Party wished revealed. 'They wanted me to lay bare my soul, to be washed clean, they said, of bourgeois thoughts, to repudiate crimes that were not crimes at all, to be redeemed of my rightist origins. Thought control was their way of keeping track of people like me, but they never convinced us, whatever they did.' Thirty-five years of brainwashing techniques had not altered her values or diminished her spirit. She was the child of her parents, not a product of the Party; a born survivor. In less resilient subjects the process of thought control met first with resistance. Gradually it wore its victims down until they realized their struggle was fruitless, and gave in. It was the most frightening aspect of the communist regime.

In the Cultural Revolution the cycle of Yulan's re-education intensified. She had married by then, a doctor with a background similar to her own, and they had two daughters. 'My family was divided by militant Red Guards who had seized control. Our daughters are twenty-one and nineteen now, so they were small at the time. We would be moved around the country independently, from farm to factory and back to farm. While I was stationed out in the countryside my husband would be kept at home, only to be sent away the moment I returned. For years they kept us apart, both from each other and from our children who were placed in state nurseries for re-education and to protect them from the "contagion of our bourgeois ideals". They taught them to spy on us and denounce our lifestyle.' Children were more easily brainwashed than adults and they kept the authorities informed.

In spite of a general Party belief that intellectuals could not make revolutionaries since they could not put their reason aside, their penal process continued. Physical privation of various kinds was imposed on millions with bourgeois leanings for whom there were no more vacancies in the labour camps, and their only escape was to accept the teachings of Mao Zedong. Almost ten years on the after-effects of factionalism persisted for they were forced to work alongside, or under, the very people who'd denounced and reviled them before.

'In spite of all that happened we were luckier than some,' Yulan reflected. 'At least we are alive, and all together now. Many marriages broke down under the strain of political indoctrination. They made us feel guilty for just being human, for having thoughts and feelings that any normal person has. We learnt to trust no one, to keep everything to ourselves. We learnt to lie to protect our families: we maintained this pretence for years.'

To survive the system required an ability to hide what one really felt and a capacity for changing tack when the Party line swung. And this Yulan refused to do. She was an object lesson in non-cooperation, opposed to the communists before they took over, opposed to their policies throughout the fifties when the system was young and most Chinese felt genuine enthusiasm for their promised reforms. And after thirty-five years of chaos, upheaval and personal humiliation she was more opposed than ever to the Party's ideals, even more resentful of its mindless control. When defeated most Chinese resigned themselves to fate. Under threat they selected the middle road and victorious they tended towards tyranny. Perhaps Yulan was atypical in the force of her resistance and resolution – it would explain why I hadn't met her like before. She was an atheist in a fraternity of agnostics and fanatics.

To those who believed, communism was a faith as fervent and inflexible as Christianity or Islam. Though by nature not spiritual (except when they wanted something) the Chinese were able to accept the imposition of a paternalistic, even messianic leadership. It was not surprising that contemporary China had produced no philosophers, for apart from the repression so absolute that questioning meanings could only deepen frustration, the Chinese character discouraged their emergence and the daily absorption in work and survival left little time over for meditation on existence or the nature of the soul. The religion of Mao was all-powerful, with its dogma and prophets and sacred texts, and its saints embalmed in a sepulchre of atheism in Tian An Men Square. Mao became god-like even in his lifetime. He defined morality, demanded submission to his political ideals. If his people doubted, the system would fail. In his final years everyone was duty-bound to salute his portrait in a morning assembly and report back each evening on the progress of the day. The sayings contained in the Little Red Book, the *Quotations from Chairman Mao Zedong*, carried by everyone in the Cultural Revolution (but which I never saw, except once in a dustbin), were a panacea for every evil, replacing the traditional 'Analects of Confucius', though many were derived, via Lenin and Marx, from Christian ethics of self-regulation, equality, good deeds, austerity, self-sacrifice and work. (Having been compiled by Lin Biao, a traitor to Mao who has since been erased from Chinese history, the Little Red Book has been removed from circulation.) Both Christ and Mao aspired to paradise, to a utopia where personal needs were forgotten in a heavenly eternity the communists called 'future'.

The ideal young communist delivered his soul to the State. In the words of O'Brien in *1984*: '. . . every human being is doomed to die, which is the greatest of all failures. But if he can make complete, utter submission, if he can escape from his identity, if he can merge himself in the Party so that he is the Party, then he is all-powerful and immortal.' Happiness depended on an ability to submerge; the Party was God.

By 1984 most surviving intellectuals (nobody knew how many had been killed, though totals could run to over a million) had been rehabilitated, albeit partly in recognition of their usefulness. Yulan's doctor husband had been sent to America to learn new techniques, but when he returned there was no means of putting his new knowledge into practice because of lack of equipment at home. 'The Party claims we are thirty-five years behind the West, but my husband believes it is more like fifty. He enjoyed America and made good friends there. He is full of compliments about Western technology and the ease of people's lives. After two years in California he longs to go back. We all long to go.'

Under Chairman Mao there was no power in China but the power of the State. Now under Deng people are being asked to dedicate their lives to the Four Modernizations, the antithesis of Mao's co-operative austerity in its claim that only individual enterprise can hope to make China modern and strong.

But after Deng what? Deng was eighty in 1984. His designated successors Zhao Ziyang as Head of Government and Hu Yaobang as Head of Party will inherit a more stable and healthy economy but will they be able to consolidate Deng's authority, to stem the influx of Western thought? Or will the leftists regain sufficient power to sabotage the economic reforms?

'Are you afraid the Cultural Revolution might happen again?' I asked Yulan.

'People with my background can never feel safe for no one knows what is going to happen next – though for seven years now there has been no swing, the longest period since the communists came to power.' The Party claimed there would not be another Cultural Revolution because the leadership had become more democratic. Most Chinese believed the leftists were too few and too scattered to organize; the followers of the Gang had either been arrested or had lost their power. Authority was being decentralized and would thus be more difficult to overthrow. To invert the current policy would require a leader far stronger than Deng, and since the workers and peasants were slightly better off they approved and supported his reforms. Perhaps the best defence against a swing back to the left was the memory of the Cultural Revolution itself.

'What do you personally feel?' I asked. 'Do you not think the current policy an improvement on what went before?' Within months of Mao's death pragmatism began to replace political ideals, specialists regained positions of power and the people had less to fear. There was more trust in Deng's leadership for it admitted mistakes and its own shortcomings. There had been a rise in living standards and a certain relaxation on all things foreign, and on foreigners themselves. But the Chinese had a habit of viewing things in extremes of black and white. Yulan was no exception: heroes (leaders of Western democracies) were unblemished and incorruptible; enemies (the Party) were the devil incarnate.

'Mao and Deng are just the same!' she cried. 'Both of them class me as bourgeois. Between them they have criticized and humiliated me for more than twenty years. The most important thing in life is freedom, and neither has allowed me to live the way I choose!' After so much socialism over almost eight months it startled me to hear such words. 'They don't want us to learn – they want to mould us in an image of themselves. They are afraid of us, and want to keep us down!'

Intellectuals had hoped for greater freedom, both political and cultural, when Deng came to power but their hopes were not to be. Underground journals were squashed in 1981, artists and writers once more attacked and dissident movements stilled. The spiritual pollution campaign in 1983 confirmed once more Deng's political views. I had often wondered where the boundary lay, whether China could still be termed communist, as claimed automatically by most Chinese, or whether it had at last 'come to its senses' and was swinging towards capitalism, as claimed by the Western press. Though the country was certainly moving away from the communism it knew in the time of Mao, socially China was still far more Marxist than recent reports would imply. Whether it was ever a truly Marxist nation – one Karl Marx would have recognized as such – is another question still: there were those who believed that Mao's communism was merely new wine in old bottles, a continuation of Imperialism ruled by a patriarch demanding obedience to a rigid set of rules.

The official line stated that China still followed Marxist–Leninist ideals but was re-evaluating its policies according to modern and Chinese needs; that it was 'socialism with Chinese characteristics'. The adoption of certain 'capitalist practices' – the foundation of the SEZs for example, and the freeing of the economy from state control – would not, it vowed, undermine the foundation of socialism, the important distinction between *ownership* of the means of production and their *use*. Though line struggles within the Party continued and viewpoints differed, according to Deng and most other leaders the purpose of socialism was to make China strong through controlled socialist growth. But did the development of productive forces conflict with the bases of socialist principles? Could a country be socialist whose leaders failed to represent the interests of its people? When they were inert, inept and not directly answerable? Was a country socialist that pulled in foreign currency by selling its art to capitalists, that opened its gates to millions of tourists, foreign experts and investors and built them luxury hotels? Was a country socialist when privilege rested on rank and status and whom one knew? Where there were those in high office who believed not a thread of Marxist theory held true? Where millions still acted as beasts of burden, pulling pedicabs, working treadmills and yoked to carts, while the privileged rode in limousines? Where the peasants still ate bitterness, and the majority were obsessed by material gain? In spite of claims of continuing Marxist fealty it was significant that the epithets 'Communist' and 'Marxist–Leninist' were being dropped from official bulletins and being replaced by the broader term 'Socialist', which could be applied to systems as diverse as British socialism and 'socialist' Albania.

At times it seemed that China had got stuck with the negative backwash of communism – the repression and control – while forsaking the good: egalitarianism and genuine dictatorship by the proletariat. Though few would admit it, the experiment had failed. While Marxism could not be trimmed and tailored to allow for the shortcomings of a billion Chinese, these same billion people could not be won round to the ideals of Marxism except through repression and thought control. Organization being by nature hierarchical, every political theory in history has ultimately led back to inequality. The communist rebels of the thirties and forties became the new bureaucracy, the new élite. By 1987 the communists would have ruled as long as the Nationalists, but in the thirty-five years up to 1984 there had been no real progress, no economic improvement, no civilizing of manners, no expanding of ideas. In those thirty-five years the system had failed in its efforts to create a stronger, more caring, more sharing society.

Yulan's family occupied one room of a traditional house in a narrow *hutong*, one of the small town lanes that threaded in a grid through old Beijing. Having smashed up their possessions the Red Guards had held a 'people's trial' in front of the neighbours and purloined three-quarters of her home. 'They said we had more space than we required and the other three rooms would be given to the people. Then three families moved in from a factory and built sheds in our courtyard and cut down our shade tree for fuel. The house is now dirty and falling apart and the yard is draped with drying clothes. Once the woodwork was painted deep green but nobody bothers any more. We never got on. The other three families invaded our privacy and they see us as class enemies. We once had a toilet but that was smashed by the Red Guards too – now we all go down the road.'

I could picture the almost windowless wall fronting the *hutong*, its soft grey brickwork, the weeds among the tiles of its low-pitched roof, the old wooden doorway slightly ajar and the stolen glimpse of the inner yard past a passageway beyond. It would be typical of houses throughout north China, unchanged in style for eight hundred years, its four large rooms looking on to the yard. But now the rooms were subdivided by partitions. There'd be wood and coal stores cluttering the yard, chickens in coops and glass in the windows where paper had been.

Beijing was once a splendid city surrounded by monolithic walls. It was entered through elaborate tiered gateways, a myriad of lanes comprising tens of thousands of low brick houses and specialist shops. Rising above them there were palaces and temples, pagodas and drum towers and dark spreading trees: the epitome of all Mao wanted to change. Since 1949 most old monuments had been destroyed and Beijing was now an ordinary place. The intention of the municipal planning authorities was to pull down what remained of the grid of *hutongs* and the 'four corners yards', as houses such as

Yulan's were called, and replace them with blocks, leaving one or two lanes in memorial to the past, to prove what conditions had been like before. Beijing would lose what was left of its charm, the tranquil walks along grey-walled lanes with their cycles and pedestrians and horse-drawn carts. But the pressing need, Yulan suggested, was for adequate housing. She would gladly sacrifice her outside yard for an inside tap and a private loo and the benefits of radiators and gas. Old houses like hers were falling apart, they were cramped and draughty and the windows were small. She had a single coal stove with which to heat the room and cook all the family's meals.

'Oh it's so dirty!' She dusted her hands of imaginary coal. 'And it takes up so much of my time. In the West you put fires against the walls but in China the stoves are in the middle of the floor!' I had thought this sensible: the room warmed evenly, greater numbers could sit close and they benefited from the heat in the flue pipe too. But Yulan knew better. 'It uses up so much precious space and you can't confine the mess. When I open the stove to add more coal smoke billows out and makes everything black!'

'Does the street committee still interfere with your home life and housekeeping?' I knew she would resent that too.

She despised the bevy of bossy old women with nothing better to fill their time than poke their noses into other people's houses and report their findings to the Party. 'If we have guests these women appear and demand to know who we're entertaining. If we want to receive a foreigner we have to apply for permission beforehand. Sometimes two or three of them bang on the door and look under the beds and investigate our cooking pots, or order us out to clean up the courtyard and sweep the *hutong*. Quite apart from the intrusion, these things take time.'

Like most educated Chinese, Yulan was acutely conscious of time. It could be because so much had been lost. It could be because her life was unfulfilling and she could feel her best years slipping away. It could be that her Westernized, cultivated background equated achievement with satisfaction and contentment. Behind her deceptively comforting smile I was beginning to perceive the tension within, the frustration, the helplessness to control her own fate. Several times on our twenty-hour journey I heard her complain about lack of time. Her daughters were occupied with college work in the evenings and her husband worked long hours in his hospital so in addition to teaching, the brunt of the housework fell on her too. Since she couldn't afford a washing machine she washed four people's clothes by hand. Since she had no fridge she went shopping for fresh food every day and it took an hour to prepare.

With bitter memories of the past, anxiety for the future and a colourless and unrelenting daily life Yulan lived under continual strain. Fearful of sharing her feelings with her friends in case they betrayed her, unable to oppose Party policy openly, all she could do was pour out her heart to a stranger on a train. Her meeting with me was a chance to unburden, to share her anger with one on whose sympathy she could rely. Being outside my personal experience her story would have much greater effect than on those around her who had heard it all before. Many Westerners in situations less demanding than hers would have sought medical or psychiatric aid. But in China stress remained unchecked, seen either as bourgeois decadence or as an unfortunate legacy of the Cultural Revolution about which nothing could be done. Psychological problems, if acknowledged at all, were treated as purely physical disorders: psychiatrists were quacks and the subject of psychology and the existence of hospitals for treating mental health were kept under cover until recent years – along with other aspects of social deviance like juvenile delinquency and sexual abnormality and black marketeering – for fear, one presumes, of a loss of national face.

Having spent eight months in close quarters with the Chinese it was clear to me that many lived close to the threshold of mental control. Arguments flared up over trivial matters, tempers exploded in virulent orgies and people gathered round to enjoy the spectacle of others making fools of themselves. The Cultural Revolution had left permanent psychological devastation with which the intellectuals could not come to terms. The perpetual cycle of unsatisfying marriages, political pressure, inadequate nutrition and difficult living and working conditions were matters beyond most people's control. I asked Yulan how the Chinese coped with tension and strain. Many smoked, she said, especially men, though there were women who smoked in the privacy of their homes. Some drank strong tea to keep them going. Others found outlets in politics or study. Some took up sport and sweated it out. Some drank, some brawled. Some escaped into the fantasy of cinema and television. More than was made public turned to crime.

Photographs of criminals were paraded in public on courtroom notice boards. The shame involved was as damaging as the punishment unless those portrayed were being taken to be executed with placards round their necks, an example to others – as their photographs were too. Ten thousand people received the death sentence in 1984, for 'counter-revolutionary activity' (not specified), for kidnapping and robbery, for the rape or sale of a woman or child, or for being a practising gay. Sometimes the pictures of ordinary criminals were accompanied by renderings depicting their crimes, pegged, like washing, to a cord. Included in one such exposé on Hainan Island was a man throwing merchandise off the back of a lorry to a pick-up truck close on its tail. There was another stealing from a woman's bag and another creeping up on a man watching television, a dagger outstretched in his hand. And another overpowering a woman by force. And another bashing a rival with a spade . . . There were punch-ups in smoke-befogged gambling dens, and muggings and gang fights, and adulterous romances, and thieves climbing walls and escaping from cells and stealing rationed rice sacks and siphoning oil from another unit's drums; as varied and imaginative a selection of crimes as might be expected anywhere. But the major story was a serial melodrama in which a man had secretly opened a brothel (scene one), engaged some girls (scene two) and begun a roaring trade. Clients came crowding through the doorway holding out banknotes (scene three). The girls were sitting on the sides of their beds in vests and bloomers (scene four), tentatively pawing men's shirts (scene five), at which point the artist retired.

It was previously assumed that Chinese born under Mao's red flag, two-thirds of the country's populace, would make better citizens, more socially motivated, more politically conscious, but the opposite was proving the case. Perhaps, like Orwell's Julia, they had 'grown up in the world of the Revolution, and knowing nothing else accepted the Party as something unalterable, like the sky, not rebelling against its authority but simply evading it, as a rabbit dodges a dog.' The young had no memory of feudal exploitation and were growing daily more restive in the knowledge of their physical, emotional and intellectual poverty by comparison with life in the West. If a communist system was superior, they asked, why was China still so poor after thirty-five years? They were tired of insufficiency, bored and alienated by politics and propaganda, angry about inadequate further education and jobs for school leavers, frustrated by the absence of privacy or free choice. Lacking cultural, spiritual and intellectual leadership they were open to all that was worst in the West. They had nowhere to go, nothing to do, and they wore their personal anomie in their behaviour and clothes. I saw them in Hangzhou, ranging the streets in bell-bottomed gangs, eyes roving restlessly, cigarettes dangling from mustachioed mouths. I saw them in Shanghai coffee shops, sitting all day with their disaffected friends, talking desultorily, getting high on a glass of bittersweet coffee. Too cold to be out in the streets sprayed with snow, too low to be alone in the joylessness of home, they hunched their shoulders and leant on their elbows and were despised as shirkers by those who had work. In desperation at the yawning gulf between expectations and reality they turned to whatever came to hand, to gambling, to alcohol, to gang feuds and sex. In our hard-berth carriage there were obscene drawings on the lavatory wall, all the more disquieting because of where we were. Addiction to opium was again taking hold, smuggled in from India, Burma and Hong Kong.

Disillusionment among the young was on the rise. Rusticated urbanites were returning to the cities, demanding reabsorption and jobs. There were riots about unemployment and housing shortages. Reports had leaked out about hooliganism at football grounds. The young were questioning their elders' views. More and more people were beginning to demand the basic human rights assumed by the world's democracies: the right to vote, the right of assembly, the right of free speech and an uncensored press, the right to education and the right of dissent.

'We don't live; we just exist!' Yulan stared through the window, seeing nothing of the pattern of the snow-filled fields. 'Everything I like is labelled "bourgeois". I enjoy Western food like butter and cheese, though I can't afford to buy it and am thought bourgeois just for liking its taste.' But there were signs of change in this direction. In its recent promotion of dairy food, long avoided by Han Chinese but believed to make people tall and strong, the Party was succeeding in popularizing yoghurt, though cheese was still suspect as it made people fat. Once something was promoted, it ceased to be bourgeois. 'I am bourgeois for liking classical European music,' Yulan continued. 'Bourgeois for having read Western books. Bourgeois for wanting to go to the ballet.' The system denied her her soul. The Party believed it a sin to be moved by a poem or a painting or a symphony or a flower, for such things were once the preserve of the rich. Instead of making them available to everyone they denied free expression to all but themselves. 'I particularly enjoy ballet and I long to go, but I haven't been able to for years – partly because I haven't the time to stand in the ticket queues. But I did try once, and when I got to the front they refused me tickets because of my background. "Not for you," they said. Anyway I could scarcely afford the two yuan it cost to get in.' As a privileged foreigner I'd not only been able to get tickets for *Swan Lake* just before the performance was due to begin, presumably from a stack reserved for foreign friends, but to wander backstage afterwards to meet the director and prima ballerina. The performers were young, and exceptionally good.

As for books, very few were available to the ordinary public, as Xiuying well knew. The official excuse was paper shortage, though when it came to the printing of political tracts there always seemed to be more than enough. On reaching Shanghai I paid a visit to the Foreign Languages Bookstore, where students were leafing through Victor Hugo, Virgil's *Aeneid* and *Robin Hood* at a small glass-topped counter while I had sole run of a fenced-off paddock comprising half the shop, containing novels in half a dozen languages and calendars and postcards and books about Chinese politics, history, scenery and arts, and safe Chinese works translated into English, most of which seemed innocuous enough but none of which the Chinese were permitted to buy. For all Deng's rhetoric about Open Policy, cultural freedom was still a faraway dream.

Mao's belief in the need for perpetual revolution had consumed surplus funds for almost thirty years and kept people struggling for mere survival. Once they got comfortable they began to think, to demand their rights. So in place of contaminated capitalist culture the Party under Deng attempted to occupy people's minds with bland hopes for the future and bland entertainment for now. For want of alternatives, contemporary Chinese culture revolved around television. I asked Yulan if she watched it much and she replied – the first to respond in this vein – that most programmes were rubbish and she rarely did. Neither would she allow her daughters to do so unless there was something worth watching.

Television being an installation on most hotel landings and a permanent background to family life which, once acquired, was rarely switched off, I absorbed its gist while visiting friends and waiting for my key in hotels. A typical programme in peak viewing hours showed ordinary people parading in a yet more ordinary park, carrying children, climbing steps, gazing at lakes, posing for photographs, pointing at flowers – all apparently, judging by the candyfloss commentary, happy and fulfilled. Then the scene might shift to a factory, not typical this time but one that was efficient and clean. The subsequent programme might be all about winter: more people in parks or cycling down streets or sweeping the pavements or gaily throwing snowballs. There might be opera or acrobats or a volleyball game. Or light entertainment in which photographic gimmicks were employed to the extent that one ceased to be aware of performer or song, bewitched instead by zooming lenses, multiple shots, starburst filters and vignetting blending every few seconds from lime to strawberry to lemon to flame.

There was a further humiliation that intellectuals still faced. It had been safer at times to conceal mental prowess rather than be pilloried as bourgeois and élitist: to a certain extent this still held true. Unqualified cadres were suspicious of those better trained than themselves, were sceptical about science, were fearful of people who thought, or held views. 'The more you learn,' Mao Zedong is reputed to have said, 'the more stupid you become.' The problem of how to train academics without creating an élite and thereby losing the revolution was the greatest dilemma the Party had faced, and one that remained unsolved. In the past all intellectuals had done spells of labour. They were still poorly paid and given little respect.

'I'm fifty-three,' Yulan confided, 'but I earn only 89 yuan a month. That's about a third less than a factory worker of similar age and less than many suburban peasants.' Wages bore no relation to aptitude or performance, only to age and Party allegiance. The same applied to doctors, artists, architects, scientists . . . I had read that intellectuals were once again being wooed for their brains and expertise, but Yulan was sceptical. 'There may be something in it,' she said. 'I have heard through the network of "little road news" that there'll be a rise in 1985. But it won't be enough,' she stated adamantly. 'Ten or twenty per cent at the most.'

The rumour was accurate. In 1985 all teachers got a rise and their pupils were commanded to show them more respect. Confucius was being rehabilitated, his moral theories reintroduced. Teacher's Day was reinstated: Jan in Changsha received a gift of mooncakes (stuffed pastries) and a bag of red apples.

All the revolutions, all the struggle and criticism and destruction had been in vain: the core of feudal mentality lived on. Thirty-five years of re-education, of the fight against tradition and selfishness had failed to change human nature. Yulan could not see why she should suffer for the good of an abstract State, an abstract proletariat; she believed her expertise was superior to field or factory work and warranted higher pay. While some 'class enemies' (landlords, rich peasants, counter-revolutionaries, renogades, spies, capitalist roaders) had given in gracefully, donned baggy cotton clothes and resigned themselves cheerfully to factory work, others still kicked and spat. Yulan *was* bourgeois. She was part of a recrystallizing intelligentsia. She held herself above the peasants and workers and uneducated cadres: she cultivated etiquette and taste. She bemoaned the habits of the labouring classes and wrote off the leaders as rural rustics with neither good manners nor sense. As the leaders were, Yulan believed, so would their people be.

'They call me bourgeois,' she complained again, 'for saying please and thank you, excuse me and sorry.' This was not the habit of peasants and workers who just stated what they wanted and barged their way through crowds.

'It's true,' I agreed. 'I hardly ever hear any of these words.' I did not add that I'd been advised – by workers – to avoid their use; such terms were rightist and feudal.

'Look how rude that man was to you, refusing to let you put your bag on the luggage rack!' I hadn't seen him since; I hadn't noticed anyone, or anything, so absorbed was I in Yulan. 'That man is clearly someone who dislikes foreigners, but it was extremely bad-mannered to show it.' That xenophobia was common I knew very well, but this was the first time a Chinese had admitted it to my face.

'A few years ago the government tried to improve people's

manners,' Yulan recalled. 'They have tried repeatedly to curb spitting as well, providing spittoons in streets and state-owned buildings and imposing low fines on people not using them. But their efforts have been futile: nothing has changed. There are many Chinese who find it abhorrent to spit in the street or in front of other people but visitors don't notice those. They assume that spitting is universal and condemn the whole nation as uncouth.' Having spent the past month in hard-seat carriages travelling from one cold, crowded, polluted northern city to the next with severe bronchitis I sympathized with people who needed to spit. Chest infections were an omnipresent curse.

'The buses in Beijing are terrible too,' Yulan went on, 'and it's not just the way people spit on the floor. Several buses will go past full before I can get on one; people push past and I'm left outside. Once on the bus and standing in the aisle I am pushed again by those around me and knocked by swinging bags and leant across and squashed against a handrail or the side. At every stop I must wait five minutes while more people try to force their way on – you've seen those queue monitors pushing in the last ones – and then the doors won't close. Everyone argues and no one will get off and still the doors won't close. People are out for themselves these days; our traditional values have almost disappeared. Children no longer respect their elders and will squeeze past old people to take the last seats. Fortunately I have a bicycle,' she said.

Yulan was the only person I met who felt no pride in being a member of the family of Chinese, who wherever they went were first and foremost Chinese, who retained their lifestyle and lived in close groups, who deserted the motherland only through necessity, who returned in their thousands to build a new China in the 1950s and again in the seventies to sort out the chaos and again in the eighties to visit as tourists; who sent back money to relatives at home and ploughed foreign currency into worthy establishments like hospitals and schools. Yulan did not partake of that peculiar Chinese patriotism, or if she once did it had been slowly crushed out of her. She had a contemporary, individual, almost Western view. It was easy for both of us to fix our sights on the system's shortcomings, to discern the persistent lack of fantasy, or honesty, or humour, or grace; more difficult to understand the less tangible but continuing benefits it had brought.

I tried once more. All day I had heard only criticism. 'What about the positive side of communism?' Most Chinese I'd met were from lowly origins and seemed to have benefited more than they had lost. They supported socialism, in principle at least, and would have felt little sympathy for people like Yulan. Wei Meng didn't think there were many of her kind, though he may have been wrong. 'What about the benefits to those who were poor? Dwellings for the homeless, food for the starving, schools in the countryside, light and piped water, better hygiene and housing, public transport, cleaner streets, a narrowing of the gulf between rich and poor, less disease, fewer beggars, fewer brothels, less corruption . . .'

Yulan shook her head. 'These things would have come whatever the system, as they have elsewhere. They are ordinary progress, not communist victory. If anything the Party has held up their development through an endless stream of avoidable mistakes – there is not much to show for thirty-five years of so-called utopian rule. Our schools are not better than schools in other countries; on the contrary, they are worse: facilities are inadequate and learning is by rote. Our hospitals are primitive, their staff poorly trained. Our artists are censored. Our factories don't produce. And our papers tell lies.'

On initial acquaintance the English-language *China Daily* had seemed a reasonable, even moderately unbiased organ of Party policy. It was only as I learned of the unprintable aspects of China's socialism – the gross bunglings in both policy and practical detail, the poverty and bitterness, the things that could have been done but had not been – that I began to read between the lines depicting a nation moving forcefully into an ever-brightening future. Yes, the paper admitted mistakes, and it acknowledged that poverty was still widespread. But the errors and the backwardness were blamed universally on the ultra-left upheaval of the Cultural Revolution, blinding many readers in the Party's opaque plea for international support.

'As for corruption,' Yulan took up my argument, 'the entire nation is corrupt. When a government controls the market and rations necessities, that's what happens. There is widespread embezzlement of state-owned equipment and communal funds and almost everyone, at some time, uses the back door. Officials take large bribes for allocating jobs or moving a peasant into a town.

Middle and high cadres – we call them "red mandarins" – appropriate cars for personal use. They have access to special shops and cinemas and medical care, and soft-berth tickets on trains. Their children go to key-point schools and later have the option of studying abroad. Their flats are larger, their clothes more expensive. They have access to Foreign Exchange Certificates and they buy foreign goods from the Friendship Stores. How they manage it I don't know; I have never even been inside a Friendship Store!'

There was no longer even a vicarious pleasure in watching the rich and influential. As I walked one morning some days before along Changan Avenue – the Avenue of Everlasting Peace – there was a siren of hooters, a deep throbbing of engines. City buses groaned to a standstill in a rattle of tin to let a cavalcade of limousines glide silently by with the pompous celebrity of a funeral cortege. The new mandarins sat corpse-like in curtain-shrouded shadows, embalmed in a fantasy of self-righteous self-esteem.

Traditionally civil servants were the best educated, most respected members of the social hierarchy, just as cadres were the most powerful ones now. The higher-ranking cadres protected each other's interests through an old-boy network in which everyone acted out of selfish interests and status was measured in back-door connections. They watched each other jealously, as most ordinary people did, to ensure that no one on a similar rung was enjoying greater privilege than themselves. Many cadres refused to grant an authorization without a hefty bribe. And not only cadres had useful connections: salespeople, drivers, workers and policemen all had access to back-door deals. Teachers were a notable exception to the rule.

For their system to succeed the leaders needed the people's support. To win their support they would have to ensure several decades of peaceful economic growth and a social climate that made corruption defunct. Open Policy brought new opportunities for high-level corruption, and since this corruption was engendered by the system itself it was not enough to try to stamp it out. Yet this was what Deng proposed to do. Early in 1986 two high-ranking cadres' sons were executed on charges of multiple rape and nefarious foreign business deals as an example to others who similarly manipulated the privilege of rank to get away with crime.

'What about your status as a woman?' I asked Yulan. 'Surely that has improved?'

'There has been no improvement,' she stated flatly. 'In my present situation I am forced to work as well as keeping house, so I have no free time. As a child of liberated parents in the forties I had almost as much freedom as my brothers did. We were happy then. We read books. We listened to music. We learnt to paint. We studied hard, but we enjoyed ourselves too. Servants did the housework. What do we have to live for now?'

Yulan was painting the opposite picture from that presented by the communists under Mao: 'Before Liberation this area was reserved for capitalists and their running dogs,' or, 'Before Liberation there was an old-fashioned factory here owned by Imperialists. The workers were exploited and very poorly paid. After Liberation the workers gained confidence since they no longer laboured for a capitalist. They are well fed and clothed and they have a say in the management. Production has increased by 300 per cent.' London's history pre-1984 had been similarly rewritten in Orwell's book, as '. . . a dark, dirty, miserable place where hardly anybody had enough to eat and where hundreds of thousands of poor people had no boots on their feet . . . The capitalists owned everything . . . and everyone else was their slave . . . They were fat, ugly men with wicked faces . . .' Chinese history was still being rewritten in 1980, with references to radical Maoist policies being erased from Party literature. Travelling round China in 1905 when the country still had an emperor, Dr King reported people looking happy, well-nourished and either busy or about to be. He saw fewer beggars than he'd noted in Europe and there were charity organizations to help people in need. If Mao inherited a devastated country, almost wholly illiterate, corrupt, diseased and dying of starvation, it had been made that way by the warlords, the Nationalists and the Japanese – and a certain embroidery of the truth.

Though her spirit had survived, Yulan's health and youth had gone. No one could give her back the lost years spent labouring in factories and fields. 'I look older than my years,' she smiled sadly, 'and my brother could pass for seventy. You can hide your suffering to a certain extent but eventually it surfaces on your face.' She had such a pleasant face it didn't matter about the lines. But it mattered to her. She played absentmindedly with the hem of her coat. Embarrassed, I looked away.

All day we talked as the train moved south. Though no one sat near us and the clatter of the wheels on the rails was quite loud, I was surprised she could talk as she did on a train.

'Are there political prisoners still?' I asked.

'Oh yes – many thousands. The Party has plain-clothes men everywhere. If they overhear you talking on a bus or in the street and you criticize the Party or one of its leaders you'll be sent to prison or labour camp. There is no defence for political crimes.'

'What about the way you are talking to me?'

'No one speaks English here,' she replied.

Snow was still falling on the bare winter fields and the sky hung low and grey. We rattled across a long steel bridge but we scarcely saw it, so engrossed were we in talk. Then a railway employee tapped Yulan's arm. 'Look at the Yangtze!' he commanded her sternly. 'This is the famous Nanjing Bridge built in 1969 during the Great Proletarian Cultural Revolution!' That her attention should have been focused on a foreigner at such a moment was a slight to the Party and the memory of Mao. Yulan turned obediently and regarded the river, rolling its brown waters beneath the bridge. It was the first time she had seen it in her life.

Yulan was a gem. I had subconsciously been searching for her, knowing she must exist somewhere. She was the other face of China, born before the revolution and dispossessed of her heritage and freedom. A great gulf yawned between her motherly smile and the heart of darkness bottled up within. But she had to keep cheerful in order to stay sane. Of the communist revolution and all that came after it, of the cadres who officiated and the peasants and workers who supported its cause, she hated every one.

14

The Ghost of China Past

Yulan was not unique in her longing for democracy. A survey of villagers in the Pearl River delta found that half would leave the Chinese mainland if they could, for Hong Kong, Macao, Taiwan or the West. In the late 1970s a quarter of a million people a year escaped illegally across the border to Hong Kong. Far more than that number were apprehended and sent to do labour, only to return for a further try when their sentence had run. Some bought their way out, paying the equivalent of four years' salary in a series of bribes. Others hiked across mountains on moonless nights, clung beneath trains, climbed barricades of coiled barbed wire, swam among sharks or built makeshift rafts, leaving families behind in their villages, staking their lives for the hope of Hong Kong, preferring capitalist exploitation to the corruption and misery of communist rule. Their time was running out. Before 1997 the successful ones must make enough money to escape once more. Few would succeed. For most the journey terminated here.

Walking the fluorescent streets of Hong Kong I played that game where someone says a word and you respond with the first thing that comes to mind. The word was 'China', and the reaction came back, as sure and effortless as a stone falls to earth: endurance. The waiting and suffering of a billion people in a world that could dissolve in a new mass campaign. Xiuying yearning for love and success. Weimin craving the chance just to learn. The Wu family toiling for their daily food. Wei Meng pining for an opportunity to paint. Yulan longing to be free.

Hong Kong. Electric, energetic, eclectic, effervescent. Economically successful; socially suffering. World's busiest harbour. World's biggest user of telex machines. World's dearest real estate and world's densest housing scheme. Where work is the ethic and money is what matters. Where a poorly paid secretary blows her salary on a horse. Where two or three families may share one room and mental strain breaks out in crime. Where squalor and poverty co-exist with luxury; where migrants mingle with millionaires, where shanties are shadowed by multiple blocks, where junks and sampans are dwarfed by tankers and racial antagonism simmers beneath the surface of the inscrutable Chinese mask.

On one hand Hong Kong seemed so Western. On the other it was still essentially Chinese, more so than China, for whereas China had been changed by Marxism–Leninism–Mao Zedong Thought, Hong Kong society still had its foundation in traditional Confucian and religious views: Hong Kong was a repository for things Chinese.

There were places and times when I could feel myself back in the world of China's Imperial past. I felt it lunching with a group of Chinese in a dim sum restaurant that seated four thousand: instead of waiters there were women trundling trolleys, shouting their contents like pedlars their wares, dispensing food that maintained its traditional opulence in appealing to sight, sound, smell and taste. I felt it in the farmland of the outlying islands, where the plots belonged to the peasants who tilled them, who were free to farm them however they pleased. I felt it when I came upon an elderly woman, her back bent low from decades of shoulder poles, her fortune on her wrist in a bangle of jade. I felt it on ferry boats, on paint-faded junks all tar and rope and cuttlefish drying like washing in the sun. I felt it in the shanties toppling on stilts, in shacks on shady boulder-strewn hillsides and in colonies of houseboats anchored in bays. I felt it walking in the narrow crowded lanes of Western, Wanchai and Yaumatei, looking through shop doorways at red satin wedding gowns, at ivory and jade, at the coloured paper models of homes and cars and boats and planes that were burnt on anniversaries to procure the comfort of departed souls. There were teashops and bird shops and pawn shops and herb shops and snake shops and wine shops such as once made up the cities of China but were now lost to the omnipotent department store. I felt it in the races on New Year's Day, in the hum of expectation I had never experienced in a Chinese parade; the fever in the smell of the horses' sweat and the crescendo of tension in the final five seconds when a bolt of electricity shot through the crowd, an almost physical thrill. And then for the first time I understood the potency of the mainland Chinese; I learnt how quiet and intelligent individuals could turn brutal as they had done in the Cultural Revolution when their passions were given legitimate rein.

So long as vision was selective and could sift through the overlay of Hong Kong's Westernness it was easy to leap into China's past. Down by the waterfront straw-hatted coolies unloaded junks, throwing basketwork crates to more ragged coolies clamouring below, jostling barrows and gesticulating, balancing timber or sacks of rice on a threadbare shoulder or swaying pole. Along the main shopping streets the destitutes trundled, barefoot, with bundles and nowhere to go, begging from the wealthy, scavenging in bins. Through windows and doorways came the clatter of mahjong tiles, the hypnotic amnesia of games lasting minutes or hours or days, as addictive as opium, as senseless as snap. Up on the hillsides the shanty towns clustered, earth-coloured, rock-scaled, their sounds almost rural: the clucking of chickens, the snuffling of pigs, the rumbling of hand-carts, the song of wild birds, the slap of wet laundry and the flap of banana leaves folding in the breeze.

In the privacy of houses and apartment blocks Confucian ethics still prevailed. Hong Kong was as conscious of class as old China, except that position was ordained not by birth, but by money and power. Whether millionaires with fleets of fast cars, or English-speaking professionals, or indigenous farmers and fishermen, or the labouring proletariat escaped from the mainland and living in slums, people were acutely aware of their place, of the appropriate behaviour pertaining to their class. Education was still the main path to success and was determined in childhood by the quality of nursery parents could afford. Most Hong Kong residents lived in close-knit families ruled by a patriarch in which traditional hierarchies endured. Men resented those women who through sheer application had risen to positions of influence and authority to undermine the old order where men were in charge. Some still kept concubines, though because of new laws they were mistresses now. To bear a male child was as paramount in the eighties as ever before; a girl was no comfort to elderly parents nor could she worship them once they were gone.

But the heart of old China was enshrined in the temples. Whereas on the mainland there were few or no real temples, only relics restored for the tourist trade, Hong Kong had six hundred places of worship, not gaudy showpieces but part of the ancient Chinese heritage going back over two thousand years. The larger temples were built in three sections, the first part the entrance, the spirit wall flanked by a large bell and drum, the second with roof vents for clearing the smoke from burnt paper offerings and incense coils, the third a row of curtained altars to the temple's principal deities. Minor shrines and the temple keeper's quarters occupied rooms on either side.

Sometimes a temple was as much a dwelling as a place of worship, the visitor a witness of family life in a setting irrevocably Chinese. In the Tam Kung Temple in Shaukiwan on a Saturday evening the temple keeper's children were playing a kind of Chinese jacks on the floor before the central shrine. While their mother nursed the baby and their grandmother mended a padded silk coat the temple keeper sat printing spirit money, brushing a woodblock with vermilion paint and pressing it on paper in coarse-cut squares. Brooms leant idly on an incense urn and an open drawer revealed palm-leaf fans. A shopping bag lay open in the middle of the floor. As day turned to dusk the aroma of the market and the cries of street pedlars flooded in through the open door.

The air in the temple was heavy with incense; the walls and altars were blackened by smoke. It gave an illusion of mellowed antiquity, subdued the brazen reds and golds and created a mysterious shadowy harmony in which nothing was fully seen. The embroidered silks and tasselled lanterns hanging from rafters were dusty and discoloured. The brass was tarnished on the bowls and oil lamps and incense stands. The life-size gods with long moustaches and floor-length gowns were tired and aged; the atmosphere was clouded by a bluish haze.

Tam Kung was a child-god who forecast the weather and was worshipped by fishermen. They gathered in thousands in the fourth lunar month to celebrate his anniversary, to convene with the spirit world, to parade, to watch the dancing of dragons and make offerings of incense and flowers at his shrine. But on this ordinary Saturday there were no more than four or five worshippers at any one time. They floated like phantoms through the eerie haze, setting light to pendulous incense coils, kneeling on cushions to mouth prayers before the shrines, throwing half-moon clappers to cast light on their destiny or shaking a cylinder of fortune sticks until one of them prised itself loose and fell. They piled fruit in bowls, jammed chrysanthemums in vases and lit bunches of incense – fat yellow joss-sticks and red wax candles – to the gilded image of Tam Kung.

In this curious interplay of mysticism and domesticity lay the ghost of China past. The Hong Kong temples were a storehouse of the arts, not in petrified form to be preserved behind glass, nor as a debased commodity to attract foreign funds, but as part of the fabric of everyday life. In addition to a distinctive architectural style they contained examples of most arts and crafts, few of them works of individual genius but expertly made and essentially Chinese. Paintings and calligraphy hung on the walls above blackwood and rosewood tables and chairs. Roof lines were embossed with ornate friezes depicting local saint-heroes and mythical beasts. The temple keeper folding silvered paper into ingots was perpetuating the crafts of woodblock printing and the manufacture of paper by hand. The life-like deities embraced the arts of sculpture, carving and costume design; their satin robes, and the curtains that enshrined them, and the pennants and banners and altar cloths, were finely embroidered with silken thread. There were musical instruments, baskets and metalwork, and bonsai trees in pots; there were paper dragons before the shrines; there were carvings of tortoiseshell, ivory and jade; so many reminders of all China had lost.

Most Hong Kong temples embodied the beliefs that together made up the folk faith that suited the Chinese temperament so well; if one set of guidelines offered no solace one could look to another for alternative views. But up in the hills there were monasteries dedicated either to Buddhism or Dao.

Ching Chung Koon was a large Daoist temple in Hong Kong's New Territories, set in terraced gardens of bonsai trees. I came across a ceremony in one of the shrine halls, where the walls were studded with ancestral tablets like a pattern of newsprint, picked out by the yellow and orange and green of fruit placed in bowls on the altars in front. Some women in one corner were fashioning a spirit house from coloured paper, doilies and slithers of bamboo, a doll's-house creation with lattice in the windows and a garden of flowers. In the centre of the shrine hall six priests gowned in saffron with black flat-topped hats were chanting from texts and banging small cymbals and long-handled drums while a seventh, clad in patchwork, was facing the altar at their head. A flautist sat a little to one side making music with the airiness of mountain-tops. Then the priest clad in patchwork threw flowers in the air – marigolds, chrysanthemums and gladioli – and handfuls of copper Qing dynasty coins to succour the spirit in the underworld, and children ran forward to gather them up.

Unlike the mainland where many urban citizens had learnt to be sceptical, almost every Hongkongese still dallied with the occult. Hence the thriving community of fortune-tellers at Wong Tai Sin: palmists, astrologers, card readers, bone feelers and diviners of sticks. Hence the fetish over numbers and the fortunes paid for 'lucky' car number plates. Hence the fear of good luck and its concealment from the gods lest they be jealous, for instance, at the birth of a boy. And hence the fear of losing blood, which people believed was part of the body's essential soul.

As had previously been the case in mainland China, nothing could be done to Hong Kong's physical environment without the approval of the *feng-shui* practitioner, the 'dragon man'. *Feng-shui* mirrors hung above doorways and goldfish aquaria were stationed in halls. If sites for the living weren't all that they should be it was at least possible to cater for the dead. People were buried on hillsides facing a valley or the sea, preferably in a grave whose horseshoe layout symbolized the protection of hills to the rear. Positive energies were collected at the grave site while malefic forces flowed by.

When a Hong Kong company moved its offices the dragon man was called in to advise. He would tell the workers which room they should use and align their desks. He might advise the installation of a goldfish tank whose circulating water would be a substitute for a stream.

A friend of mine worked in an office block with particularly unwholesome *feng-shui*. The windows faced north along a one-way street whose traffic bore energy away from the block; the sea was invisible and Victoria Peak lay behind to the south. Most of the offices were still unlet, for in spite of a lack of available office space few Chinese firms dared take the risk of openly defying ill fate.

When new buildings were designed a dragon man was asked to vet the plans: in the instance of the Hong Kong–Shanghai bank he shifted the escalators and proposed a pair of carved stone lions for a guard at the front. When a friend designed a garden and the dragon man failed to find fault with it, to prove his worth he said it must be built within a week. Of course it wasn't, so work had to stop while the owner moved in. He then moved out to enable the contractors to finish the scheme.

No one could question a dragon man. He was not an engineer to whom one could say, 'Why does it have to be like this?' An engineer might answer, 'Because of the building regulations,' but he could not get away without a reply, or surround his work with secrecy. It was *feng-shui* Raj in Hong Kong.

Hong Kong villagers manipulated *feng-shui* as a means of extorting compensation from the government. Whatever the planners proposed to do there'd be a local outcry: 'You can't put a road here, this is an important *feng-shui* rock!', or 'It wouldn't be possible to build just there because that's a *feng-shui* tree which cannot be felled!' The villagers got their money and the government got its way. The Hong Kong landscape was spiritually violated and visibly desecrated by new buildings and roads. Summits were chopped off, hillsides carved up, thousands of acres levelled for construction. Old blocks were demolished and new ones built. I turned my eyes away from the ugliness and focused on the memory of China past.

Three places haunt my memories of Hong Kong, each symptomatic of a side of China that once existed, but that I had never seen. On Christmas Day I walked in warm sunshine along the leafy Bowen Road to the Maiden's Stone. Below, through the trees, there were panoramic views of the city and the sea. The Maiden's Stone is mentioned in guide books but only briefly, for it is special to the locals, attributed with the power of making barren women fertile.

The steep wooded hillside studded with boulders was a romantic setting for the numerous small shrines. They were garlanded with offerings, of fruit and flowers and oil and incense and plastic windmills and paper cut-outs of a maiden on a horse, most profuse and decorative about a shallow blackened cave where incense spirals hung from a ledge and small brass deities shone in the glow of a miniature lamp. It reminded me, as Hong Kong temples did, of India. There seemed to be an affinity between the Chinese folk faith and Hinduism, in the polytheistic worship of images, in the abundance of small shrines in both landscape and towns and of gods related to different aspects of life, in the offerings of incense and flowers and food, in the alerting of the deities with bells and gongs and their parading in chariots on festival days, in the reds and golds of temple decoration, and in the mode of worship being predominantly personal and material.

Only the first of these memories would make any sense on a tourist map, for my second concerned a refugee camp. According to tradition only five relationships were considered significant: master and servant, friend and friend, brother and sister, husband and wife and parent and child. There was nothing in the Analects to suggest people's conduct in relation to strangers; I'd seen the outcome of that when Rosy was ill.

Bounded by a seven-foot chain-link fence topped with strands of barbed wire and a further wire roll, the camp personified this lack of sympathy for those who don't belong. It was invisible from the streets and closed – understandably – to visitors, but the man at the gate mistook me for the girl who came to teach English and waved me inside. By the time I was discovered I'd already seen more than I should have done and was feeling shattered, for the conditions of the two and a half thousand Vietnamese in buildings intended to accommodate five hundred were the worst I had ever seen. They were worse than the teeming tenement blocks, worse than the shanties rotting on stilts, worse than the camp beds set beneath flyovers; for not only were people grossly overcrowded, they were also rigidly controlled.

Those with expertise had already been absorbed and the remainder were unskilled workers and fishermen with small hope of resettlement abroad. Aware of their fate they turned in on themselves; it was every man for himself. They cheated each other for minor privilege. They fought, they stole, they sought freedom in heroin. They defecated in the corridors and outside yards. They spat on the floors. They threw rubbish from the windows and it hung there limply, suspended on bars projecting from the walls, and spattered the corrugations of lean-to roofs in the yards below, and decomposed in corners and blocked the drains. They walled themselves in from each other and the world, from the grim dereliction of their barrack-block home. Windows were broken, plaster was crumbling: rats ran down the corridors. Water lay on floors and trickled down walls. To clean the blocks the authorities hosed them down.

The refugees walled themselves in. Each family was allocated a box-like berth (or maybe two), an iron grid frame with a boarded floor 6 feet by 5 feet by 3 feet high, one of a tier of three. They walled themselves in with cardboard and cloth, retreated into safety with their televisions and toddlers and cooking rings and shrines.

The administration blamed the Vietnamese, one of the happiest, cleanest peoples in the world. The camp provided kitchens but people wouldn't use them. The same applied to the block of loos. Yet in conditions of such squalor it was simpler to withdraw, to flow with the tide. It was easier to retreat to the tiny cells and pull the hardboard tight behind. Most refugees despised the people in charge. The rules were strict: no alcohol was allowed within the camp and the gates were locked at night. The Hong Kong government refused to rent its subsidized flats to Vietnamese. Since those who had jobs were the lowest paid workers they had no choice but to remain where they were.

The third of my memories was more disturbing still.

They called it the walled city, yet it had no walls, at least none that one could see. It was walled instead by legend and fear. No one was prepared to accompany me, so I went alone.

Kowloon's walled city had never come under the jurisdiction of British rule and was still beyond the reach of the law. As the stronghold of the Triads, a secret society of the type which pervaded the mainland's past, it may still be the most dangerous place in the Chinese subcontinent and was consequently specially alluring. Visitors were warned to keep out.

From outside the walled city seemed much like any other Kowloon tenement, with a basketry of balconies in front of the windows and an artillery of aerials up on the roofs; except that it looked impenetrable. I plunged into darkness through an opening between blocks no wider than a door, down a slit of passageway lined with small shops. As my eyes grew accustomed to the artificial light I realized the city was almost self-contained, a mafia of clinics, dentists and laundries, bakeries and noodle stalls, tailors and workshops; if one lived there, or was hiding, one need never go out. And once inside I understood the epithet: the old Chinese quarter was nothing *but* walls, discoloured, constricting walls full of foreboding, defining the alleys that twisted, turned, stepped and sloped through a labyrinth pregnant with unseen threat. The walls towered eighty or a hundred feet high with sometimes less than a foot between. Looking upwards there were distant ribbons of light latticed by window frames slightly ajar and criss-crossed by washing drying on poles. Elsewhere the walls became half-lit tunnels, grey with grime and mossy with dust, threaded with sinister pipes and wires. To the left and right there were padlocked doors, and side turnings narrower and darker still, and shadowy recesses, leading nowhere.

The walls engulfed me like a nightmare. Though I met almost no one I could feel the presence of ears and eyes. Though empty it felt crowded, like a darkened theatre before the curtain rose. Though I sensed no real danger, yet nothing was normal. A hum of hostility issued from windows and electric wires. Water gurgled in gulches, murky and ominous as the River Styx. It slithered down walls and plopped from pipes. Rubbish rotted in gulleys or clung damply in drains.

I crossed the walled city four times. Sometimes I turned back when I reached a dead end; sometimes I retreated when the rats in my path were too large, or lacked fear. I felt more and more like the helpless Tom Kitten lost in a world of wainscots and flues. The feeling of underworld began to gnaw at my sanity, to alter my perception of what I thought of as real.

One night I stayed at the Buddhist monastery of Po Lin. I caught a ferry to Lantau and set off walking, steeply uphill. Low cloud enveloped the mountainside and soaked my clothes and skin. All I could see were tufts of pine at the edge of the road and red-brown grasses beaded with dew. In that strange silent world my mind drifted back to the moments in China when I had been quiet and at peace; such times had been few and I remembered them well. There was an hour on the shores of Hangzhou Lake, that time past day that was not yet night when the sky and the lake and the hills in the distance were an equal slate-blue and the moon shone silver and huge. Tendrils of willow twig tickled the water and bats inked the sky in looping trails, like scrolls of cursive calligraphy.

On the night of the full moon the month before, I slept out on a sacred mountainside. As the light began to fade I settled by a tree starred white with flowers to wait for night and anonymity; it was against the rules to sleep outside. Across the valley, range upon range of rounded hills faded into peach-bloom haze. Their flanks were striped with terraces, sickle-shaped field plots emerald with wheat, blue-green with broad beans, frothy with peas, lacy with kale, red-brown-fallow, pink-brown-flooded, scattered with groves of spindly trees. For such moments does one travel. Once darkness had fallen I set about finding a place to sleep, not a simple task in that garden land where every last inch was farmed. But I came upon a rock, concealed two terraces down from the road at the head of the darkening valley. Three terraces below it a man was still ploughing with a buffalo in the moonlight, guiding it, cajoling it, his feet splashing bare in the mud. As the moon rose higher the flooded fields shone in a jigsaw of silver, and the air was warm and still.

Walking up the hillside to Po Lin monastery in that cloud-drenched silence, as the road curved on and up and on between pine trees and grasses and thick walls of mist, continually climbing and never arriving, it felt as if the planet had been deserted. It felt as though I were the last one left on earth.

Coming out of China the final time I paused in Shenzhen, searching for something on which to spend my last few pence. Rejecting china and souvenirs I came at last on a box of silk anemones, crushed and faded, rejected in their turn by the manager of the store. Their cost was minimal so I bought them all. It was the last thing I did, to fill my bags with flowers, in memoriam.